Microlocal and
Time-Frequency Analysis

Microlocal and Time-Frequency Analysis

Editors

Elena Cordero
S. Ivan Trapasso

MDPI • Basel • Beijing • Wuhan • Barcelona • Belgrade • Manchester • Tokyo • Cluj • Tianjin

Editors
Elena Cordero
Dipartimento di Matematica "G. Peano"
Università di Torino
Torino
Italy

S. Ivan Trapasso
Dipartimento di Matematica (DIMA)
Università di Genova
Genova
Italy

Editorial Office
MDPI
St. Alban-Anlage 66
4052 Basel, Switzerland

This is a reprint of articles from the Special Issue published online in the open access journal *Mathematics* (ISSN 2227-7390) (available at: www.mdpi.com/journal/mathematics/special_issues/time-frequency-analysis).

For citation purposes, cite each article independently as indicated on the article page online and as indicated below:

LastName, A.A.; LastName, B.B.; LastName, C.C. Article Title. *Journal Name* **Year**, *Volume Number*, Page Range.

ISBN 978-3-0365-3173-1 (Hbk)
ISBN 978-3-0365-3172-4 (PDF)

© 2022 by the authors. Articles in this book are Open Access and distributed under the Creative Commons Attribution (CC BY) license, which allows users to download, copy and build upon published articles, as long as the author and publisher are properly credited, which ensures maximum dissemination and a wider impact of our publications.

The book as a whole is distributed by MDPI under the terms and conditions of the Creative Commons license CC BY-NC-ND.

Contents

Preface to "Microlocal and Time-Frequency Analysis" vii

Alexandre Arias Junior and Marco Cappiello
On the Sharp Gårding Inequality for Operators with Polynomially Bounded and Gevrey Regular Symbols
Reprinted from: *Mathematics* **2020**, *8*, 1938, doi:10.3390/math8111938 1

Divyang G. Bhimani and Saikatul Haque
Norm Inflation for Benjamin–Bona–Mahony Equation in Fourier Amalgam and Wiener Amalgam Spaces with Negative Regularity
Reprinted from: *Mathematics* **2021**, *9*, 3145, doi:10.3390/math9233145 25

Maurice A. de Gosson
The Pauli Problem for Gaussian Quantum States: Geometric Interpretation
Reprinted from: *Mathematics* **2021**, *9*, 2578, doi:10.3390/math9202578 39

Hans G. Feichtinger
Homogeneous Banach Spaces as Banach Convolution Modules over $M(G)$
Reprinted from: *Mathematics* **2022**, *10*, 364, doi:10.3390/ math10030364 49

Jose M. Machorro-Lopez, Juan P. Amezquita-Sanchez, Martin Valtierra-Rodriguez, Francisco J. Carrion-Viramontes, Juan A. Quintana-Rodriguez and Jesus I. Valenzuela-Delgado
Wavelet Energy Accumulation Method Applied on the Rio Papaloapan Bridge for Damage Identification
Reprinted from: *Mathematics* **2021**, *9*, 422, doi:10.3390/math9040422 71

Jaime Navarro-Fuentes, Salvador Arellano-Balderas and Oscar Herrera-Alcántara
Local Convergence of the Continuous and Semi-Discrete Wavelet Transform in $L^p(\mathbb{R})$
Reprinted from: *Mathematics* **2021**, *9*, 522, doi:10.3390/math9050522 101

Stevan Pilipović, Nenad Teofanov and Filip Tomić
Boundary Values in Ultradistribution Spaces Related to Extended Gevrey Regularity
Reprinted from: *Mathematics* **2021**, *9*, 7, doi:10.3390/math9010007 117

Preface to "Microlocal and Time-Frequency Analysis"

The present volume collects the contributions selected for publication in the Special Issue entitled and Time-Frequency Analysis of the journal *Mathematics*, for which we served as guest editors over 2020 and 2021.

The focus of this Special Issue lies in two fascinating areas of modern mathematics with a broad spectrum of applications ranging from theoretical physics to signal processing, namely, microlocal and time-frequency analysis. The fruitful interaction between the two disciplines is witnessed by the vast body of literature published in recent decades. It is worth mentioning the following problems among several which have benefited from this joint perspective, without any claim of being exhaustive: properties of quantization rules, as well as pseudodifferential and Fourier integral operators; algebras of sparse operators in phase space; well-posedness of nonlinear dispersive PDEs and representation of their solutions; wave front sets; and the propagation of singularities.

In order to further explore these research trends, we invited and solicited original, high-quality articles on microlocal and time-frequency analysis and their diverse applications. As a matter of fact, the resulting contributions provide a wide and interesting selection of topics and problems that we are going to briefly outline below, in alphabetic order, as they appear in the book.

The paper entitled *On the Sharp Gårding Inequality for Operators with Polynomially Bounded and Gevrey Regular Symbols*, by Alexandre Arias Junior and Marco Cappiello, offers novel interesting applications of the sharp Gårding inequality to p-evolution equations. These results rely on the asymptotic regularity analysis of suitable pseudodifferential operators.

In the paper *Norm Inflation for Benjamin–Bona–Mahony Equation in Fourier Amalgam and Wiener Amalgam Spaces with Negative Regularity* by Divyang G. Bhimani and Saikatul Haque, the authors study the problem of strong ill-posedness (through the subtle phenomenon of norm inflation) for the so-called BBM equation using techniques and function spaces of Fourier analysis.

Maurice A. de Gosson is the author of the article *The Pauli Problem for Gaussian Quantum States: Geometric Interpretation*, where a beautiful and fruitful combination of ideas from convex geometry and harmonic analysis eventually leads to the solution of the Pauli tomography problem for Gaussian signals.

We are particularly happy to host in this collection the latest addition to a research agenda that Hans G. Feichtinger has been developing over the recent years, entitled *Homogeneous Banach Spaces as Banach Convolution Modules over M(G)*. This program is aimed at providing an alternative, yet elementary, approach to the fundamental notions and results of modern Fourier analysis.

From the perspective of applied mathematics, we have the contribution *Wavelet Energy Accumulation Method Applied on the Rio Papaloapan Bridge for Damage Identification*, by Jose M. Machorro-Lopez, Juan P. Amezquita-Sanchez, Martin Valtierra-Rodriguez, Francisco J. Carrion-Viramontes, Juan A. Quintana-Rodriguez, and Jesus I. Valenzuela-Delgado. The authors introduce a wavelet-based method to detect, locate and quantify damage in vehicular bridges, with potential applications to be further explored.

In the paper *Local Convergence of the Continuous and Semi-Discrete Wavelet Transform in $L^p(\mathbb{R})$*, the authors (namely, Jaime Navarro-Fuentes, Salvador Arellano-Balderas and Oscar Herrera-Alcántara) provide a nice characterization of the regularity of functions in standard Lebesgue spaces in terms of the local convergence of continuous and semi-discrete wavelet transforms.

Finally, the focus of the contribution entitled *Boundary Values in Ultradistribution Spaces Related to*

Extended Gevrey Regularity by Stevan Pilipović, Nenad Teofanov and Filip Tomić is on the design of novel intermediate spaces between those of Schwartz distributions and any space of Gevrey ultradistributions as boundary values of analytic functions. The non-trivial technical difficulties arising from this effort are handled in great detail by the authors.

There is reason for us to be very satisfied with the quality and the variety of these contributions. We take this occasion to thank the authors for responding to our call for papers, certain that their work will help to attract more attention to the manifold aspects and intriguing problems of microlocal and time-frequency analysis.

Elena Cordero, S. Ivan Trapasso
Editors

Article

On the Sharp Gårding Inequality for Operators with Polynomially Bounded and Gevrey Regular Symbols

Alexandre Arias Junior [1] and Marco Cappiello [2],*

1. Department of Mathematics, Federal University of Paraná, Curitiba 81531-980, Brazil; arias@ufpr.br
2. Department of Mathematics, University of Turin, Via Carlo Alberto 10, 10123 Turin, Italy
* Correspondence: marco.cappiello@unito.it

Received: 29 September 2020; Accepted: 29 October 2020; Published: 3 November 2020

Abstract: In this paper, we analyze the Friedrichs part of an operator with polynomially bounded symbol. Namely, we derive a precise expression of its asymptotic expansion. In the case of symbols satisfying Gevrey estimates, we also estimate precisely the regularity of the terms in the asymptotic expansion. These results allow new and refined applications of the sharp Gårding inequality in the study of the Cauchy problem for p-evolution equations.

Keywords: pseudodifferential operators; Gevrey regularity; sharp Gårding inequality; p-evolution equations

MSC: 35S05; 46F05; 35S10

---

1. Introduction

The sharp Gårding inequality for a pseudodifferential operator was first proved by Hörmander [1] and by Lax and Nirenberg [2] for symbols in the Kohn–Nirenberg class $S^m(\mathbb{R}^{2n})$, namely satisfying the following estimates

$$|\partial_\xi^\alpha \partial_x^\beta p(x,\xi)| \leq C_{\alpha\beta} \langle \xi \rangle^{m-|\alpha|}, \quad \alpha,\beta \in \mathbb{N}_0^n,$$

for some positive constant $C_{\alpha\beta}$, where $\langle \xi \rangle := \sqrt{1+|\xi|^2}$ for every $\xi \in \mathbb{R}^n$ and $\mathbb{N}_0^n$ stands for the set of all multi-indices of length n. In its original form, this result states that, if $p \in S^m(\mathbb{R}^{2n})$, for some $m \in \mathbb{R}$, is such that $\operatorname{Re} p(x,\xi) \geq 0$, then the corresponding operator $p(x,D)$ satisfies the following estimate

$$\operatorname{Re}(p(x,D)u,u)_{L^2} \geq -C\|u\|^2_{\frac{m-1}{2}}, \quad u \in \mathscr{S}(\mathbb{R}^n), \tag{1}$$

for some $C \in \mathbb{R}$, where $\|\cdot\|_{\frac{m-1}{2}}$ denotes the standard norm in the Sobolev space $H^{\frac{m-1}{2}}(\mathbb{R}^n)$. Later on, several different proofs and extensions of this result have been provided by many authors (cf. [3–6]). In particular, the inequality has been extended to symbols defined in terms of a general metric (cf. [4], Theorem 18.6.7) and to matrix valued pseudo-differential operators (cf. [4], Lemma 18.6.13, and [5], Theorem 4.4 page 134). In all the proofs of the sharp Gårding inequality, the operator $p(x,D)$ is decomposed as the sum of a positive definite part and a remainder term providing the inequality (1). In the approach proposed in [5], this positive definite part p_F is called *Friedrichs* part and satisfies the following conditions:

(i) $(p_F u, v)_{L^2} = (u, p_F v)_{L^2}$ if $p(x,\xi)$ is real;
(ii) $(p_F u, u)_{L^2} \geq 0$ if $p(x,\xi) \geq 0$; and
(iii) $\operatorname{Re}(p_F u, u)_{L^2} \geq 0$ if $\operatorname{Re} p(x,\xi) \geq 0$.

Although the results in [4] are extremely general and sharp, in some applications, more detailed information on the remainder term is needed. In particular, it is important to state not only the order

but also the asymptotic expansion of $p - p_F$. This is needed in particular in the analysis of the so called
p-evolution equations, namely equations of the form

$$D_t u + a_p(t) D_x^p + \sum_{j=0}^{p-1} a_j(t,x) D_x^j u = f(t,x), \qquad t \in [0,T], \qquad (2)$$

where p is a positive integer and $a_p(t)$ is a real valued function (cf. [7,8]). This large class of equations
includes for instance strictly hyperbolic equations ($p = 1$) and Schrödinger-type equations ($p = 2$).
The classical approach to study the Cauchy problem for these equations is based on a reduction
to an auxiliary problem via a suitable change of variable and on a repeated application of sharp
Gårding inequality which needs at every step to understand the precise form of all the remainder
terms (cf. [9]). When the coefficients $a_j(t,x)$ are uniformly bounded with respect to x, this is possible
using Theorem 4.2 in [5], where the asymptotic expansion of $p_F - p$ is given in the frame of classical
Kohn–Nirenberg classes. In this way, under suitable assumptions on the behavior of the coefficients
$a_j(t,x), j = 0, \ldots, p-1$, for $|x| \to \infty$, well posedness with loss of derivatives has been proved in
$H^\infty = \cap_{m \in \mathbb{R}} H^m$ (see [9]).

In fact, for equations of the form (2), the loss of derivatives can be avoided by choosing the data
of the Cauchy problem with a certain decay at infinity (cf. [10]). This motivated us to study the initial
value problem for (2) in a weighted functional setting admitting also polynomially bounded coefficients,
which cannot be treated in the theory of standard Kohn–Nirenberg classes but are included in the
so-called **SG** classes (see the definition below). For this purpose we need a variant of [5] (Theorem 4.2)
for **SG** operators with a precise information on the asymptotic expansion of $p - p_F$.

Another challenging issue is to study Equation (2) on Gelfand–Shilov spaces of type $\mathcal{S}$ (cf. [11]).
A first step in this direction has been done in the case $p = 2$, that is for Schrödinger-type equations
(see [12]), and for $p = 3$ (see [13]). In both cases, it is sufficient to apply the sharp Gårding inequality
only once. To treat p-evolution equations for $p > 3$, however, we need to apply the iterative procedure
described above. In addition, a precise estimate of the Gevrey regularity of the terms in the asymptotic
expansion of $p - p_F$ is also needed.

In this paper, we provide appropriate tools for both the aforementioned issues. This is achieved by
defining in a suitable way the Friedrichs part of our operators and by studying in detail its asymptotic
expansion and its regularity. With this purpose, we prove two separate results for the following classes
of symbols. Fixing $m = (m_1, m_2) \in \mathbb{R}^2$, we denote by $\mathbf{SG}^m(\mathbb{R}^{2n})$ the space of all functions $p \in C^\infty(\mathbb{R}^{2n})$
satisfying for any $\alpha, \beta \in \mathbb{N}_0^n$ the following condition

$$|\partial_\xi^\alpha \partial_x^\beta p(x,\xi)| \leq C_{\alpha\beta} \langle \xi \rangle^{m_1 - |\alpha|} \langle x \rangle^{m_2 - |\beta|}, \quad x, \xi \in \mathbb{R}^n, \qquad (3)$$

for some positive constant $C_{\alpha,\beta}$. These symbols have been treated by a large number of authors along
the years (see [14–21]). We are moreover interested in the subclass of $\mathbf{SG}^m(\mathbb{R}^{2n})$ given by the **SG**
symbols possessing a Gevrey-type regularity. Namely, for $\mu, \nu \geq 1$, we say that a symbol $p(x, \xi)$
belongs to the class $\mathbf{SG}^m_{(\mu,\nu)}(\mathbb{R}^{2n})$ if there are constants $C, C_1 > 0$ satisfying

$$|\partial_\xi^\alpha \partial_x^\beta p(x,\xi)| \leq C_1 C^{|\alpha|+|\beta|} \alpha!^\mu \beta!^\nu \langle \xi \rangle^{m_1 - |\alpha|} \langle x \rangle^{m_2 - |\beta|}, \qquad (4)$$

for every $\alpha, \beta \in \mathbb{N}_0^n, x, \xi \in \mathbb{R}^n$.

This work is organized as follows. In Section 2, we recall some results concerning **SG**
pseudodifferential operators. In Section 3, we discuss the concepts of oscillatory integrals and double
symbols, which are fundamental tools in the present work. Finally, in Section 4, we study the Friedrichs
part of symbols belonging to the classes $\mathbf{SG}^m$ and $\mathbf{SG}^m_{(\mu,\nu)}$ and we prove the main results of this paper,
namely Theorems 4 and 6.

2. SG Pseudodifferential Operators

In this section, we recall some basic facts about **SG** pseudodifferential operators which are used in the sequel. Although for our applications we are interested to prove the main results for the classes defined by inequalities (3) and (4), in order to prove them, we need to consider more general classes of symbols which are defined as follows.

Definition 1. *Given $m = (m_1, m_2) \in \mathbb{R}^2, \rho = (\rho_1, \rho_2) \in (0,1]^2, \delta = (\delta_1, \delta_2) \in [0,1)^2$, with $\delta_j < \rho_j, j = 1, 2$, we denote by $\mathbf{SG}^m_{\rho,\delta}$ the space of all functions $p \in C^\infty(\mathbb{R}^{2n})$ such that*

$$\sup_{(x,\xi) \in \mathbb{R}^{2n}} |\partial^\alpha_\xi \partial^\beta_x p(x,\xi)| \langle \xi \rangle^{-m_1 + \rho_1|\alpha| - \delta_1|\beta|} \langle x \rangle^{-m_2 + \rho_2|\beta| - \delta_2|\alpha|} < \infty. \quad (5)$$

We recall that $\mathbf{SG}^m_{\rho,\delta}$ is a Fréchet space endowed with the seminorms

$$|p|_\ell := \sup_{\substack{(x,\xi) \in \mathbb{R}^{2n} \\ |\alpha + \beta| \leq \ell}} |\partial^\alpha_\xi \partial^\beta_x p(x,\xi)| \langle \xi \rangle^{-m_1 + \rho_1|\alpha| - \delta_1|\beta|} \langle x \rangle^{-m_2 + \rho_2|\beta| - \delta_2|\alpha|},$$

for $\ell \in \mathbb{N}_0$. The class $\mathbf{SG}^m_{\rho,\delta}$ is included in the general theory by Hörmander [4]. A specific calculus for this class can be found in [22]. Pseudodifferential operators with symbols in $\mathbf{SG}^m_{\rho,\delta}$ are linear and continuous from $\mathscr{S}(\mathbb{R}^n)$ to $\mathscr{S}(\mathbb{R}^n)$ and extend to linear and continuous maps from $\mathscr{S}'(\mathbb{R}^n)$ to $\mathscr{S}'(\mathbb{R}^n)$. Moreover, denoting by $H^s(\mathbb{R}^n)$ with $s = (s_1, s_2) \in \mathbb{R}^2$ the weighted Sobolev space

$$H^s(\mathbb{R}^n) := \{u \in \mathscr{S}'(\mathbb{R}^n) : \langle x \rangle^{s_2} \langle D_x \rangle^{s_1} u \in L^2(\mathbb{R}^n)\},$$

we know that an operator with symbol in $\mathbf{SG}^m_{\rho,\delta}$ extends to a linear and continuous map from $H^s(\mathbb{R}^n)$ to $H^{s-m}(\mathbb{R}^n)$ for every $s \in \mathbb{R}^2$.

Definition 2. *Let, for $j \in \mathbb{N}_0$, $p_j \in SG^{(m_{1,j}, m_{2,j})}_{\rho,\delta}$, where $m_{1,j}, m_{2,j}$ are nonincreasing sequences and $m_{1,j} \to -\infty$, $m_{2,j} \to -\infty$, when $j \to \infty$. We say that $p \in C^\infty(\mathbb{R}^{2n})$ has the asymptotic expansion*

$$p(x,\xi) \sim \sum_{j \in \mathbb{N}_0} p_j(x,\xi)$$

if for any $N \in \mathbb{N}$ we have

$$p(x,\xi) - \sum_{j=0}^{N-1} p_j(x,\xi) \in SG^{(m_{1,N}, m_{2,N})}_{\rho,\delta}.$$

Given $p_j \in \mathbf{SG}^{(m_{1,j}, m_{2,j})}_{\rho,\delta}$ as in the previous definition, we can find $p \in \mathbf{SG}^{(m_{1,0}, m_{2,0})}_{\rho,\delta}$ such that $p \sim \sum p_j$. Furthermore, if there is q such that $q \sim \sum p_j$, then $p - q \in \mathbf{SG}^{-\infty} := \cap_{m \in \mathbb{R}^2} \mathbf{SG}^m_{\rho,\delta} = \mathscr{S}(\mathbb{R}^{2n})$ (cf. [22], Theorem 2). The class $\mathbf{SG}^m_{\rho,\delta}$ is closed under adjoints. Namely, given $p \in \mathbf{SG}^m_{\rho,\delta}$ and denoting by P^* the L^2 adjoint of $p(x, D)$, we can write $P^* = p^*(x, D) + R$, where p^* is a symbol in $\mathbf{SG}^m_{\rho,\delta}$ admitting the asymptotic expansion

$$p^*(x,\xi) \sim \sum_{\alpha \in \mathbb{N}_0^n} \alpha!^{-1} \partial^\alpha_\xi D^\alpha_x \overline{p(x,\xi)}$$

and $R : \mathscr{S}'(\mathbb{R}^n) \to \mathscr{S}(\mathbb{R}^n)$. The class $\mathbf{SG}_{\rho,\delta}^\infty := \cup_{m \in \mathbb{R}^2} \mathbf{SG}_{\rho,\delta}^m$ possesses algebra properties with respect to composition. Namely, given $p \in \mathbf{SG}_{\rho,\delta}^m$ and $q \in \mathbf{SG}_{\rho,\delta}^{m'}$, there exists a symbol $s \in \mathbf{SG}_{\rho,\delta}^{m+m'}$ such that $p(x,D)q(x,D) = s(x,D) + R'$ where R' is a smoothing operator $\mathscr{S}'(\mathbb{R}^n) \to \mathscr{S}(\mathbb{R}^n)$. Moreover,

$$s(x,\xi) \sim \sum_{\alpha \in \mathbb{N}_0^n} \alpha!^{-1} \partial_\xi^\alpha p(x,\xi) D_x^\alpha q(x,\xi)$$

(cf. [22], Theorem 3).

We now consider Gevrey regular symbols.

Definition 3. *Fixing $C > 0$, we denote by $\mathbf{SG}_{\rho,\delta;(\mu,\nu)}^m(\mathbb{R}^{2n}; C)$ the space of all smooth functions $p(x,\xi)$ such that*

$$|p|_C := \sup_{\alpha,\beta \in \mathbb{N}_0^n} C^{-|\alpha|-|\beta|} \alpha!^{-\mu} \beta!^{-\nu} \sup_{x,\xi \in \mathbb{R}^n} \langle \xi \rangle^{-m_1 + \rho_1|\alpha| - \delta_1|\beta|} \langle x \rangle^{-m_2 + \rho_2|\beta| - \delta_2|\alpha|} |\partial_\xi^\alpha \partial_x^\beta p(x,\xi)| < +\infty.$$

We set $\mathbf{SG}_{\rho,\delta;(\mu,\nu)}^m(\mathbb{R}^{2n}) = \cup_{C>0} \mathbf{SG}_{\rho,\delta;(\mu,\nu)}^m(\mathbb{R}^{2n}; C)$.

Equipping $\mathbf{SG}_{\rho,\delta;(\mu,\nu)}^m(\mathbb{R}^{2n}; C)$ with the norm $|\cdot|_C$ we obtain a Banach space and we can endow $\mathbf{SG}_{\rho,\delta;(\mu,\nu)}^m(\mathbb{R}^{2n})$ with the topology of inductive limit of Banach spaces. A complete calculus for operators with symbols in this class can be found in [23]. Here, we recall only the main results. Since $\mathbf{SG}_{\rho,\delta;(\mu,\nu)}^m \subset \mathbf{SG}_{\rho,\delta}^m$, the previous mapping properties on the Schwartz and weighted Sobolev spaces hold true for operators with symbols in $\mathbf{SG}_{\rho,\delta;(\mu,\nu)}^m$. By the way, the most natural functional setting for these operators is given by the Gelfand–Shilov spaces of type $\mathcal{S}$. We recall that, fixing $\mu > 0, \nu > 0$, the Gelfand–Shilov space $\mathcal{S}_\nu^\mu(\mathbb{R}^n)$ is defined as the space of all functions $f \in C^\infty(\mathbb{R}^n)$ such that for some constant $C > 0$

$$\sup_{\alpha,\beta \in \mathbb{N}_0^n} C^{-|\alpha+\beta|} (\alpha!)^{-\nu} (\beta!)^{-\mu} \sup_{x \in \mathbb{R}^n} |x^\alpha \partial^\beta f(x)| < +\infty. \tag{6}$$

For every $\mu' \geq \mu/(1-\delta_2), \nu' \geq \nu/(1-\delta_1)$, an operator with symbol in $\mathbf{SG}_{\rho,\delta;(\mu,\nu)}^m$ is linear and continuous from $\mathcal{S}_{\mu'}^{\nu'}(\mathbb{R}^n)$ to itself and extends to a linear continuous map from the dual space $(\mathcal{S}_{\mu'}^{\nu'})'(\mathbb{R}^n)$ into itself (see [23], Theorem A.4).

The notion of asymptotic expansion for symbols in $\mathbf{SG}_{\rho,\delta;(\mu,\nu)}^m$ can be defined in terms of formal sums (cf. [23]). Here, to obtain our results, we need to use a refined notion of formal sum introduced in [13] for the case $\rho = (1,1), \delta = (0,0)$. All the next statements can be transferred to the case of general ρ and δ without changing the argument, thus we refer to [13] for the proofs.
For $t_1, t_2 \geq 0$, set

$$Q_{t_1,t_2} = \{(x,\xi) \in \mathbb{R}^{2n} : \langle x \rangle < t_1 \text{ and } \langle \xi \rangle < t_2\}$$

and $Q_{t_1,t_2}^e = \mathbb{R}^{2n} \setminus Q_{t_1,t_2}$. When $t_1 = t_2 = t$, we simply write Q_t and Q_t^e.

Definition 4. *Let $\tilde{\sigma}_j = (k_j, \ell_j)$ be a sequence such that $k_0 = \ell_0 = 0$, k_j, ℓ_j are strictly increasing, $k_{j+N} \geq k_j + k_N$, $\ell_{j+N} \geq \ell_j + \ell_N$, for $j, N \in \mathbb{N}_0$, and $k_j \geq \Lambda_1 j, \ell_j \geq \Lambda_2 j$ for $j \geq 1$, for some $\Lambda_1, \Lambda_2 > 0$. We say that $\sum_{j \geq 0} p_j \in F_{\tilde{\sigma}} SG_{\rho,\delta;(\mu,\nu)}^m$ if $p_j \in C^\infty(\mathbb{R}^{2n})$ and there are $C, c, B > 0$ satisfying*

$$|\partial_\xi^\alpha \partial_x^\beta p_j(x,\xi)| \leq C^{|\alpha|+|\beta|+2j+1} \alpha!^\mu \beta!^\nu j!^{\mu+\nu-1} \langle \xi \rangle^{m_1 - \rho_1|\alpha|+\delta_1|\beta|-k_j} \langle x \rangle^{m_2 - \rho_2|\beta|+\delta_2|\alpha|-\ell_j}$$

for $\alpha, \beta \in \mathbb{N}_0^n, j \geq 0$ and $(x,\xi) \in Q_{B_2(j),B_1(j)}^e$, where $B_i(j) = (Bj^{\mu+\nu-1})^{\frac{1}{\Lambda_i}}, i = 1, 2$.

Definition 5. *Given* $\sum_{j\geq 0} p_j, \sum_{j\geq 0} q_j \in F_{\tilde{\sigma}}SG^m_{\mu,\nu}$, *we say that* $\sum_{j\geq 0} p_j \sim \sum_{j\geq 0} q_j$ *in* $F_{\tilde{\sigma}}SG^m_{\rho,\delta;(\mu,\nu)}$ *if there are* $C, c, B > 0$ *satisfying*

$$\left|\partial_\xi^\alpha \partial_x^\beta \sum_{j<N}(p_j - q_j)(x,\xi)\right| \leq C^{|\alpha|+|\beta|+2N+1}\alpha!^\mu \beta!^\nu N!^{\mu+\nu-1}\langle\xi\rangle^{m_1-\rho_1|\alpha|+\delta_1|\beta|-k_N}\langle x\rangle^{m_2-\rho_2|\beta|+\delta_2|\alpha|-\ell_N}$$

for $\alpha, \beta \in \mathbb{N}_0^n, N \geq 1$ *and* $(x,\xi) \in Q^\varrho_{B_2(N),B_1(N)}$.

Remark 1. *If* $k_j = (\rho_1 - \delta_1)j$, $\ell_j = (\rho_2 - \delta_2)j$ *and* $\Lambda_i = \rho_i - \delta_i, i = 1, 2$, *we simply write* $FSG^m_{\rho,\delta;(\mu,\nu)}$ *and we recover the usual definitions presented under different notation in* [23]. *If moreover* $\rho = (1,1), \delta = (0,0)$, *we use the notation* $FSG^m_{(\mu,\nu)}$.

Remark 2. *If* $\sum_{j\geq 0} p_j \in F_{\tilde{\sigma}}SG^m_{\rho,\delta;(\mu,\nu)}$, *then* $p_0 \in SG^m_{\rho,\delta;(\mu,\nu)}$. *Given* $p \in SG^m_{\rho,\delta;(\mu,\nu)}$ *and setting* $p_0 = p$, $p_j = 0$, $j \geq 1$, *we have* $p = \sum_{j\geq 0} p_j$. *Hence, we can consider* $SG^m_{\rho,\delta;(\mu,\nu)}$ *as a subset of* $F_{\tilde{\sigma}}SG^m_{\rho,\delta;(\mu,\nu)}$.

Proposition 1. *Given* $\sum_{j\geq 0} p_j \in F_{\tilde{\sigma}}SG^m_{\rho,\delta;(\mu,\nu)}$, *there exists* $p \in SG^m_{\rho,\delta;(\mu,\nu)}$ *such that* $p \sim \sum_{j\geq 0} p_j$ *in* $F_{\tilde{\sigma}}SG^m_{\rho,\delta;(\mu,\nu)}$.

Proposition 2. *Let* $p \in SG^{(0,0)}_{\rho,\delta;(\mu,\nu)}$ *such that* $p \sim 0$ *in* $F_{\tilde{\sigma}}SG^{(0,0)}_{\rho,\delta;(\mu,\nu)}$. *Then,* $p \in \mathcal{S}_r(\mathbb{R}^{2n})$ *for* $r \geq \max\{\frac{1}{\tilde{\Lambda}}(\mu + \nu - 1), \mu + \nu - 1\}$, *where* $\tilde{\Lambda} = \min\{\Lambda_1, \Lambda_2\}$.

Proposition 3. *Let* $p \in SG^m_{\rho,\delta;(\mu,\nu)}$ *and let* P^* *be the* L^2 *adjoint of* $p(x,D)$. *Then, there exists a symbol* $p^* \in SG^m_{\rho,\delta;(\mu,\nu)}$ *such that* $P^* = p^*(x,D) + R$, *where* R *is a* $\mathcal{S}_r$-*regularizing operator for any* $r \geq \frac{\mu+\nu-1}{\min\{\varrho_1-\delta_1,\varrho_2-\delta_2\}}$. *Moreover,*

$$p^*(x,\xi) \sim \sum_{j\geq 0}\sum_{|\alpha|=j} \alpha!^{-1}\partial_\xi^\alpha D_x^\alpha \overline{p(x,\xi)} \quad \text{in} \quad FSG^m_{\rho,\delta;(\mu,\nu)}.$$

Proposition 4. *Let* $p \in SG^m_{\rho,\delta;(\mu,\nu)}, q \in SG^{m'}_{\rho,\delta;(\mu,\nu)}$. *Then, there exists a symbol* $s \in SG^{m+m'}_{\rho,\delta;(\mu,\nu)}$ *such that* $p(x,D)q(x,D) = s(x,D) + R'$ *where* R' *is a* $\mathcal{S}_r$-*regularizing operator for any* $r \geq \frac{\mu+\nu-1}{\min\{\varrho_1-\delta_1,\varrho_2-\delta_2\}}$. *Moreover,*

$$s(x,\xi) \sim \sum_{j\geq 0}\sum_{|\alpha|=j} \alpha!^{-1}\partial_\xi^\alpha p(x,\xi) D_x^\alpha q(x,\xi) \quad \text{in} \quad FSG^{m+m'}_{\rho,\delta;(\mu,\nu)}.$$

3. Oscillatory Integrals and Operators with Double Symbols

To define the Friedrichs part of an operator, it is necessary to extend the notion of pseudodifferential operator as in [5] by considering more general symbols called *double symbols*. Quantizations of these symbols are defined as oscillatory integrals.

3.1. Amplitudes and Oscillatory Integrals

Definition 6 (Amplitudes). *For* $m \in \mathbb{R}^2$ *and* $\delta \in [0,1)^2$, *we define* $\mathcal{A}^m_\delta(\mathbb{R}^{2n})$ *as the space of all smooth functions* $a(\eta, y)$ *such that*

$$|\partial_\eta^\alpha \partial_y^\beta a(\eta, y)| \leq C_{\alpha,\beta}\langle\eta\rangle^{m_1+\delta_1|\beta|}\langle y\rangle^{m_2+\delta_2|\alpha|}, \quad \eta, y \in \mathbb{R}^n.$$

For $\ell \in \mathbb{N}_0$ *and* $a \in \mathcal{A}^m_\delta(\mathbb{R}^{2n})$, *the seminorms*

$$|a|_\ell = \max_{|\alpha+\beta|\leq \ell} \sup_{\eta,y\in\mathbb{R}^n} \{|\partial_\eta^\alpha \partial_y^\beta a(\eta,y)|\langle\eta\rangle^{-(m_1+\delta_1|\beta|)}\langle y\rangle^{-(m_2+\delta_2|\alpha|)}\},$$

turn $\mathcal{A}^m_\delta(\mathbb{R}^{2n})$ into a Fréchet space.

Remark 3. *In [5] (Chapter 1, Section 6), the special case $\mathcal{A}^{(m,\tau)}_{(\delta,0)}(\mathbb{R}^n)$, where $m \in \mathbb{R}$, $\tau > 0$ and $\delta \in [0,1)$, is treated.*

Definition 7 (Oscillatory Integral). *For $a \in \mathcal{A}^m_{\delta,\tau}$, we define*

$$Os - [e^{-i\eta y} a(\eta,y)] = Os - \iint e^{-i\eta y} a(\eta,y) dy d\eta$$
$$:= \lim_{\varepsilon \to 0} \iint e^{-i\eta y} \chi_\varepsilon(\eta,y) a(\eta,y) dy d\eta,$$

where $\chi_\varepsilon(\eta,y) = \chi(\varepsilon\eta,\varepsilon y)$ and χ is a Schwartz function on $\mathbb{R}^{2n}$ such that $\chi(0,0) = 1$.

Theorem 1. *Let $a \in \mathcal{A}^m_\delta(\mathbb{R}^{2n})$. If $\ell, \ell' \in \mathbb{N}_0$ satisfy*

$$-2\ell(1-\delta_1) + m_1 < -n, \quad -2\ell'(1-\delta_2) + m_2 < -n,$$

then $|\langle y \rangle^{-2\ell'} \langle D_\eta \rangle^{2\ell'} \{\langle \eta \rangle^{-2\ell} \langle D_y \rangle^{2\ell} a(\eta,y)\}|$ belongs to $L^1(\mathbb{R}^{2n})$ and we have

$$Os - [e^{-i\eta y} a(\eta,y)] = \iint e^{-i\eta y} \langle y \rangle^{-2\ell'} \langle D_\eta \rangle^{2\ell'} \{\langle \eta \rangle^{-2\ell} \langle D_y \rangle^{2\ell} a(\eta,y)\} dy d\eta.$$

Furthermore, there is $C_{\ell,\ell'} > 0$ independent of $a \in \mathcal{A}^m_{\delta,\tau}(\mathbb{R}^{2n})$ such that

$$|Os - [e^{-i\eta y} a(\eta,y)]| \leq C_{\ell,\ell'} |a|_{2(\ell+\ell')}. \tag{7}$$

Proof. Integration by parts gives

$$Os - [e^{-i\eta y} a] = \lim_{\varepsilon \to 0} \iint e^{-i\eta y} \langle y \rangle^{-2\ell'} \langle D_\eta \rangle^{2\ell'} \{\langle \eta \rangle^{-2\ell} \langle D_y \rangle^{2\ell} (a\chi_\varepsilon)\} dy d\eta,$$

where $\chi_\varepsilon(\eta,y) = \chi(\varepsilon\eta,\varepsilon y)$. Since

$$\langle D_\eta \rangle^{2\ell'} = \sum_{\ell'_0+|L'|=\ell'} \frac{\ell'!}{\ell'_0! L'!} D_\eta^{2L'}, \quad \langle D_y \rangle^{2\ell} = \sum_{\ell_0+|L|=\ell} \frac{\ell!}{\ell_0! L!} D_y^{2L},$$

where $L' = (\ell'_1, \ldots, \ell'_n)$ and $L = (\ell_1, \ldots, \ell_n)$, we have

$$\langle D_\eta \rangle^{2\ell'} \{\langle \eta \rangle^{-2\ell} \langle D_y \rangle^{2\ell} (\chi_\varepsilon a)\} = \sum_{\ell'_0+|L'|=\ell'} \frac{\ell'!}{\ell'_0! L'!} D_\eta^{2L'} \{\langle \eta \rangle^{-2\ell} \langle D_y \rangle^{2\ell} (\chi_\varepsilon a)\}$$

$$= \sum_{\ell'_0+|L'|=\ell'} \frac{\ell'!}{\ell'_0! L'!} \sum_{\alpha_1+\alpha_2=2L'} \frac{(2L')!}{\alpha_1! \alpha_2!} D_\eta^{\alpha_1} \langle \eta \rangle^{-2\ell} \cdot D_\eta^{\alpha_2} \langle D_y \rangle^{2\ell} (\chi_\varepsilon a)$$

$$= \sum_{\ell'_0+|L'|=\ell'} \frac{\ell'!}{\ell'_0! L'!} \sum_{\alpha_1+\alpha_2=2L'} \frac{(2L')!}{\alpha_1! \alpha_2!} D_\eta^{\alpha_1} \langle \eta \rangle^{-2\ell}$$

$$\times \sum_{\ell_0+|L|=\ell} \frac{\ell!}{\ell_0! L!} D_\eta^{\alpha_2} D_y^{2L} (\chi_\varepsilon a)$$

$$= \sum_{\ell'_0+|L'|=\ell'} \frac{\ell'!}{\ell'_0! L'!} \sum_{\alpha_1+\alpha_2=2L'} \frac{(2L')!}{\alpha_1! \alpha_2!} D_\eta^{\alpha_1} \langle \eta \rangle^{-2\ell} \sum_{\ell_0+|L|=\ell} \frac{\ell!}{\ell_0! L!}$$

$$\times \sum_{\alpha'_1+\alpha'_2=\alpha_2} \sum_{\beta_1+\beta_2=2L} \frac{\alpha_2!}{\alpha'_1! \alpha'_2!} \frac{(2L)!}{\beta_1! \beta_2!} D_\eta^{\alpha'_1} D_y^{\beta_1} \chi_\varepsilon D_\eta^{\alpha'_2} D_y^{\beta_2} a.$$

Hence, we obtain the following estimates, for ε in $[0,1]$,

$$|\langle D_\eta\rangle^{2\ell'}\{\langle\eta\rangle^{-2\ell}\langle D_y\rangle^{2\ell}(\chi_\varepsilon a)\}|\leq \sum_{\ell'_0+|L'|=\ell'}\frac{\ell'!}{\ell'_0!L'!}\sum_{\alpha_1+\alpha_2=2L'}\frac{(2L')!}{\alpha_1!\alpha_2!}$$

$$\times C_0^{|\alpha_1|+1}\alpha_1!\langle\eta\rangle^{-2\ell-|\alpha_1|}\sum_{\ell_0+|L|=\ell}\frac{\ell!}{\ell_0!L!}\sum_{\alpha'_1+\alpha'_2=\alpha_2}\sum_{\beta_1+\beta_2=2L}\frac{\alpha_2!}{\alpha'_1!\alpha'_2!}\frac{(2L)!}{\beta_1!\beta_2!}$$

$$\times \varepsilon^{|\alpha'_1+\beta_1|}C_\chi^{|\alpha'_1|+|\beta_1|+1}\alpha'_1!^\mu\beta_1!^\nu|a|_{|\alpha'_2+\beta_2|}\langle\eta\rangle^{m_1+\delta_1|\beta_2|}\langle y\rangle^{m_2+\delta_2|\alpha'_2|}$$

$$\leq C_{\ell,\ell'}|a|_{2(\ell+\ell')}\langle\eta\rangle^{m-2\ell(1-\delta_1)}\langle y\rangle^{m_2+2\ell'\delta_2},$$

and

$$\langle y\rangle^{-2\ell'}|\langle D_\eta\rangle^{2\ell'}\{\langle\eta\rangle^{-2\ell}\langle D_y\rangle^{2\ell}(\chi_\varepsilon a)\}|$$

$$\leq C_{\ell,\ell'}|a|_{2(\ell+\ell')}\langle\eta\rangle^{m_1-2\ell(1-\delta_1)}\langle y\rangle^{m_2-2\ell'(1-\delta_2)}.$$

Finally, by Lemma 6.3 on Page 47 of [5] and Lebesgue dominated convergence theorem, we obtain

$$Os - [e^{-i\eta y}a] = \iint e^{-i\eta y}\langle y\rangle^{-2\ell'}\langle D_\eta\rangle^{2\ell'}\{\langle\eta\rangle^{-2\ell}\langle D_y\rangle^{2\ell}a\}dy\mathchar'26\mkern-12mud\eta,$$

$$|Os - [e^{-i\eta y}a]| \leq C_{\ell,\ell'}|a|_{2(\ell+\ell')}\iint \langle\eta\rangle^{m_1-2\ell(1-\delta_1)}\langle y\rangle^{m_2-2\ell'(1-\delta_2)}dy\mathchar'26\mkern-12mud\eta.$$

□

Following the ideas in the proofs of Theorems 6.7 and 6.8 of [5] (Chapter 1, Section 6), one can obtain the following result.

Proposition 5. *Let $a \in \mathcal{A}^m_\delta(\mathbb{R}^{2n})$, $\alpha, \beta \in \mathbb{N}_0$ and $\eta_0, y_0 \in \mathbb{R}^n$. Then,*

(i) $Os - [e^{-i\eta y}y^\alpha a] = Os - [(-D_\eta)^\alpha e^{-i\eta y}a] = Os - [e^{-i\eta y}D_\eta^\alpha a];$

(ii) $Os - [e^{-i\eta y}\eta^\beta a] = Os - [(-D_y)^\beta e^{-i\eta y}a] = Os - [e^{-i\eta y}D_y^\beta a];$ and

(iii) $Os - [e^{-i\eta y}a(\eta, y)] = Os - [e^{-i(\eta-\eta_0)(y-y_0)}a(\eta-\eta_0, y-y_0)].$

3.2. Operators with Double Symbols

Definition 8. *Let $m = (m_1, m_2), m' = (m'_1, m'_2) \in \mathbb{R}^2$ and $\rho = (\rho_1, \rho_2), \delta = (\delta_1, \delta_2)$ such that $0 \leq \delta_j < \rho_j \leq 1, j = 1, 2$. We denote by $\mathbf{SG}^{m,m'}_{\rho,\delta}(\mathbb{R}^{4n})$ the space of all functions $p \in C^\infty(\mathbb{R}^{4n})$ such that for any $\alpha, \alpha', \beta, \beta' \in \mathbb{N}_0^n$ there is $C^{\alpha',\beta'}_{\alpha,\beta} > 0$ for which*

$$|p^{\alpha,\alpha'}_{\beta,\beta'}(x,\xi,x',\xi')| \leq C^{\alpha',\beta'}_{\alpha,\beta}\langle\xi\rangle^{m_1-\rho_1|\alpha|}\langle\xi'\rangle^{m'_1-\rho_1|\alpha'|}\langle\xi;\xi'\rangle^{\delta_1|\beta+\beta'|}\langle x\rangle^{m_2-\rho_2|\beta|}\langle x'\rangle^{m'_2-\rho_2|\beta'|}\langle x;x'\rangle^{\delta_2|\alpha+\alpha'|} \quad (8)$$

for every $x, x', \xi, \xi' \in \mathbb{R}^n$, where $p^{\alpha,\alpha'}_{\beta,\beta'} = \partial^\alpha_\xi \partial^{\alpha'}_{\xi'} D^\beta_x D^{\beta'}_{x'} p$ and $\langle z; z'\rangle = \sqrt{1+|z|^2+|z'|^2}$ for $z, z' \in \mathbb{R}^n$.

Denoting by $|p|^{m,m'}_{\alpha,\alpha',\beta,\beta'}$ the supremum over $x, \xi, x', \xi' \in \mathbb{R}^n$ of

$$|p^{\alpha,\alpha'}_{\beta,\beta'}(x,\xi,x',\xi')|\langle\xi\rangle^{-m_1+\rho_1|\alpha|}\langle\xi'\rangle^{-m'_1+\rho_1|\alpha'|}\langle\xi;\xi'\rangle^{-\delta_1|\beta+\beta'|}\langle x\rangle^{-m_2+\rho_2|\beta|}\langle x'\rangle^{-m'_2+\rho_2|\beta'|}\langle x;x'\rangle^{-\delta_2|\alpha+\alpha'|},$$

the space $\mathbf{SG}^{m,m'}_{\rho,\delta}$ is a Fréchet space whose topology is defined by the family of seminorms

$$|p|^{m,m'}_\ell := \sup_{|\alpha+\beta+\alpha'+\beta'|\leq\ell}|p|^{m,m'}_{\alpha,\alpha',\beta,\beta'}.$$

Definition 9. Let $m = (m_1, m_2), m' = (m_1', m_2') \in \mathbb{R}^2$, $\rho = (\rho_1, \rho_2)$, $\delta = (\delta_1, \delta_2)$ such that $0 \leq \delta_j < \rho_j \leq 1, j = 1, 2$, and let $\mu, \nu \geq 1$. We denote by $\mathbf{SG}_{\rho,\delta;(\mu,\nu)}^{m,m'}(\mathbb{R}^{4n})$ the space of all functions $p \in C^\infty(\mathbb{R}^{4n})$ such that for some $C > 0$:

$$|p_{\beta,\beta'}^{\alpha,\alpha'}(x,\xi,x',\xi')| \leq C^{|\alpha+\beta+\alpha'+\beta'|}(\alpha!\alpha'!)^\mu (\beta!\beta'!)^\nu \langle\xi\rangle^{m_1-\rho_1|\alpha|} \langle\xi'\rangle^{m_1'-\rho_1|\alpha'|} \langle\xi;\xi'\rangle^{\delta_1|\beta+\beta'|} \quad (9)$$
$$\times \langle x\rangle^{m_2-\rho_2|\beta|} \langle x'\rangle^{m_2'-\rho_2|\beta'|} \langle x;x'\rangle^{\delta_2|\alpha+\alpha'|}.$$

For $C > 0$, the space $\mathbf{SG}_{\rho,\delta;(\mu,\nu)}^{m,m'}(\mathbb{R}^{4n};C)$ of all smooth functions $p(x,\xi,x',\xi')$, such that (9) holds for a fixed $C > 0$, is a Banach space with norm

$$|p|_C^{m,m'} := \sup_{\alpha,\alpha',\beta,\beta' \in \mathbb{N}_0^n} C^{-|\alpha+\alpha'+\beta+\beta'|}(\alpha!\alpha'!)^{-\mu}(\beta!\beta'!)^{-\nu}|p|_{\alpha,\alpha',\beta,\beta'}^{m,m'}.$$

After that, we define $\mathbf{SG}_{\rho,\delta;(\mu,\nu)}^{m,m'} = \bigcup_{C>0} \mathbf{SG}_{\rho,\delta;(\mu,\nu)}^{m,m'}(\mathbb{R}^{4n};C)$ as an inductive limit of Banach spaces.

Definition 10. For $p \in \mathbf{SG}_{\rho,\delta}^{m,m'}$, we define

$$p(x, D_x, x', D_{x'}) u(x) := \int e^{i\xi(x-x')} e^{i\xi'(x'-x'')} p(x,\xi,x',\xi') u(x'') dx'' d\xi' dx' d\xi$$
$$= \int e^{i\xi(x-x')} e^{i\xi'x'} p(x,\xi,x',\xi') \hat{u}(\xi') d\xi' dx' d\xi,$$

for every $u \in \mathscr{S}(\mathbb{R}^n)$.

Lemma 1. Let $p \in \mathbf{SG}_{\rho,(0,\delta_2)}^{m,m'}(\mathbb{R}^{4n})$. For any multi-indices $\alpha, \alpha', \beta, \beta'$, set $q = p_{\beta,\beta'}^{\alpha,\alpha'}$, and, for $\theta \in [-1,1]$, define

$$q_\theta(x,\xi) = Os - \iint e^{-i\eta y} q(x, \xi + \theta\eta, x+y, \xi) dy d\eta, \quad x, \xi \in \mathbb{R}^n.$$

Then, $\{q_\theta\}_{|\theta| \leq 1}$ is bounded in $\mathbf{SG}_{\rho,(0,\delta_2)}^{\tau}(\mathbb{R}^{2n})$, where $\tau = (\tau_1, \tau_2)$, $\tau_1 = m_1 + m_1' - \rho_1|\alpha + \alpha'|$, $\tau_2 = m_2 + m_2' - \rho_2|\beta + \beta'| + \delta_2|\alpha + \alpha'|$. Furthermore, for any $\ell \in \mathbb{N}_0$, there are $\ell' := \ell'(\ell) \in \mathbb{N}_0$ and $C_{\ell,\ell'} > 0$ independent of θ such that

$$|q_\theta|_\ell^\tau \leq C_{\ell,\ell'} |p|_{\ell'}^{m,m'}.$$

Proof. First, notice that $q(x, \xi + \theta\eta, x+y, \xi) \in \mathcal{A}_{(0,\delta_2)}^{(m_1, m_2' + \delta_2|\alpha+\alpha'|)}(\mathbb{R}_{\eta,y}^{2n})$, therefore $q_\theta(x,\xi)$ is well defined for any fixed ξ, x, θ. Given $\gamma, \mu \in \mathbb{N}_0^n$, we may write, omitting the variables $(x, \xi + \theta\eta, x+y, \xi)$,

$$\partial_x^\gamma \partial_\xi^\mu q = \sum_{\substack{\mu' \leq \mu \\ \gamma' \leq \gamma}} \frac{\mu!}{\mu'!(\mu-\mu')!} \frac{\gamma!}{\gamma'!(\gamma-\gamma')!} p_{(\beta+\gamma',\beta'+\gamma-\gamma')}^{(\alpha+\mu',\alpha'+\mu-\mu')}. \quad (10)$$

To prove that $\{q_\theta\}_{|\theta| \leq 1}$ is bounded in $\mathbf{SG}_{\rho,(0,\delta_2)}^{\tau}(\mathbb{R}^{2n})$, it is sufficient to show that

$$|q_\theta(x,\xi)| \leq C_1 |p|_{\ell_1}^{m,m'} \langle\xi\rangle^{\tau_1} \langle x\rangle^{\tau_2} \quad (11)$$

for some $C_1 > 0$ and $\ell_1 \in \mathbb{N}_0$ depending on $\alpha, \beta, \alpha', \beta'$. Indeed, if (11) holds, then we can estimate the derivatives of q_θ as follows:

$$\begin{aligned}
|\partial_x^\gamma \partial_\xi^\mu q_\theta(x,\xi)| &= \left| Os - \iint e^{-iy\eta} \partial_x^\gamma \partial_\xi^\mu q(x, \xi + \theta\eta, x+y, \xi) dy d\eta \right| \\
&\leq \sum_{\substack{\gamma' \leq \gamma \\ \mu' \leq \mu}} \binom{\mu}{\mu'}\binom{\gamma}{\gamma'} \left| Os - \iint e^{-iy\eta} p_{(\beta+\gamma', \beta'+\gamma-\gamma')}^{(\alpha+\mu', \alpha'+\mu-\mu')}(x, \xi+\theta\eta, x+y, \xi) dy d\eta \right| \\
&\leq \sum_{\substack{\gamma' \leq \gamma \\ \mu' \leq \mu}} \binom{\mu}{\mu'}\binom{\gamma}{\gamma'} C_1(\alpha, \alpha', \beta, \beta', \gamma, \mu) |p|_{\ell_1}^{m,m'} \\
&\quad \times \langle \xi \rangle^{m_1+m_1'-\rho_1|\alpha+\mu'+\alpha'+\mu-\mu'|} \langle x \rangle^{m_2+m_2'-\rho_2|\beta+\gamma'+\beta'+\gamma-\gamma'|+\delta_2|\alpha+\mu'+\alpha'+\mu-\mu'|} \\
&\leq C|p|_{\ell_1}^{m,m'} \langle \xi \rangle^{m_1+m_1'-\rho_1|\alpha+\alpha'+\mu|} \langle x \rangle^{m_2+m_2'-\rho_2|\beta+\beta'+\gamma|+\delta_2|\alpha+\alpha'+\mu|}
\end{aligned}$$

where C and ℓ_1 depend of $\alpha, \alpha', \beta, \beta', \gamma, \mu$ and does not depend of θ.

Now, we show that (11) holds true. Observe that

$$e^{-iy\eta} = (1 + \langle x \rangle^{2\delta_2}|\eta|^2)^{-\ell}(1 - \langle x \rangle^{2\delta_2}\Delta_y)^\ell e^{-iy\eta},$$

therefore

$$q_\theta(x,\xi) = Os - \iint e^{-iy\eta} r_\theta(x, \xi; \eta, y) dy d\eta,$$

where

$$r_\theta(x, \xi; \eta, y) = (1 + \langle x \rangle^{2\delta_2}|\eta|^2)^{-\ell}(1 - \langle x \rangle^{2\delta_2}\Delta_y)^\ell q(x, \xi+\theta\eta, x+y, \xi).$$

If we take ℓ satisfying $2\ell > |m_1| + n$, then r_θ is integrable with respect to η. Now, consider a cutoff function $\chi(y)$ such that $\chi(y) = 1$ for $|y| \leq 4^{-1}\langle x \rangle$ and $\chi(y) = 0$ for $|y| \geq 2^{-1}\langle x \rangle$. Then, we can write

$$Os - \iint e^{-iy\eta} r_\theta(x, \xi; \eta, y) dy d\eta = I_1 + I_2 + I_3,$$

where

$$I_1 = \int_{\mathbb{R}_\eta^n} \int_{|y| \leq 4^{-1}\langle x \rangle^{\delta_2}} e^{-iy\eta} r_\theta(x, \xi; \eta, y) \chi(y) dy d\eta,$$

$$I_2 = \int_{\mathbb{R}_\eta^n} \int_{4^{-1}\langle x \rangle^{\delta_2} \leq |y| \leq 2^{-1}\langle x \rangle} e^{-iy\eta} r_\theta(x, \xi; \eta, y) \chi(y) dy d\eta,$$

$$I_3 = Os - [e^{-iy\eta} r_\theta(x, \xi; \eta, y)(1 - \chi(y))].$$

Let us obtain a useful inequality when $|y| \leq 2^{-1}\langle x \rangle$. Since

$$|\langle x+y \rangle - \langle x \rangle| \leq \int_0^1 \left| \frac{d}{dt} \langle x+ty \rangle \right| dt \leq \int_0^1 |y| \frac{|x+ty|}{\langle x+ty \rangle} dt \leq |y|,$$

for $|y| \leq 2^{-1}\langle x \rangle$, we have

$$\frac{1}{2}\langle x \rangle \leq \langle x+y \rangle \leq \frac{3}{2}\langle x \rangle, \quad \langle x; x+y \rangle \leq \langle x \rangle + |x+y| \leq \frac{5}{2}\langle x \rangle.$$

Now, we proceed to estimate I_1, I_2, I_3. We begin with I_1. With aid of Petree's inequality and using the fact that $\rho_2 > \delta_2$, we obtain, for $|y| \leq 4^{-1}\langle x \rangle^{\delta_2}$ and $|\theta| \leq 1$,

$$|r_\theta(x,\xi;\eta,y)| \leq (1+\langle x\rangle^{2\delta_2}|\eta|^2)^{-\ell} \sum_{\ell_0+|L|=\ell} \frac{\ell!}{\ell_0! L!} \langle x\rangle^{2\delta_2|L|} |p^{(\alpha,\alpha')}_{(\beta,\beta'+2L)}|$$

$$\leq (1+\langle x\rangle^{2\delta_2}|\eta|^2)^{-\ell} \langle x\rangle^{2\delta_2|L|} \sum_{\ell_0+|L|=\ell} \frac{\ell!}{\ell_0! L!} |p|^{m,m'}_{|\alpha+\alpha'|+\beta+\beta'|+2\ell}$$

$$\times \langle \xi+\theta\eta\rangle^{m_1-\rho_1|\alpha|} \langle \xi\rangle^{m'_1-\rho_1|\alpha'|} \langle x\rangle^{m_2-\rho_2|\beta|} \langle x+y\rangle^{m'_2-\rho_2|\beta'|+2L} \langle x;x+y\rangle^{\delta_2|\alpha+\alpha'|}$$

$$\leq C^k |p|^{m,m'}_k \langle \xi\rangle^{\tau_1} \langle x\rangle^{\tau_2} (1+\langle x\rangle^{2\delta_2}|\eta|^2)^{-\ell} \langle \eta\rangle^{|m_1|+\rho_1|\alpha|},$$

where $k = |\alpha+\beta+\alpha'+\beta'|+2\ell$. Therefore, for $2\ell > |m_1|+\rho_1|\alpha|+n$,

$$|I_1| = \left| \int_{\mathbb{R}^n_\eta} \int_{|y|\leq 4^{-1}\langle x\rangle^{\delta_2}} e^{-iy\eta} r_\theta(x,\xi;\eta,y) \chi(y) dy d\eta \right|$$

$$\leq C^k |p|^{m,m'}_k \langle \xi\rangle^{\tau_1} \langle x\rangle^{\tau_2} \int (1+\langle x\rangle^{2\delta_2}|\eta|^2)^{-\ell} \langle \eta\rangle^{|m_1|+\rho_1|\alpha|} d\eta \int_{|y|\leq \frac{\langle x\rangle^{\delta_2}}{4}} dy$$

$$\leq C^k |p|^{m,m'}_k \langle \xi\rangle^{\tau_1} \langle x\rangle^{\tau_2} \int \langle \eta\rangle^{-2\ell} \langle \langle x\rangle^{-\delta_2}\eta\rangle^{|m_1|+\rho_1|\alpha|} d\eta \int_{|y|\leq \frac{\langle x\rangle^{\delta_2}}{4}} \langle x\rangle^{-\delta_2 n} dy$$

$$\leq C^k |p|^{m,m'}_k \langle \xi\rangle^{\tau_1} \langle x\rangle^{\tau_2} \int \langle \eta\rangle^{-2\ell+|m_1|+\rho_1|\alpha|} d\eta \prod_{j=1}^n \int_{|y_j|\leq \frac{\langle x\rangle^{\delta_2}}{4}} \langle x\rangle^{-\delta_2 n} dy_j$$

$$\leq C^k \int \langle \eta\rangle^{-n} d\eta |p|^{m,m'}_k \langle \xi\rangle^{\tau_1} \langle x\rangle^{\tau_2}.$$

To estimate I_2 and I_3, it is useful to study $|\Delta^{\ell_1}_\eta r_\theta|$. We have

$$|\Delta^{\ell_1}_\eta r_\theta| \leq \sum_{|Q|=\ell_1} \frac{\ell_1!}{Q!} \sum_{Q_1+Q_2=2Q} \frac{(2Q)!}{Q_1! Q_2!} |\partial^{Q_1}_\eta (1+\langle x\rangle^{2\delta_2}|\eta|^2)^{-\ell}| \cdot |(1-\langle x\rangle^{2\delta_2}\Delta_y)^\ell \partial^{Q_2}_\eta q|$$

$$\leq \sum_{|Q|=\ell_1} \frac{\ell_1!}{Q!} \sum_{Q_1+Q_2=2Q} \frac{(2Q)!}{Q_1! Q_2!} C^{|Q_1|+\ell+1} \langle x\rangle^{\delta_2|Q_1|} Q_1! (1+\langle x\rangle^{2\delta_2}|\eta|^2)^{-\ell-|Q_1|} |\theta|^{|Q_2|}$$

$$\times |(1-\langle x\rangle^{2\delta_2}\Delta_y)^\ell p^{(\alpha+Q_2,\alpha')}_{(\beta,\beta')}|.$$

Noticing that

$$|(1-\langle x\rangle^{2\delta_2}\Delta_y)^\ell p^{(\alpha+Q_2,\alpha')}_{(\beta,\beta')}| \leq \sum_{\ell_0+|L|=\ell} \frac{\ell!}{\ell_0! L!} \langle x\rangle^{2\delta_2|L|} |p^{(\alpha+Q_2,\alpha')}_{(\beta,\beta'+2L)}|$$

$$\leq \sum_{\ell_0+|L|=\ell} \frac{\ell!}{\ell_0! L!} \langle x\rangle^{2\delta_2|L|} |p|^{m,m'}_{\tilde{k}} \langle \xi+\theta\eta\rangle^{m_1-\rho_1|\alpha+Q_2|} \langle \xi\rangle^{m'_1-\rho_1|\alpha'|}$$

$$\times \langle x\rangle^{m_2-\rho_2|\beta|} \langle x+y\rangle^{m'_2-\rho_2|\beta'|+2L} \langle x;x+y\rangle^{\delta_2|\alpha+\alpha'+Q_2|},$$

where $\tilde{k} = |\alpha+\alpha'+\beta+\beta'|+2(\ell_1+\ell)$, we obtain

$$|\Delta^{\ell_1}_\eta r_\theta| \leq \sum_{|Q|=\ell_1} \frac{\ell_1!}{Q!} \sum_{Q_1+Q_2=2Q} \frac{(2Q)!}{Q_1! Q_2!} C^{|Q_1|+\ell+1} \langle x\rangle^{\delta_2|Q_1|} Q_1!$$

$$\times (1+\langle x\rangle^{2\delta_2}|\eta|^2)^{-\ell-|Q_1|} \sum_{\ell_0+|L|=\ell} \frac{\ell!}{\ell_0! L!} \langle x\rangle^{2\delta_2|L|} |p|^{m,m'}_{\tilde{k}} \langle \xi+\theta\eta\rangle^{m_1-\rho_1|\alpha+Q_2|}$$

$$\times \langle \xi\rangle^{m'_1-\rho_1|\alpha'|} \langle x\rangle^{m_2-\rho_2|\beta|} \langle x+y\rangle^{m'_2-\rho_2|\beta'|+2L} \langle x;x+y\rangle^{\delta_2|\alpha+\alpha'+Q_2|}.$$

Now, we proceed with the estimate for I_2. If $|y| \leq 2^{-1}\langle x \rangle$, we get

$$|\Delta_\eta^\ell r_\theta| \leq C^{\tilde{k}+1}|p|_{\tilde{k}}^{m,m'}\langle \xi \rangle^{\tau_1}\langle x \rangle^{\tau_2+2\delta_2\ell}(1+\langle x \rangle^{2\delta_2}|\eta|^2)^{-\ell}\langle \eta \rangle^{|m_1|+\rho_1|\alpha|},$$

therefore, using integration by parts and assuming $2\ell > |m_1| + \rho_1|\alpha| + 2n$,

$$|I_2| \leq C^{\tilde{k}+1}|p|_{\tilde{k}}^{m,m'}\langle \xi \rangle^{\tau_1}\langle x \rangle^{\tau_2+\delta_2(2\ell-n)} \int_{\frac{\langle x \rangle^{\delta_2}}{4} \leq |y| \leq \frac{\langle x \rangle}{2}} |y|^{-2\ell} dy.$$

For $|y| \geq 4^{-1}\langle x \rangle^{\delta_2}$, we may write

$$|y|^{-2\ell} \leq 2^{2\ell} \prod_{j=1}^{n}(|y_j| + \frac{\langle x \rangle^{\delta_2}}{4})^{-\frac{2\ell}{n}},$$

and then

$$\int_{\frac{\langle x \rangle^{\delta_2}}{4} \leq |y| \leq \frac{\langle x \rangle}{2}} |y|^{-2\ell} dy \leq 2^{2\ell} \prod_{j=1}^{n} \int (|y_j| + \frac{\langle x \rangle^{\delta_2}}{4})^{-\frac{2\ell}{n}} dy_j \leq C^\ell \langle x \rangle^{\delta_2(n-2\ell)}.$$

After that,

$$|I_2| \leq \tilde{C}^{\tilde{k}+1}|p|_{\tilde{k}}^{m,m'}\langle \xi \rangle^{\tau_1}\langle x \rangle^{\tau_2}.$$

Finally, we take care of I_3. If $|y| \geq 4^{-1}\langle x \rangle$, we have $\langle x+y \rangle \leq 5|y|$ and $\langle x; x+y \rangle \leq 9|y|$. Hence, for $|y| \geq 4^{-1}\langle x \rangle$, we may write

$$|\Delta_\eta^{\ell_1} r_\theta| \leq C^{\tilde{k}+1}|p|_{\tilde{k}}^{m,m'}\langle \xi \rangle^{\tau_1}\langle \eta \rangle^{|m_1|+\rho_1|\alpha|}\langle x \rangle^{m_2-\rho_2|\beta|}|y|^{|m_2'|+\delta_2|\alpha+\alpha'|+2\delta_2(\ell+\ell_1)}$$

and therefore, choosing $\ell, \ell_1 \in \mathbb{N}_0$ satisfying $2\ell > |m_1| + \rho_1|\alpha| + 2n$ and $2\ell_1(1-\delta_2) \geq |m_2'| + \delta_2|\alpha + \alpha'| + 2\delta_2\ell + 2n$,

$$|I_3| \leq C^{\tilde{k}+1}|p|_{\tilde{k}}^{m,m'}\langle \xi \rangle^{\tau_1}\langle x \rangle^{m_2-\rho_2|\beta|-\delta_2n} \int \langle \eta \rangle^{|m_1|+\rho_1|\alpha|-2\ell} d\eta$$
$$\times \int_{|y| \geq 4^{-1}\langle x \rangle} |y|^{|m_2'|+\delta_2|\alpha+\alpha'|+2\delta_2\ell-2\ell_1(1-\delta_2)} dy.$$

Setting $r = 2\ell_1(1-\delta_2) - |m_2'| - \delta_2|\alpha + \alpha'| - 2\delta_2\ell$, we obtain

$$|I_3| \leq C^{\tilde{k}+1}|p|_{\tilde{k}}^{m,m'}\langle \xi \rangle^{\tau_1}\langle x \rangle^{m_2-\rho_2|\beta|} \int \langle \eta \rangle^{-2n} d\eta \langle x \rangle^{n(1-\delta_2)-r}.$$

Choosing ℓ_1 such that $r > -m_2 + \rho_2|\beta'| - \delta_2|\alpha + \alpha'| + n(1-\delta_2)$, we get

$$|I_3| \leq C^{\tilde{k}+1}|p|_{\tilde{k}}^{m,m'}\langle \xi \rangle^{\tau_1}\langle x \rangle^{\tau_2} \int \langle \eta \rangle^{-2n} d\eta.$$

Gathering all the previous computations and choosing $\ell, \ell_1 \in \mathbb{N}_0$ satisfying $2\ell \geq |m_1| + \rho_1|\alpha| + 2n$,

$$2\ell_1(1-\delta_2) \geq 2|m_2'| + \rho_2|\beta'| + \delta_2|\alpha + \alpha'| + 2\delta_2\ell + 2n,$$

we have

$$|q_\theta(x,\xi)| \leq C^{\tilde{k}}|p|_{\tilde{k}}^{m,m'}\langle \xi \rangle^{\tau_1}\langle x \rangle^{\tau_2},$$

where $\tilde{k} = |\alpha + \beta + \alpha' + \beta'| + 2(\ell + \ell_1)$. This concludes the proof. □

Remark 4. Let $a \in C^\infty(\mathbb{R}^n)$ such that $|\partial_x^\beta a(x)| \leq C_\beta \langle x \rangle^{m_2 - |\beta|}$, for $\beta \in \mathbb{N}_0^n$. For each fixed x, we can look at $a(x + \cdot)$ as an amplitude in $\mathcal{A}_{(0,0)}^{(0,|m_2|)}(\mathbb{R}^{2n})$ and, for $\chi \in \mathcal{S}(\mathbb{R}^n)$, $\chi(0) = 1$,

$$\begin{aligned} Os - [e^{-i\eta y} a(x+y)] &= Os - [e^{-i\eta(y-x)} a(y)] \\ &= \lim_{\varepsilon \to 0} \iint e^{-i\eta(y-x)} \chi(\varepsilon \eta) \chi(\varepsilon y) a(y) dy d\eta \\ &= \lim_{\varepsilon \to 0} \int a(y) \chi(\varepsilon y) \varepsilon^{-n} \mathcal{F}^{-1}(\chi)(\varepsilon^{-1}(x-y)) dy \\ &= \lim_{\varepsilon \to 0} \int a(x - \varepsilon y) \chi(\varepsilon(x - \varepsilon y)) \mathcal{F}^{-1}(\chi)(y) dy \\ &= a(x) \int \mathcal{F}^{-1} \chi(y) dy = a(x). \end{aligned}$$

Theorem 2. Let $p(x, \xi, x', \xi') \in SG_{\rho,(0,\delta_2)}^{m,m'}$ and set

$$p_L(x, \xi) = Os - \iint e^{-i\eta y} p(x, \xi + \eta, x + y, \xi) dy d\eta, \quad x, \xi \in \mathbb{R}^n.$$

Then, $p_L \in SG_{\rho,(0,\delta_2)}^{m+m'}$, $p(x, D_x, x', D_{x'}) = p_L(x, D_x)$ and

$$p_L(x, \xi) \sim \sum_{j \in \mathbb{N}_0} \sum_{|\alpha|=j} \frac{1}{\alpha!} (\partial_\xi^\alpha D_{x'}^\alpha p)(x, \xi, x, \xi)$$

Furthermore, given $\ell \in \mathbb{N}_0$, there is $\ell_0 := \ell_0(\ell) \in \mathbb{N}_0$ such that

$$|p_L|_\ell^{m+m'} \leq C_{\ell, \ell_0} |p|_{\ell_0}^{(m,m')}.$$

Proof. First, we notice that, repeating the ideas in the proof of [5] (Lemma 2.3, Page 65), we can conclude that $p_L = p$ as operators.

Applying Lemma 1 for $\alpha = \alpha' = \beta' = \beta = 0$, we obtain that $p_L \in SG_{\rho,(0,\delta_2)}^{m+m'}$.

Now, by Taylor formula, we may write

$$\begin{aligned} p(x, \xi + \eta, x + y, \xi) &= \sum_{|\alpha|<N} \frac{\eta^\alpha}{\alpha!} (\partial_\xi^\alpha p)(x, \xi, x + y, \xi) \\ &+ N \sum_{|\gamma|=N} \frac{\eta^\gamma}{\gamma!} \int_0^1 (1-\theta)^{N-1} (\partial_\xi^\gamma p)(x, \xi + \theta \eta, x + y, \xi) d\theta. \end{aligned}$$

Integration by parts and Remark 4 give

$$\begin{aligned} Os - [e^{-i\eta y} \eta^\alpha (\partial_\xi^\alpha p)(x, \xi, x + y, \xi)] &= Os - [e^{-i\eta y} D_y^\alpha (\partial_\xi^\alpha p)(x, \xi, x + y, \xi)] \\ &= (\partial_\xi^\alpha D_{x'}^\alpha p)(x, \xi, x, \xi) \end{aligned}$$

and

$$Os - [e^{-i\eta y} \eta^\gamma \int_0^1 (1-\theta)^{N-1} (\partial_\xi^\gamma p)(x, \xi + \theta \eta, x + y, \xi) d\theta] = $$
$$Os - [e^{-i\eta y} \int_0^1 (1-\theta)^{N-1} (\partial_\xi^\gamma D_{x'}^\gamma p)(x, \xi + \theta \eta, x + y, \xi) d\theta].$$

Hence

$$p_L(x, \xi) = \sum_{|\alpha|<N} \frac{1}{\alpha!} (\partial_\xi^\alpha D_{x'}^\alpha p)(x, \xi, x, \xi) + r_N(x, \xi),$$

and Lemma 1 implies $r_N \in \mathbf{SG}^{m+m'-N(\rho-(0,\delta_2))}_{\rho,(0,\delta_2)}$. □

To obtain the same kind of result for the classes $\mathbf{SG}^{m,m'}_{\rho,(0,\delta_2);(\mu,\nu)}$, we need an analog of Lemma 1 with a precise estimate of the Gevrey regularity.

Lemma 2. *Let $p \in \mathbf{SG}^{m,m'}_{\rho,(0,\delta_2);(\mu,\nu)}(\mathbb{R}^{4n};A)$ for some $A > 0$. For any multi-indices $\alpha, \alpha', \beta, \beta'$ set $q = p^{\alpha,\alpha'}_{\beta,\beta'}$ and for $\theta \in [-1,1]$, consider q_θ as in Lemma 1. Then,*

$$|\partial_\xi^\sigma \partial_x^\gamma q_\theta(x,\xi)| \leq |p|^{m,m'}_A (CA^r)^k (\alpha!\alpha'!\sigma!)^{\tilde{\mu}} (\beta!\beta'!\gamma!)^{\tilde{\nu}} \langle x \rangle^{\tau_2 - \rho_2|\gamma| + \delta_2|\sigma|} \langle \xi \rangle^{\tau_1 - \rho_1|\sigma|} \qquad (12)$$

where $k = |\alpha + \beta + \alpha' + \beta' + \sigma + \gamma|$, $\tilde{\mu} = (1 + \frac{\rho_1 + \delta_2}{1 - \delta_2})\mu + \rho_1 \nu$, $\tilde{\nu} = \frac{\rho_2}{1 - \delta_2}\mu + \nu$, τ_1 and τ_2 are as in Lemma 1 and C, r are positive constants depending only on $\rho, \delta, m, m', \mu, \nu$ and n.

Proof. Following the ideas presented in the proof of Lemma 1 and using standard factorial inequalities, we obtain

$$|q_\theta(x,\xi)| \leq |p|^{m,m'}_A (CA)^{\tilde{k}} \ell!^{2\nu} \ell_1!^{2\mu} (\alpha!\alpha'!)^\mu (\beta!\beta'!)^\nu \langle \xi \rangle^{\tau_1} \langle x \rangle^{\tau_2},$$

where $C > 0$ depends only of μ, ν, n, m_1, $\tilde{k} = |\alpha + \beta + \alpha' + \beta'| + 2(\ell + \ell_1)$ and ℓ, ℓ_1 are positive integers satisfying $2\ell \geq |m_1| + \rho_1|\alpha| + 2n$, and

$$2\ell_1(1 - \delta_2) \geq 2|m_2'| + \rho_2|\beta'| + \delta_2|\alpha + \alpha'| + 2\delta_2 \ell + 2n.$$

In particular, if we choose

$$\ell = \left\lfloor \frac{|m_1|}{2} + \frac{\rho_1}{2}|\alpha| \right\rfloor + n + 1,$$

$$\ell_1 = \left\lfloor \frac{1}{1-\delta_2}\left(|m_2'| + \delta_2 \ell + \frac{\rho_2}{2}|\beta'| + \frac{\delta_2}{2}|\alpha + \alpha'|\right) \right\rfloor + n + 1,$$

where $\lfloor \cdot \rfloor$ stands for the floor function, then we obtain

$$|q_\theta(x,\xi)| \leq |p|^{m,m'}_A (CA^r)^{|\alpha+\beta+\alpha'+\beta'|} \alpha!^{\tilde{\mu}} \alpha'!^{\mu(1+\frac{\delta_2}{1-\delta_2})} \beta!^\nu \beta'!^{\tilde{\nu}} (\beta!\beta'!)^\nu \langle \xi \rangle^{\tau_1} \langle x \rangle^{\tau_2}.$$

From the last estimate and (10), we get (12). □

As a consequence of Lemma 2, we have the following result.

Theorem 3. *Let $p \in \mathbf{SG}^{m,m'}_{\rho,(0,\delta_2);(\mu,\nu)}(\mathbb{R}^{4n})$. Then, p_L belongs to $\mathbf{SG}^{m+m'}_{\rho,(0,\delta_2);(\tilde{\mu},\tilde{\nu})}$ and*

$$p_L(x,\xi) \sim \sum_{j \in \mathbb{N}_0^n} p_j(x,\xi) \quad \text{in} \quad FSG^{m+m'}_{\rho,(0,\delta_2);(\tilde{\mu},\tilde{\nu})},$$

where

$$p_j(x,\xi) = \sum_{|\alpha|=j} \alpha!^{-1}(\partial_\xi^\alpha D_{x'}^\alpha p)(x,\xi,x,\xi)$$

and $\tilde{\mu}$ and $\tilde{\nu}$ are as in Lemma 2.

Theorem 3 states that p_L has a lower Gevrey regularity than p since $\tilde{\mu} > \mu$ and $\tilde{\nu} > \nu$. However, we observe that, if $p \in \mathbf{SG}^{m,m'}_{\rho,(0,\delta_2);(\mu,\nu)}$, then $\sum_{j \in \mathbb{N}_0} p_j \in FSG^{m+m'}_{\rho,(0,\delta_2);(\mu,\nu)}$. Thus, by Proposition 1, there exists $q \in \mathbf{SG}^{m+m'}_{\rho,(0,\delta_2);(\mu,\nu)}$ such that $q \sim \sum p_j$ in $FSG^{m+m'}_{\rho,(0,\delta_2);(\mu,\nu)}$. On the other hand, we have $p_L \sim \sum p_j$ in $\mathbf{FS}^{m+m'}_{\rho,(0,\delta_2);(\tilde{\mu},\tilde{\nu})}$. Hence, $p_L - q \sim 0$ in $FSG^{m+m'}_{\rho,(0,\delta_2);(\tilde{\mu},\tilde{\nu})}$, which implies that $p_L = q + r$, where r belongs to the Gelfand–Shilov space $\mathcal{S}_{\tilde{\mu}+\tilde{\nu}-1}(\mathbb{R}^{2n})$. This means that we can write p_L as the sum of a symbol with the same orders and regularity as p plus a remainder term which has a lower Gevrey regularity but with orders small as we want. This is a crucial in the applications to the Cauchy problem for p-evolution equations because in the energy estimates the remainder terms can be neglected and does not affect the regularity of the solution (cf. [12]).

4. The Friedrichs Part

Fix $q \in C_0^\infty(\mathbb{R}^n; \mathbb{R})$ supported on $Q = \{\sigma \in \mathbb{R}^n : |\sigma| \leq 1\}$, such that q is even, $\int q(\sigma)^2 d\sigma = 1$ and $|\partial_\sigma^\alpha q(\sigma)| \leq C_q^{|\alpha|+1} \alpha!^s$, where $1 < s \leq \min\{\mu, \nu\}$. In this section, we consider $\mu, \nu > 1$.

Lemma 3. *For $\tau, \tau' \in (0,1)$, set $F : \mathbb{R}^{3n} \to \mathbb{R}$ given by*

$$F(x, \xi, \zeta) = q(\langle x \rangle^{\tau'} \langle \xi \rangle^{-\tau}(\zeta - \xi)) \langle \xi \rangle^{-\frac{\tau n}{2}} \langle x \rangle^{\frac{\tau' n}{2}}, \tag{13}$$

for $x, \xi, \zeta \in \mathbb{R}^n$. Then, for any $\alpha, \beta \in \mathbb{N}_0^n$, we have

$$
\begin{aligned}
\partial_\xi^\alpha \partial_x^\beta F(x, \xi, \zeta) &= \langle x \rangle^{\frac{\tau' n}{2}} \langle \xi \rangle^{-\frac{\tau n}{2}} \sum_{\substack{|\gamma| \leq |\alpha| \\ \gamma_1 \leq \gamma}} \sum_{|\delta| \leq |\beta|} \psi_{\alpha \gamma \gamma_1}(\xi) \phi_{\beta \delta \gamma \gamma_1}(x) \\
&\quad \times (\langle x \rangle^{\tau'} \langle \xi \rangle^{-\tau}(\zeta - \xi))^{\gamma_1 + \delta} (\partial^{\gamma+\delta} q)(\langle x \rangle^{\tau'} \langle \xi \rangle^{-\tau}(\zeta - \xi)),
\end{aligned}
$$

where $\psi_{\alpha \gamma \gamma_1}$ and $\phi_{\beta \delta \gamma \gamma_1}$ satisfy the following estimates:

$$|\partial_\xi^\mu \psi_{\alpha \gamma \gamma_1}(\xi)| \leq C_{\alpha \mu} \langle \xi \rangle^{-|\alpha|+(1-\tau)|\gamma-\gamma_1|-|\mu|}, \tag{14}$$

$$|\partial_x^\nu \phi_{\beta \delta \gamma \gamma_1}(x)| \leq C_{\beta \nu} \langle x \rangle^{-|\beta|+\tau'|\gamma-\gamma_1|-|\nu|}, \tag{15}$$

for every $\mu, \nu \in \mathbb{N}_0^n$.

The lemma can be proved by induction on $|\alpha + \beta|$ following the same argument as in the proof of [5] [Lemma 4.1 page 129]. Observing that $|\gamma - \gamma_1| \leq |\gamma| \leq |\alpha|$ we have $\psi_{\alpha \gamma \gamma_1}(\xi) \phi_{\beta \delta \gamma \gamma_1}(x) \in \mathbf{SG}^{(-\tau|\alpha|, -|\beta|+\tau'|\alpha|)}(\mathbb{R}^{2n})$. Finally, we remark that, for $\alpha = \beta = 0$, we have $\psi_{\alpha \gamma \gamma_1} \equiv \phi_{\beta \delta \gamma \gamma_1} \equiv 1$.

Definition 11. *Let $p \in \mathbf{SG}^m$. Moreover, let $F(x, \xi, \zeta)$ be defined by (13) with $\tau = \tau' = \frac{1}{2}$. We define the Friedrichs part of p by*

$$p_F(\xi, x', \xi') = \int F(x', \xi, \zeta) p(x', \zeta) F(x', \xi', \zeta) \, d\zeta, \quad x', \xi, \xi' \in \mathbb{R}^n.$$

The following properties can be proved as in [5]. We leave the details to the reader.

Proposition 6. *Let $p \in \mathbf{SG}^m$ and let p_F be its Friedrichs part. For $u, v \in \mathscr{S}(\mathbb{R}^n)$, the following conditions hold:*

(i) *If $p(x, \xi)$ is real, then $(p_F u, v)_{L^2} = (u, p_F v)_{L^2}$.*
(ii) *If $p(x, \xi) \geq 0$, then $(p_F u, u)_{L^2} \geq 0$.*
(iii) *If $p(x, \xi)$ is purely imaginary, then $(p_F u, v)_{L^2} = -(u, p_F v)_{L^2}$.*
(iv) *If $\operatorname{Re} p(x, \xi) \geq 0$, then $\operatorname{Re}(p_F u, u)_{L^2} \geq 0$.*

Theorem 4. *Let $p \in \mathbf{SG}^m(\mathbb{R}^{2n})$ and let p_F be its Friedrichs part. Then, $p_{F,L} \in \mathbf{SG}^m(\mathbb{R}^{2n})$ and $p_{F,L} - p \in \mathbf{SG}^{m-(1,1)}(\mathbb{R}^{2n})$. Moreover,*

$$p_{F,L}(x, \xi) - p(x, \xi) \sim \sum_{|\beta|=1} q_{0,\beta}(x, \xi) + \sum_{|\alpha+\beta| \geq 2} q_{\alpha, \beta}(x, \xi),$$

where, for $|\beta| = 1$,

$$q_{0,\beta}(x,\xi) = \sum_{\beta_1+\beta_2+\beta_3=\beta} D_x^{\beta_3} p(x,\xi) \sum_{|\gamma|\leq|\beta|} \sum_{|\delta|\leq|\beta_1|} \psi_{\beta\gamma\gamma}(\xi) \phi_{\beta_1\delta\gamma\gamma}(x)$$
$$\times \sum_{|\delta'|\leq|\beta_2|} \phi_{\beta_2\delta'00}(x) \int \sigma^{\gamma+\delta+\delta'} (\partial^{\gamma+\delta}q)(\sigma)(\partial^{\delta'}q)(\sigma)d\sigma,$$

with $\psi_{\beta\gamma\gamma}\phi_{\beta_1\delta\gamma\gamma} \in SG^{(-|\beta|,-|\beta_1|)}(\mathbb{R}^{2n})$, $\phi_{\beta_2\delta'00} \in SG^{(0,-|\beta_2|)}(\mathbb{R}^{2n})$ and, for $|\alpha+\beta| \geq 2$:

$$q_{\alpha,\beta}(x,\xi) = \sum_{\beta_1+\beta_2+\beta_3=\beta} \frac{(\langle\xi\rangle^{\frac{1}{2}}\langle x\rangle^{-\frac{1}{2}})^{|\alpha|}}{\alpha!\beta_1!\beta_2!\beta_3!}$$
$$\times \sum_{\substack{|\gamma|\leq|\beta| \\ \gamma_1\leq\gamma}} \sum_{|\delta|\leq|\beta_1|} \psi_{\beta\gamma\gamma_1}(\xi) \phi_{\beta_1\delta\gamma\gamma_1}(x) \sum_{|\delta'|\leq|\beta_2|} \phi_{\beta_2\delta'00}(x)$$
$$\times \int_Q \sigma^{\alpha+\gamma_1+\delta_1+\delta'_1} (\partial^{\gamma+\delta}q)(\sigma)(\partial^{\delta'}q)(\sigma)\,d\sigma \cdot \partial_\xi^\alpha D_x^{\beta_3} p(x,\xi).$$

with $\psi_{\beta\gamma\gamma_1}\phi_{\beta_1\delta\gamma\gamma_1} \in SG^{(-\frac{1}{2}|\beta|,-|\beta_1|+\frac{1}{2}|\beta|)}(\mathbb{R}^{2n})$, $\phi_{\beta_2\delta'00} \in SG^{(0,-|\beta_2|)}(\mathbb{R}^{2n})$.

We need the following technical lemma whose proof follows by a compactness argument.

Lemma 4. *For $\tau \in (0,1)$, there is $C > 0$ such that*

$$C^{-1}\langle\xi\rangle \leq \langle\xi + \zeta\langle\xi\rangle^\tau\rangle \leq C\langle\xi\rangle,$$

for every $\xi \in \mathbb{R}^n$ and $|\zeta| \leq 1$.

Proof of Theorem 4. From Leibniz formula and Cauchy–Schwartz inequality, we get

$$|\partial_\xi^\alpha \partial_{\xi'}^{\alpha'} \partial_{x'}^{\beta'} p_F(\xi,x',\xi')|$$
$$\leq \sum_{\beta'_1+\beta'_2+\beta'_3=\beta'} \frac{\beta'!}{\beta'_1!\beta'_2!\beta'_3!} \left[\int |\partial_\xi^\alpha \partial_{x'}^{\beta'_1} F(x',\xi,\zeta)|^2 d\zeta\right]^{\frac{1}{2}} \cdot \left[\int |\partial_{x'}^{\beta'_2} p(x',\zeta) \partial_\xi^{\alpha'} \partial_{x'}^{\beta'_3} F(x',\xi',\zeta)|^2 d\zeta\right]^{\frac{1}{2}}.$$

Now, by changing variables, we obtain

$$|\partial_\xi^\alpha \partial_{\xi'}^{\alpha'} \partial_{x'}^{\beta'} p_F(\xi,x',\xi')|$$
$$\leq \langle\xi\rangle^{\frac{n}{4}} \langle x'\rangle^{-\frac{n}{2}} \langle\xi'\rangle^{\frac{n}{4}} \sum_{\beta'_1+\beta'_2+\beta'_3=\beta'} \frac{\beta'!}{\beta'_1!\beta'_2!\beta'_3!} \left[\int_Q |(\partial_\xi^\alpha \partial_{x'}^{\beta'_1} F)(x',\xi,\langle x'\rangle^{-\frac{1}{2}}\langle\xi\rangle^{\frac{1}{2}}\sigma + \xi)|^2 d\sigma\right]^{\frac{1}{2}}$$
$$\times \left[\int_Q |(\partial_{\xi'}^{\alpha'} \partial_{x'}^{\beta'_2} F)(x',\xi',\langle x'\rangle^{-\frac{1}{2}}\langle\xi'\rangle^{\frac{1}{2}}\sigma + \xi')(\partial_{x'}^{\beta'_3} p)(x',\langle x'\rangle^{-\frac{1}{2}}\langle\xi'\rangle^{\frac{1}{2}}\sigma + \xi')|^2 d\sigma\right]^{\frac{1}{2}}.$$

Applying Lemma 3, we obtain

$$|\partial_\xi^\alpha \partial_{\xi'}^{\alpha'} \partial_{x'}^{\beta'} p_F(\xi, x', \xi')|$$

$$\leq \sum_{\beta_1' + \beta_2' + \beta_3' = \beta'} \frac{\beta'!}{\beta_1'! \beta_2'! \beta_3'!} \left[\int \sum_{\substack{|\gamma| \leq |\alpha| \\ \gamma_1 \leq \gamma}} \sum_{|\delta| \leq |\beta_1'|} \left| \psi_{\alpha\gamma\gamma_1}(\xi) \phi_{\beta_1'\delta\gamma\gamma_1}(x') \sigma^{\gamma_1 + \delta} (\partial^{\gamma + \delta} q)(\sigma) \right|^2 d\sigma \right]^{\frac{1}{2}}$$

$$\times \left[\int \sum_{\substack{|\gamma| \leq |\alpha'| \\ \gamma_1 \leq \gamma}} \sum_{|\delta| \leq |\beta_2'|} \left| \psi_{\alpha'\gamma\gamma_1}(\xi') \phi_{\beta_2'\delta\gamma\gamma_1}(x') \sigma^{\gamma_1 + \delta} (\partial^{\gamma + \delta} q)(\sigma) \right|^2 \left| \partial_{x'}^{\beta_3'} p(x', \langle x' \rangle^{-\frac{1}{2}} \langle \xi' \rangle^{\frac{1}{2}} \sigma + \xi') \right|^2 d\sigma \right]^{\frac{1}{2}}.$$

We now observe that by Lemma 4

$$\left| \partial_{x'}^{\beta_3'} p(x', \langle x' \rangle^{-\frac{1}{2}} \langle \xi' \rangle^{\frac{1}{2}} \sigma + \xi') \right| \leq C_{\beta_3'} \langle \xi' \rangle^{m_1} \langle x' \rangle^{m_2 - |\beta_3'|}.$$

Since $\psi_{\alpha\gamma\gamma_1} \phi_{\beta_1'\delta\gamma\gamma_1} \in \mathbf{SG}^{(-\frac{|\alpha|}{2}, -|\beta_1'| + \frac{|\alpha|}{2})}$ and $\psi_{\alpha'\gamma\gamma_1} \phi_{\beta_2'\delta\gamma\gamma_1} \in \mathbf{SG}^{(-\frac{|\alpha'|}{2}, -|\beta_2'| + \frac{|\alpha'|}{2})}$ we obtain

$$|\partial_\xi^\alpha \partial_{\xi'}^{\alpha'} \partial_{x'}^{\beta'} p_F(\xi, x', \xi')| \leq C_{\alpha\alpha'\beta'} \langle \xi \rangle^{-\frac{|\alpha|}{2}} \langle \xi' \rangle^{m_1 - \frac{|\alpha'|}{2}} \langle x' \rangle^{m_2 - |\beta'| + \frac{|\alpha + \alpha'|}{2}},$$

that is $p_F \in \mathbf{SG}_{(1/2,1),(0,1/2)}^{(0,0),(m_1,m_2)}$. Then, by Theorem 2, $p_{F,L} \in \mathbf{SG}_{(1/2,1),(0,1/2)}^m$ and

$$p_{F,L}(x, \xi) \sim \sum_\beta \frac{1}{\beta!} (\partial_\xi^\beta D_{x'}^\beta p_F)(\xi, x, \xi) = \sum_\beta \tilde{p}_\beta(x, \xi),$$

which implies that $p_{F,L} - \sum_{|\beta| < N} \tilde{p}_\beta \in \mathbf{SG}_{(1/2,1),(0,1/2)}^{m - \frac{N}{2}(1,1)}$ for every $N \in \mathbb{N}$. To improve this result, let us study more carefully the above asymptotic expansion. Note that

$$\tilde{p}_\beta(x, \xi) = \sum_{\beta_1 + \beta_2 + \beta_3 = \beta} \frac{1}{\beta_1! \beta_2! \beta_3!} \int \partial_\xi^\beta D_x^{\beta_1} F(x, \xi, \zeta) D_x^{\beta_3} p(x, \zeta) D_x^{\beta_2} F(x, \xi, \zeta) d\zeta$$

$$= \sum_{\beta_1 + \beta_2 + \beta_3 = \beta} \frac{1}{\beta_1! \beta_2! \beta_3!} \sum_{\substack{|\gamma| \leq |\beta| \\ \gamma_1 \leq \gamma}} \sum_{|\delta| \leq |\beta_1|} \psi_{\beta\gamma\gamma_1}(\xi) \phi_{\beta_1\delta\gamma\gamma_1}(x) \sum_{|\delta'| \leq |\beta_2|} \psi_{\beta_2\delta'00}(x)$$

$$\times \int_Q (D_x^{\beta_3} p)(x, \langle \xi \rangle^{\frac{1}{2}} \langle x \rangle^{-\frac{1}{2}} \sigma + \xi) \sigma^{\gamma_1 + \delta + \delta'} (\partial^{\gamma + \delta} q)(\sigma) (\partial^{\delta'} q)(\sigma) d\sigma.$$

By Taylor formula, we can write

$$D_x^{\beta_3} p(x, \langle \xi \rangle^{\frac{1}{2}} \langle x \rangle^{-\frac{1}{2}} \sigma + \xi) = \sum_{|\alpha| < N} \frac{(\langle \xi \rangle^{\frac{1}{2}} \langle x \rangle^{-\frac{1}{2}})^{|\alpha|} \sigma^\alpha}{\alpha!} \partial_\xi^\alpha D_x^{\beta_3} p(x, \xi)$$

$$+ N \sum_{|\alpha| = N} \frac{\langle \xi \rangle^{\frac{N}{2}} \langle x \rangle^{-\frac{N}{2}} \sigma^\alpha}{\alpha!} \int_0^1 (1 - \theta)^{N-1} (\partial_\xi^\alpha D_x^{\beta_3} p)(x, \theta \langle \xi \rangle^{\frac{1}{2}} \langle x \rangle^{-\frac{1}{2}} \sigma + \xi) d\theta.$$

Then, we get

$$\tilde{p}_\beta(x,\xi) = \sum_{\beta_1+\beta_2+\beta_3=\beta} \sum_{|\alpha|<N} \frac{(\langle\xi\rangle^{\frac{1}{2}}\langle x\rangle^{-\frac{1}{2}})^{|\alpha|}}{\alpha!\beta_1!\beta_2!\beta_3!}$$
$$\times \sum_{\substack{|\gamma|\leq|\beta|\\ \gamma_1\leq\gamma}} \sum_{|\delta|\leq|\beta_1|} \psi_{\beta\gamma\gamma_1}(\xi)\phi_{\beta_1\delta\gamma\gamma_1}(x) \sum_{|\delta'|\leq|\beta_2|} \phi_{\beta_2\delta'00}(x)$$
$$\times \int_Q \sigma^{\alpha+\gamma_1+\delta+\delta'} \partial^{\gamma+\delta}q(\sigma)\partial^{\delta'}q(\sigma)\,d\sigma \cdot \partial_\xi^\alpha D_x^{\beta_3}p(x,\xi) + r_{\beta,N}(x,\xi)$$

where

$$r_{\beta,N}(x,\xi) = \sum_{\beta_1+\beta_2+\beta_3=\beta} \sum_{|\alpha|=N} \frac{N}{\alpha!} \cdot \frac{(\langle\xi\rangle^{\frac{1}{2}}\langle x\rangle^{-\frac{1}{2}})^N}{\beta_1!\beta_2!\beta_3!} \sum_{\substack{|\gamma|\leq|\beta|\\ \gamma_1\leq\gamma}} \sum_{|\delta|\leq|\beta_1|} \psi_{\beta\gamma\gamma_1}(\xi)\phi_{\beta_1\delta\gamma\gamma_1}(x) \sum_{|\delta'|\leq|\beta_2|} \phi_{\beta_2\delta'00}(x)$$
$$\times \int_Q \sigma^{\gamma_1+\delta+\delta'+\alpha}\partial^{\gamma+\delta}q(\sigma)\partial^{\delta'}q(\sigma) \int_0^1 (1-\theta)^{N-1}(\partial_\xi^\alpha D_x^{\beta_3}p)(x,\theta\langle\xi\rangle^{\frac{1}{2}}\langle x\rangle^{-\frac{1}{2}}\sigma+\xi)\,d\theta d\sigma. \quad (16)$$

Using Lemma 4, we get that $r_{\beta,N}$ belongs to $\mathbf{SG}^{(m_1-\frac{1}{2}(N+|\beta|),m_2-\frac{1}{2}(|\beta|+N))}$, whereas

$$q_{\alpha,\beta}(x,\xi) = \sum_{\beta_1+\beta_2+\beta_3=\beta} \frac{(\langle\xi\rangle^{\frac{1}{2}}\langle x\rangle^{-\frac{1}{2}})^{|\alpha|}}{\alpha!\beta_1!\beta_2!\beta_3!}$$
$$\times \sum_{\substack{|\gamma|\leq|\beta|\\ \gamma_1\leq\gamma}} \sum_{|\delta|\leq|\beta_1|} \psi_{\beta\gamma\gamma_1}(\xi)\phi_{\beta_1\delta\gamma\gamma_1}(x) \sum_{|\delta'|\leq|\beta_2|} \phi_{\beta_2\delta'00}(x)$$
$$\times \int_Q \sigma^{\alpha+\gamma_1+\delta_1+\delta_1'}\partial^{\gamma+\delta}q(\sigma)\partial^{\delta'}q(\sigma)\,d\sigma \cdot \partial_\xi^\alpha D_x^{\beta_3}p(x,\xi)$$

belongs to $\mathbf{SG}^{(m_1-\frac{1}{2}(|\alpha|+|\beta|),m_2-\frac{1}{2}(|\beta|+|\alpha|))}$. Hence,

$$\sum_{|\alpha+\beta|=j} q_{\alpha,\beta} \in \mathbf{SG}^{m-\frac{1}{2}(j,j)}.$$

Then, we can find a symbol $t(x,\xi)$ such that

$$t(x,\xi) \sim \sum_{j\in\mathbb{N}_0} \sum_{|\alpha+\beta|=j} q_{\alpha,\beta}(x,\xi).$$

Since, for every $N \in \mathbb{N}$,

$$\tilde{p}_\beta(x,\xi) - \sum_{|\alpha|<N} q_{\alpha,\beta}(x,\xi) \in \mathbf{SG}^{m-\frac{1}{2}(N+|\beta|,N+|\beta|)}_{(\frac{1}{2},1),(0,\frac{1}{2})}(\mathbb{R}^{2n}),$$

we obtain that $p_{F,L} - t \in \mathscr{S}(\mathbb{R}^{2n})$, and therefore

$$p_{F,L}(x,\xi) \sim \sum_{j\in\mathbb{N}_0} \sum_{|\alpha+\beta|=j} q_{\alpha,\beta}(x,\xi).$$

To finish the proof, let us analyze more carefully the functions $q_{\alpha,\beta}(x,\xi)$ when $|\alpha+\beta| \leq 1$. First, we notice that if $\alpha = \beta = 0$, we have $q_{0,0}(x,\xi) = p(x,\xi)$. If $|\alpha| = 1$ and $\beta = 0$,

$$q_{\alpha,0}(x,\xi) = \frac{\langle\xi\rangle^{\frac{|\alpha|}{2}}\langle x\rangle^{-\frac{|\alpha|}{2}}}{\alpha!} \int \sigma^\alpha q(\sigma)^2 d\sigma = 0,$$

because $\sigma^\alpha q^2(\sigma)$ is an odd function. In the case $|\alpha|=0$ and $|\beta|=1$, we have

$$q_{0,\beta}(x,\xi) = \sum_{\beta_1+\beta_2+\beta_3=\beta} D_x^{\beta_3} p(x,\xi) \sum_{\substack{|\gamma|\le|\beta|\\|\gamma_1|\le|\gamma|}} \sum_{|\delta|\le|\beta_1|} \psi_{\beta\gamma\gamma_1}(\xi)\phi_{\beta_1\delta\gamma\gamma_1}(x)$$
$$\times \sum_{|\delta'|\le|\beta_2|} \phi_{\beta_2\delta'00}(x) \int \sigma^{\gamma_1+\delta+\delta'}(\partial^{\gamma+\delta}q)(\sigma)(\partial^{\delta'}q)(\sigma)d\sigma.$$

If $|\gamma_1|<|\gamma|$ in the above formula, we have $\gamma_1=0$ and $|\gamma|=1$, and, since q is even,

$$\int \sigma^{\delta+\delta'}(\partial^{e_j+\delta}q)(\sigma)(\partial^{\delta'}q)(\sigma)d\sigma = 0, \; j=1,\ldots,n.$$

Therefore,

$$q_{0,\beta}(x,\xi) = \sum_{\beta_1+\beta_2+\beta_3=\beta} D_x^{\beta_3} p(x,\xi) \sum_{|\gamma|\le|\beta|} \sum_{|\delta|\le|\beta_1|} \psi_{\beta\gamma\gamma}(\xi)\phi_{\beta_1\delta\gamma\gamma}(x)$$
$$\times \sum_{|\delta'|\le|\beta_2|} \phi_{\beta_2\delta'00}(x) \int \sigma^{\gamma+\delta+\delta'}(\partial^{\gamma+\delta}q)(\sigma)(\partial^{\delta'}q)(\sigma)d\sigma,$$

and by Lemma 3 $q_{0,\beta}\in \mathbf{SG}^{m-(1,1)}(\mathbb{R}^{2n})$. Hence

$$p_{F,L}(x,\xi) - p(x,\xi) \sim \sum_{|\beta|=1} q_{0,\beta}(x,\xi) + \sum_{|\alpha+\beta|\ge 2} q_{\alpha,\beta}(x,\xi)$$

and in particular that $p_{F,L}-p\in \mathbf{SG}^{m-(1,1)}(\mathbb{R}^{2n})$. □

Proposition 6 and Theorem 4 imply the well known sharp Gårding inequality.

Theorem 5. *Let $p\in SG^m(\mathbb{R}^{2n})$. If $\operatorname{Re} p(x,\xi)\ge 0$, then*

$$\operatorname{Re}(p(x,D)u,u)_{L^2} \ge -C\|u\|^2_{H^{\frac{1}{2}(m-(1,1))}} \qquad u\in \mathscr{S}(\mathbb{R}^n),$$

for some positive constant C.

Proof. Setting $q=p-p_{F,L}\in \mathbf{SG}^{m-(1,1)}(\mathbb{R}^{2n})$ and recalling that p_F and $p_{F,L}$ define the same operator, we may write, by (iv) of Proposition 6:

$$\operatorname{Re}(p(x,D)u,u)_{L^2} = \operatorname{Re}(q(x,D)u,u)_{L^2} + \operatorname{Re}(p_F u,u)_{L^2} \ge \operatorname{Re}(q(x,D)u,u)_{L^2}.$$

Now, observe that for any $s=(s_1,s_2)\in \mathbb{R}^2$

$$|(q(x,D)u,u)_{L^2}| = |(\langle x\rangle^{s_2}\langle D_x\rangle^{s_1} q(x,D)u, \langle x\rangle^{-s_2}\langle D_x\rangle^{-s_1} u)_{L^2}|$$
$$\le \|q(x,D)u\|_{H^s}\|u\|_{H^{-s}} \le C\|u\|_{H^{s+m-(1,1)}}\|u\|_{H^{-s}}.$$

Choosing $s=\frac{1}{2}[(1,1)-m]$, we conclude that

$$\operatorname{Re}(p(x,D)u,u)_{L^2} \ge -C\|u\|^2_{H^{\frac{1}{2}(m-(1,1))}}.$$

□

To study the Friedrichs part of symbols satisfying Gevrey estimates, we need the Faà di Bruno formula. Given smooth functions $g : \mathbb{R}^n \to \mathbb{R}^p$, $g = (g_1, \ldots, g_p)$, $f : \mathbb{R}^p \to \mathbb{R}$ and $\gamma \in \mathbb{N}_0^n - \{0\}$, we have

$$\partial^\gamma (f \circ g)(x) = \sum \frac{\gamma!}{k_1! \ldots k_\ell!} (\partial^{k_1 + \cdots + k_n} f)(g(x)) \prod_{j=1}^{\ell} \prod_{i=1}^{p} \left[\frac{1}{\delta_j!} \partial^{\delta_j} g_i(x) \right]^{k_{ji}}, \qquad (17)$$

where the sum is taken over all $\ell \in \mathbb{N}$, all sets $\{\delta_1, \ldots, \delta_\ell\}$ of ℓ distinct elements of $\mathbb{N}_0^n - \{0\}$ and all $(k_1, \ldots, k_\ell) \in (\mathbb{N}_0^p - \{0\})^\ell$, such that

$$\gamma = \sum_{s=1}^{\ell} |k_s| \delta_s.$$

It is possible to show that there is a constant $C > 0$ such that

$$\sum \frac{(k_1 + \ldots + k_\ell)!}{k_1! \ldots k_\ell!} \leq C^{|\gamma|+1}, \quad \gamma \in \mathbb{N} - \{0\},$$

and $|k_1 + \ldots + k_\ell|! \leq |\gamma|!$, where the summation and $k_1, \ldots, k_\ell$ are as in (17). For a proof of these assertions, we refer to Proposition 4.3 (Page 9), Corollary 4.5 (Page 11) and Lemma 4.8 (Page 12) of [24].

Let $p \in \mathbf{SG}^m_{(\mu,\nu)}$. We already know that $p_F \in \mathbf{SG}^{(0,0),(m_1,m_2)}_{(\frac{1}{2},1),(0,\frac{1}{2})}$. Now, we want to obtain a precise information about the Gevrey regularity of p_F. By Faà di Bruno formula,

$$\partial_x^\beta \partial_\xi^\alpha q(\langle \xi \rangle^{-\frac{1}{2}} \langle x \rangle^{\frac{1}{2}} (\zeta - \xi)) = \partial_x^\beta \sum_{\ell, k_1, \ldots, k_\ell} \frac{\alpha!}{k_1! \ldots k_\ell!}$$

$$\times (\partial^{k_1 + \cdots + k_\ell} q)(\langle \xi \rangle^{-\frac{1}{2}} \langle x \rangle^{\frac{1}{2}} (\zeta - \xi)) \prod_{j=1}^{\ell} \langle x \rangle^{\frac{|k_j|}{2}} \prod_{i=1}^{n} \left[\frac{1}{\delta_j!} \partial_\xi^{\delta_j} \{\langle \xi \rangle^{-\frac{1}{2}} (\zeta_i - \xi_i)\} \right]^{k_{ji}}$$

$$= \sum_{\ell, k_1, \ldots, k_\ell} \frac{\alpha!}{k_1! \ldots k_\ell!} \sum_{\beta_1 + \beta_2 = \beta} \frac{\beta!}{\beta_1! \beta_2!} \partial_x^{\beta_1} (\partial^{k_1 + \cdots + k_\ell} q)(\langle \xi \rangle^{-\frac{1}{2}} \langle x \rangle^{\frac{1}{2}} (\zeta - \xi))$$

$$\times \partial_x^{\beta_2} \prod_{j=1}^{\ell} \langle x \rangle^{\frac{|k_j|}{2}} \prod_{i=1}^{n} \left[\frac{1}{\delta_j!} \partial_\xi^{\delta_j} \{\langle \xi \rangle^{-\frac{1}{2}} (\zeta_i - \xi_i)\} \right]^{k_{ji}}$$

$$= \sum_{\ell, k_1, \ldots, k_\ell} \frac{\alpha!}{k_1! \ldots k_\ell!} \sum_{\beta_1 + \beta_2 = \beta} \frac{\beta!}{\beta_1! \beta_2!} \sum_{\ell', k'_1, \ldots, k'_{\ell'}} \frac{\beta_1!}{k'_1! \ldots k'_{\ell'}!}$$

$$\times (\partial^{(k_1 + \cdots + k_\ell) + (k'_1 + \cdots + k'_{\ell'})} q)(\langle \xi \rangle^{-\frac{1}{2}} \langle x \rangle^{\frac{1}{2}} (\zeta - \xi))$$

$$\times \prod_{j'=1}^{\ell'} \prod_{i'=1}^{n} \left[\frac{1}{\delta'_{j'}!} \partial_x^{\delta'_{j'}} \langle \xi \rangle^{-\frac{1}{2}} \langle x \rangle^{\frac{1}{2}} (\zeta_{i'} - \xi_{i'}) \right]^{k'_{j'i'}}$$

$$\times \sum_{\sigma_1 + \ldots + \sigma_\ell = \beta_2} \frac{\beta_2!}{\sigma_1! \ldots \sigma_\ell!} \prod_{j=1}^{\ell} \partial_x^{\sigma_j} \langle x \rangle^{\frac{|k_j|}{2}} \prod_{i=1}^{n} \left[\frac{1}{\delta_j!} \partial_\xi^{\delta_j} \{\langle \xi \rangle^{-\frac{1}{2}} (\zeta_i - \xi_i)\} \right]^{k_{ji}},$$

hence

$$\partial_x^\beta \partial_\zeta^\alpha q(\langle\zeta\rangle^{-\frac{1}{2}}\langle x\rangle^{\frac{1}{2}}(\zeta-\xi)) = \sum_{\ell,k_1,\ldots,k_\ell} \frac{\alpha!}{k_1!\ldots k_\ell!} \sum_{\beta_1+\beta_2=\beta} \frac{\beta!}{\beta_1!\beta_2!}$$

$$\times \sum_{\ell',k'_1,\ldots,k'_{\ell'}} \frac{\beta_1!}{k'_1!\ldots k'_{\ell'}!} (\partial^{(k_1+\ldots+k_\ell)+(k'_1+\ldots+k'_{\ell'})} q)(\langle\zeta\rangle^{-\frac{1}{2}}\langle x\rangle^{\frac{1}{2}}(\zeta-\xi))$$

$$\times \prod_{j'=1}^{\ell'} \prod_{i'=1}^{n} \left[\frac{1}{\delta'_{j'}!} \partial_x^{\delta'_{j'}} \langle x\rangle^{\frac{1}{2}} \langle x\rangle^{-\frac{1}{2}} \right]^{k'_{j'i'}} \left[\langle\zeta\rangle^{-\frac{1}{2}}\langle x\rangle^{\frac{1}{2}}(\zeta_{i'}-\xi_{i'}) \right]^{k'_{j'i'}}$$

$$\times \sum_{\sigma_1+\ldots+\sigma_\ell=\beta_2} \frac{\beta_2!}{\sigma_1!\ldots\sigma_\ell!} \prod_{j=1}^{\ell} \partial_x^{\sigma_j} \langle x\rangle^{\frac{1}{2}|k_j|} \prod_{i=1}^{n} \left[\frac{1}{\delta_j!} \{\partial_\zeta^{\delta_j}\langle\zeta\rangle^{-\frac{1}{2}}(\zeta_i-\xi_i) - \delta_{ji}\partial_\zeta^{\delta_j-e_i}\langle\zeta\rangle^{-\frac{1}{2}}\} \right]^{k_{ji}}.$$

Noticing that $\langle x\rangle^{\frac{1}{2}}\langle\zeta\rangle^{-\frac{1}{2}}|\zeta-\xi| \leq 1$ on the support of q, we have

$$|\partial_x^\beta \partial_\zeta^\alpha q(\langle\zeta\rangle^{-\frac{1}{2}}\langle x\rangle^{\frac{1}{2}}(\zeta-\xi))| \leq \tilde{C}_{q,s}^{|\alpha+\beta|+1}(\alpha!\beta!)^s \langle x\rangle^{\frac{|\alpha|}{2}-|\beta|}\langle\zeta\rangle^{-\frac{|\alpha|}{2}}.$$

We now apply the above inequality to estimate the derivatives of F. We have

$$|\partial_\zeta^\alpha \partial_x^\beta F(x,\xi,\zeta)| \leq \sum_{\substack{\alpha_1+\alpha_2=\alpha \\ \beta_1+\beta_1=\beta}} \frac{\alpha!\beta!}{\alpha_1!\beta_1!\alpha_2!\beta_2!} \partial_\zeta^{\alpha_1}\langle\zeta\rangle^{-\frac{n}{4}} \partial_x^{\beta_1}\langle x\rangle^{\frac{n}{4}} |\partial_\zeta^{\alpha_2}\partial_x^{\beta_2} q(\langle\zeta\rangle^{-\frac{1}{2}}\langle x\rangle^{\frac{1}{2}}(\zeta-\xi))|$$

$$\leq C_{q,s}^{|\alpha+\beta|+1}(\alpha!\beta!)^s \langle\zeta\rangle^{-\frac{n}{4}-\frac{|\alpha|}{2}}\langle x\rangle^{\frac{n}{4}+\frac{|\alpha|}{2}-|\beta|}. \qquad (18)$$

Finally we proceed with the estimates for p_F. Denoting

$$Q_{x,\xi} = \{\zeta \in \mathbb{R}^n : \langle x\rangle^{\frac{1}{2}}\langle\zeta\rangle^{-\frac{1}{2}}|\zeta-\xi| < 1\}, \quad x,\xi \in \mathbb{R}^n,$$

we obtain

$$|\partial_\xi^\alpha \partial_{\xi'}^{\alpha'} \partial_{x'}^{\beta'} p_F(\xi,x',\xi')| \leq \sum_{\beta_1+\beta_2+\beta_2=\beta} \frac{\beta!}{\beta_1!\beta_2!\beta_3!} \left[\int_{Q_{x,\xi}} |\partial_\xi^\alpha \partial_x^{\beta_1} F(\xi,x',\zeta)|^2 d\zeta \right]^{\frac{1}{2}}$$

$$\times \left[\int_{Q_{x',\xi'}} |\partial_x^{\beta_3} p(x',\zeta) \partial_\xi^{\alpha'} \partial_x^{\beta_2'} F(x',\xi',\zeta)|^2 d\zeta \right]^{\frac{1}{2}}$$

$$\leq \sum_{\beta_1+\beta_2+\beta_2=\beta} \frac{\beta!}{\beta_1!\beta_2!\beta_3!} C_{q,s}^{|\alpha+\alpha'+\beta_1'+\beta_2'|+2} (\alpha!\alpha'!\beta_1'!\beta_2'!)^s \langle\xi\rangle^{-\frac{|\alpha|}{2}}\langle\xi'\rangle^{-\frac{|\alpha'|}{2}}$$

$$\times \langle x\rangle^{\frac{1}{2}|\alpha+\alpha'|-|\beta_1'+\beta_2'|} \left[\int_{Q_{x,\xi}} \langle\xi\rangle^{-\frac{n}{2}}\langle x'\rangle^{\frac{n}{2}} d\zeta \right]^{\frac{1}{2}} \cdot \left[\int_{Q_{x',\xi'}} \langle\xi'\rangle^{-\frac{n}{2}}\langle x'\rangle^{\frac{n}{2}} |\partial_x^{\beta_3'} p(x',\zeta)|^2 d\zeta \right]^{\frac{1}{2}}$$

$$\leq \sum_{\beta_1+\beta_2+\beta_2=\beta} \frac{\beta!}{\beta_1!\beta_2!\beta_3!} C_{q,s}^{|\alpha+\alpha'+\beta_1'+\beta_2'|+2} (\alpha!\alpha'!\beta_1'!\beta_2'!)^s \langle\xi\rangle^{-\frac{|\alpha|}{2}}\langle\xi'\rangle^{-\frac{|\alpha'|}{2}}$$

$$\times \langle x\rangle^{\frac{|\alpha+\alpha'|}{2}-|\beta_1'+\beta_2'|} \left[\int_{|\zeta|<1} d\zeta \right]^{\frac{1}{2}} \left[\int_{|\zeta|<1} |\partial_x^{\beta_3'} p(x',\langle x'\rangle^{-\frac{1}{2}}\langle\xi\rangle^{\frac{1}{2}}\zeta+\xi')|^2 d\zeta \right]^{\frac{1}{2}}.$$

Using Lemma 4 and recalling that $s \leq \min\{\mu,\nu\}$,

$$|\partial_\xi^\alpha \partial_{\xi'}^{\alpha'} \partial_{x'}^{\beta'} p_F| \leq C^{|\alpha+\alpha'+\beta'|+1} (\alpha!\alpha'!)^\mu \beta'!^\nu \langle x\rangle^{m_2-|\beta'|+\frac{1}{2}|\alpha+\alpha'|}\langle\xi\rangle^{-\frac{|\alpha|}{2}}\langle\xi'\rangle^{m_1-\frac{|\alpha'|}{2}},$$

which means $p_F \in \mathbf{SG}^{(0,0),(m_1,m_2)}_{(\frac{1}{2},1),(0,\frac{1}{2});(\mu,\nu)}(\mathbb{R}^{4n}).$

Now, we discuss the asymptotic expansion of p_F, when $p \in \mathbf{SG}^m_{(\mu,\nu)}$. In the following, we use the notation of the proof of Theorem 4. We have

$$p_{F,L}(x,\xi) \sim \sum_\beta \tilde{p}_\beta(x,\xi) \text{ in } FSG^m_{(\frac{1}{2},1),(0,\frac{1}{2});(\tilde{\mu},\tilde{\nu})},$$

and, by Lemma 2 and Taylor formula, we may write

$$\left|\partial_\xi^\theta \partial_x^\sigma \left(p_{F,L} - \sum_{|\beta|<N} \tilde{p}_\beta\right)(x,\xi)\right| \leq C^{|\theta+\sigma|+2N+1}\theta!^{\tilde{\mu}}\sigma!^{\tilde{\nu}} N!^{\tilde{\mu}+\tilde{\nu}-1}\langle\xi\rangle^{m_1-\frac{|\theta|}{2}-\frac{N}{2}}\langle x\rangle^{m_2-|\sigma|+\frac{|\theta|}{2}-\frac{N}{2}} \quad (19)$$

for every $\theta,\sigma \in \mathbb{N}_0^n$, $x,\xi \in \mathbb{R}^n$ and $N \in \mathbb{N}$, where $\tilde{\mu} = 3\mu + \frac{1}{2}\nu$ and $\tilde{\nu} = \nu + 2\mu$. We also have, for every $\beta \in \mathbb{N}_0^n$ and $N \in \mathbb{N}$,

$$\tilde{p}_\beta(x,\xi) - \sum_{|\alpha|<N} q_{\alpha,\beta}(x,\xi) = r_{\beta,N}(x,\xi).$$

where $r_{\beta,N}$ is given as in (16).

Changing variables and setting $\sigma = (\zeta - \xi)\langle x\rangle^{\frac{1}{2}}\langle\xi\rangle^{-\frac{1}{2}}$, we obtain

$$r_{\beta,N}(x,\xi) = \sum_{\beta_1+\beta_2+\beta_3=\beta} \sum_{|\alpha|=N} \frac{N}{\alpha!} \cdot \frac{(\langle\xi\rangle^{\frac{1}{2}}\langle x\rangle^{-\frac{1}{2}})^N}{\beta_1!\beta_2!\beta_3!}$$

$$\times \sum_{\substack{|\gamma|\leq|\beta| \\ \gamma_1 \leq \gamma}} \sum_{|\delta|\leq|\beta_1|} \psi_{\beta\gamma\gamma_1}(\xi)\phi_{\beta_1\delta\gamma\gamma_1}(x) \sum_{|\delta'|\leq|\beta_2|} \phi_{\beta_2\delta'00}(x)$$

$$\times \int_{Q_{x,\xi}} ((\zeta-\xi)\langle x\rangle^{\frac{1}{2}}\langle\xi\rangle^{-\frac{1}{2}})^{\gamma_1+\delta+\delta'+\alpha}\partial^{\gamma+\delta}q((\zeta-\xi)\langle x\rangle^{\frac{1}{2}}\langle\xi\rangle^{-\frac{1}{2}})\partial^{\delta'}q((\zeta-\xi)\langle x\rangle^{\frac{1}{2}}\langle\xi\rangle^{-\frac{1}{2}})$$

$$\cdot \int_0^1 (1-\theta)^{N-1}(\partial_\xi^\alpha D_x^{\beta_3}p)(x,\theta\zeta+(1-\theta)\xi)\,d\theta\langle x\rangle^{\frac{n}{2}}\langle\xi\rangle^{-\frac{n}{2}}d\zeta.$$

By Lemma 3, we get

$$r_{\beta,N}(x,\xi) = \sum_{\beta_1+\beta_2+\beta_3=\beta} \sum_{|\alpha|=N} \frac{N}{\alpha!} \cdot \frac{(\langle\xi\rangle^{\frac{1}{2}}\langle x\rangle^{-\frac{1}{2}})^N}{\beta_1!\beta_2!\beta_3!}$$

$$\times \int_{Q_{x,\xi}} (\partial_\xi^\beta \partial_x^{\beta_1}F)(x,\xi,\zeta)(\partial_x^{\beta_2}F)(x,\xi,\zeta)\int_0^1 (1-\theta)^{N-1}(\partial_\xi^\alpha D_x^{\beta_3}p)(x,\theta\zeta+(1-\theta)\xi)\,d\theta d\zeta.$$

Now, there exists $K > 0$ such that

$$K^{-1}\langle\xi\rangle \leq \langle\theta\zeta+(1-\theta)\xi\rangle \leq K\langle\xi\rangle, \quad |\theta|<1, \zeta \in Q_{x,\xi}, x,\xi \in \mathbb{R}^n.$$

Then, using (18), since $s \leq \min\{\mu,\nu\}$, we obtain

$$|\partial_\xi^\gamma \partial_x^\delta r_{\beta,N}(x,\xi)| \leq C^{|\gamma+\delta|+2(N+|\beta|)+1}\gamma!^\mu \delta!^\nu \beta!^{s+\nu-1}N!^{\mu-1}$$

$$\times \langle\xi\rangle^{m_1-|\gamma|-\frac{N+|\beta|}{2}}\langle x\rangle^{m_2-|\delta|-\frac{N+|\beta|}{2}} \underbrace{\int_{Q_{x,\xi}} \langle\xi\rangle^{-\frac{n}{2}}\langle x\rangle^{\frac{n}{2}}d\sigma}_{=\int_{|\sigma|\leq 1}d\sigma}$$

$$\leq C^{|\gamma+\delta|+2(N+|\beta|)+1}\gamma!^\mu \delta!^\nu \beta!^{s+\nu-1}N!^{\mu-1}\langle\xi\rangle^{m_1-|\gamma|-\frac{N+|\beta|}{2}}\langle x\rangle^{m_2-|\delta|-\frac{N+|\beta|}{2}}, \quad (20)$$

for every $\gamma,\delta \in \mathbb{N}_0^n$, $x,\xi \in \mathbb{R}^n$ and $N \in \mathbb{N}$. Now, by (19) and (20), we get

$$p_{F,L}(x,\xi) \sim \sum_{j \in \mathbb{N}_0}\sum_{|\alpha+\beta|=j} q_{\alpha,\beta}(x,\xi) \text{ in } FSG^m_{(\frac{1}{2},1),(0,\frac{1}{2});(\tilde{\mu},\tilde{\nu})}.$$

To improve the above asymptotic expansion, note that, for $j \geq 2$,

$$|\partial_\xi^\gamma \partial_x^\delta \sum_{|\alpha+\beta|=j} q_{\alpha,\beta}(x,\xi)| \leq C^{|\gamma+\delta|+2j+1} \gamma!^\mu \delta!^\nu j!^{\mu+\nu-1} \langle x \rangle^{m_2-|\delta|-\frac{j}{2}} \langle \xi \rangle^{m_1-|\gamma|-\frac{j}{2}},$$

and

$$|\partial_\xi^\gamma \partial_x^\delta \sum_{|\beta|=1} q_{0,\beta}(x,\xi)| \leq C^{|\theta+\sigma|+2j+1} \gamma!^\mu \delta!^\nu j!^{\mu+\nu-1} \langle x \rangle^{m_2-|\delta|-1} \langle \xi \rangle^{m_1-|\gamma|-1},$$

for every $\gamma, \delta \in \mathbb{N}_0^n$, $x, \xi \in \mathbb{R}^n$, hence

$$\sum_{j \in \mathbb{N}_0} \sum_{|\alpha+\beta|=j} q_{\alpha,\beta}(x,\xi) \in F_{(k_j,\ell_j)} SG_{(\mu,\nu)}^m,$$

where $k_0 = \ell_0 = 0$, $k_1 = \ell_1 = 1$, $k_j = \ell_j = \frac{j}{2}$. Then, there exists $q \in \mathbf{SG}_{(\mu,\nu)}^m(\mathbb{R}^{2n})$ such that

$$q(x,\xi) \sim \sum_{\alpha,\beta} q_{\alpha,\beta}(x,\xi) \quad \text{in } F_{(k_j,\ell_j)} SG_{(\mu,\nu)}^m.$$

Repeating the argument at the end of Section 3, we can write $p_{F,L}(x,\xi) = q(x,\xi) + r(x,\xi)$, where r belongs to the Gelfand–Shilov space $\mathcal{S}_{\tilde{\mu}+\tilde{\nu}-1}(\mathbb{R}^{2n})$. Summing up, we obtain the following result.

Theorem 6. *Let $p \in SG_{(\mu,\nu)}^m$ and p_F be its Friedrichs part. Then, we can write $p_{F,L} = q + r$, with $r \in \mathcal{S}_{\tilde{\mu}+\tilde{\nu}-1}(\mathbb{R}^{2n})$ and*

$$q(x,\xi) \sim p(x,\xi) + \sum_{|\beta|=1} q_{0,\beta}(x,\xi) + \sum_{|\alpha+\beta|\geq 2} q_{\alpha,\beta}(x,\xi) \quad \text{in } F_{(k_j,\ell_j)} SG_{(\mu,\nu)}^m$$

where $k_0 = \ell_0 = 0$, $k_1 = \ell_1 = 1$, $k_j = \ell_j = \frac{j}{2}$. Moreover, the symbols $q_{0,\beta} \in \mathbf{SG}_{(\mu,\nu)}^{m-(1,1)}(\mathbb{R}^{2n})$ and $q_{\alpha,\beta} \in \mathbf{SG}_{(\mu,\nu)}^{m-\frac{|\alpha+\beta|}{2}(1,1)}(\mathbb{R}^{2n})$ are the same as in Theorem 4.

Author Contributions: Conceptualization, A.A.J. and M.C.; methodology, A.A.J. and M.C.; formal analysis, A.A.J. and M.C.; investigation, A.A.J. and M.C.; writing–original draft preparation, A.A.J. and M.C.; writing–review and editing, A.A.J. and M.C. All authors have read and agreed to the published version of the manuscript.

Funding: This research received no external funding.

Acknowledgments: The first author would like to thank Fundação Araucária for the financial support during the development of this paper.

Conflicts of Interest: The authors declare no conflict of interest.

References

1. Hörmander, L. Pseudo-differential operators and non-elliptic noundary problems. *Ann. Math.* **1966**, *83*, 129–209. [CrossRef]
2. Lax, P.D.; Nirenberg, L. On stability for difference scheme: A sharp form of Gårding inequality. *Commun. Pure Appl. Math.* **1966**, *19*, 473–492. [CrossRef]
3. Friedrichs, K.O. *Pseudo-Differential Operators*; Lecture Note; Courant Inst. Math. Sci. New York Univ.: New York, NY, USA, 1968.
4. Hörmander, L. *The Analysis of Linear Partial Differential Operators III*; Springer: Berlin/Heidelberg, Germany, 1985.
5. Kumano-Go, H. *Pseudo-Differential Operators*; The MIT Press: Cambridge, UK; London, UK, 1982.
6. Nagase, M. A new proof of sharp Gårding inequality. *Funkc. Ekvacioj* **1977**, *20*, 259–271.
7. Cicognani, M.; Colombini, F. The Cauchy problem for p-evolution equations. *Trans. Am. Math. Soc.* **2010**, *362*, 4853–4869. [CrossRef]

8. Cicognani, M.; Reissig, M. Well-posedness for degenerate Schrödinger equations. *Evol. Equ. Control Theory* **2014**, *3*, 15–33. [CrossRef]
9. Ascanelli, A.; Boiti, C.; Zanghirati, L. Well-posedness of the Cauchy problem for p-evolution equations. *J. Differ. Equ.* **2012**, *253* 2765–2795. [CrossRef]
10. Ascanelli, A.; Cappiello, M. Weighted energy estimates for p-evolution equations in **SG**classes. *J. Evol. Equ.* **2015**, *15*, 583–607. [CrossRef]
11. Gelfand, I.M.; Shilov, G.E. *Generalized Functions*; Academic Press: New York, NY, USA; London, UK, 1967; Volume 2.
12. Ascanelli, A.; Cappiello, M. Schrödinger-type equations in Gefand-Shilov spaces. *J. Math. Pures Appl.* **2019**, *132*, 207–250. [CrossRef]
13. Arias, A., Jr.; Ascanelli, A.; Cappiello, M. The Cauchy problem for 3-evolutions equations with data in Gelfand-Shilov spaces. *arXiv* **2020**, arXiv:2009.10366.
14. Cappiello, M.; Rodino, L. **SG**-pseudodifferential operators and Gelfand-Shilov spaces. *Rocky Mt. J. Math.* **2006**, *36*, 1118–1148. [CrossRef]
15. Cordes, H.O. *The Technique of Pseudo-Differential Operators*; Cambridge Univ. Press: Cambridge, UK, 1995.
16. Coriasco, S. Fourier integral operators in SG classes.I. Composition theorems and action on SG-Sobolev spaces. *Rend. Sem. Mat. Univ. Pol. Torino* **1999**, *57*, 249–302.
17. Coriasco, S. Fourier integral operators in SG classes.II. Application to SG hyperbolic Cauchy problems. *Ann. Univ. Ferrara Sez VII* **1998**, *44*, 81–122.
18. Egorov, Y.V.; Schulze, B.-W. *Pseudo-Differential Operators, Singularities, Applications*; Operator Theory: Advances and Applications 93; Birkhäuser Verlag: Basel, Switzerland, 1997.
19. Nicola, F.; Rodino, L. *Global Pseudo-Differential Calculus on Euclidean Spaces*; Birkhäuser: Basel, Switzerland, 2010; Volume 4.
20. Parenti, C. Operatori pseudodifferenziali in $\mathbb{R}^n$ e applicazioni. *Ann. Mat. Pura Appl.* **1972**, *93*, 359–389. [CrossRef]
21. Schrohe, E. Spaces of weighted symbols and weighted Sobolev spaces on manifolds. In *Proceedings, Oberwolfach, 1256*; Cordes, H.O., Gramsch, B., Widom, H., Eds.; Springer: New York, NY, USA, 1986; pp. 360–377.
22. Camperi, I. Global hypoellipticity and Sobolev estimates for generalized SG-pseudo-differential operators. *Rend. Sem. Mat. Univ. Pol. Torino* **2008**, *66*, 99–112.
23. Cappiello, M.; Gramchev, T.; Rodino, L. Sub-exponential decay and uniform holomorphic extensions for semilinear pseudodifferential equations. *Commun. Partial Differ. Equ.* **2010**, *35*, 846–877. [CrossRef]
24. Bierstone, E.; Milman, P.D. Resolution of singularities in Denjoy-Carleman classes. *Sel. Math.* **2004**, *10*, 1. [CrossRef]

Publisher's Note: MDPI stays neutral with regard to jurisdictional claims in published maps and institutional affiliations.

 © 2020 by the authors. Licensee MDPI, Basel, Switzerland. This article is an open access article distributed under the terms and conditions of the Creative Commons Attribution (CC BY) license (http://creativecommons.org/licenses/by/4.0/).

Article

Norm Inflation for Benjamin–Bona–Mahony Equation in Fourier Amalgam and Wiener Amalgam Spaces with Negative Regularity

Divyang G. Bhimani [1],* and Saikatul Haque [2]

[1] Department of Mathematics, Indian Institute of Science Education and Research, Dr. Homi Bhabha Road, Pune 411008, India
[2] Department of Mathematics, Harish-Chandra Research Institute, Allahabad 2110019, India; saikatulhaque@hri.res.in
* Correspondence: divyang.bhimani@iiserpune.ac.in

Abstract: We consider the Benjamin–Bona–Mahony (BBM) equation of the form $u_t + u_x + uu_x - u_{xxt} = 0, (x,t) \in \mathcal{M} \times \mathbb{R}$ where $\mathcal{M} = \mathbb{T}$ or $\mathbb{R}$. We establish norm inflation (NI) with infinite loss of regularity at general initial data in Fourier amalgam and Wiener amalgam spaces with negative regularity. This strengthens several known NI results at zero initial data in $H^s(\mathbb{T})$ established by Bona–Dai (2017) and the ill-posedness result established by Bona–Tzvetkov (2008) and Panthee (2011) in $H^s(\mathbb{R})$. Our result is sharp with respect to the local well-posedness result of Banquet–Villamizar–Roa (2021) in modulation spaces $M_s^{2,1}(\mathbb{R})$ for $s \geqslant 0$.

Keywords: BBM equation; ill-posedness; Fourier amalgam spaces; Wiener amalgam spaces; Fourier-Lebesgue spaces; modulation spaces

MSC: 35Q53; 35R25 (primary); 42B35 (secondary)

1. Introduction

We study strong ill-posedness for the Benjamin–Bona–Mahony (BBM) equation of the form

$$\begin{cases} u_t + u_x + uu_x - u_{xxt} = 0 \\ u(x,0) = u_0(x) \end{cases} \tag{1}$$

where $u: \mathcal{M} \times \mathbb{R} \to \mathbb{R}$ unknown function and $\mathcal{M} = \mathbb{T}$ or $\mathbb{R}$. The BBM (1) can be written as

$$iu_t = \varphi(D_x)u + \frac{1}{2}\varphi(D_x)u^2, \quad u(x,0) = u_0(x) \tag{2}$$

where $\varphi(\xi) = \frac{\xi}{1+\xi^2}, D_x = \frac{1}{i}\partial_x$ and $\varphi(D_x)$ is the Fourier multiplier operator defined by

$$\mathcal{F}[\varphi(D_x)u](\xi) = \varphi(\xi)\hat{u}(\xi).$$

This BBM (1) model is the regularized counterpart of the Korteweg–de Vries (KdV) equation. This is extensively studied in the literature; see [1–5]. BBM equation (1) is well-suited for modeling wave propagation on star graphs; see [6]. This model gave a good description of the propagation of surface water waves in a channel; see [5].

The aim of this paper is to establish the following strong ill-posedness (norm inflation at general initial data with infinite loss of regularity) for (1) in Fourier amalgam $\hat{w}_s^{p,q}(\mathcal{M})$ and Wiener amalgam $W_s^{p,q}(\mathcal{M})$ spaces (to be defined in Section 2). We recall that

$$\widehat{w}_s^{p,q}(\mathcal{M}) = \begin{cases} \mathcal{F}L_s^q(\mathcal{M}) \text{ (Fourier–Lebesgue spaces)} & \text{if } p = q \\ M_s^{2,q}(\mathcal{M}) \text{ (modulation spaces)} & \text{if } p = 2 \\ M_s^{2,2}(\mathcal{M}) = W_s^{2,2}(\mathcal{M}) = H^s(\mathcal{M}) \text{ (Sobolev spaces)} & \text{if } p = q = 2 \\ \mathcal{F}L_s^q(\mathcal{M}) = M_s^{p,q}(\mathcal{M}) = W_s^{p,q}(\mathcal{M}) & \text{if } \mathcal{M} = \mathbb{T}^d. \end{cases}$$

These time–frequency spaces are proven to be very fruitful in handling various problems in analysis and have gained prominence in nonlinear dispersive PDEs, e.g., [7–15]. We now state our main theorem.

Theorem 1. *Assume that* $1 \leq p, q \leq \infty, s < 0$ *and let*

$$X_s^{p,q}(\mathcal{M}) = \begin{cases} \widehat{w}_s^{p,q}(\mathbb{R}) \text{ or } W_s^{2,q}(\mathbb{R}) \text{ for } \mathcal{M} = \mathbb{R} \\ \mathcal{F}L_s^q(\mathbb{T}) \text{ for } \mathcal{M} = \mathbb{T}. \end{cases}$$

Then, norm inflation with infinite loss of regularity occurs to (1) *everywhere in* $X_s^{p,q}(\mathcal{M})$, *i.e., for any* $u_0 \in X_s^{p,q}(\mathcal{M})$, $\theta \in \mathbb{R}$ *and* $\varepsilon > 0$, *there exists a smooth* $u_{0,\varepsilon} \in X_s^{p,q}(\mathcal{M})$ *and* $T > 0$ *satisfying*

$$\|u_0 - u_{0,\varepsilon}\|_{X_s^{p,q}} < \varepsilon, \quad 0 < T < \varepsilon$$

such that the corresponding smooth solution u_ε *to* (1) *with data* $u_{0,\varepsilon}$ *exists on* $[0, T]$ *and*

$$\|u_\varepsilon(T)\|_{X_\theta} > \frac{1}{\varepsilon}.$$

In particular, for any $T > 0$, *the solution map* $X_s^{p,q}(\mathcal{M}) \ni u_0 \mapsto u \in C([0,T], X_\theta^{p,q}(\mathcal{M}))$ *for* (1) *is discontinuous everywhere in* $X_s^{p,q}(\mathcal{M})$ *for all* $\theta \in \mathbb{R}$.

In [3], Bona and Tzvetkov proved that (1) is globally well-posed in $H^s(\mathbb{R})$ for $s \geq 0$. Moreover, they also proved that (1) is ill-posed for $s < 0$ in the sense that the solution map $u_0 \mapsto u(t)$ is not C^2 from $H^s(\mathbb{R})$ to $C([0,T], H^s(\mathbb{R}))$. Later, in [16], Panthee proved that it is discontinuous at the origin from $H^s(\mathbb{R})$ to $\mathcal{D}'(\mathbb{R})$. Recently, Bona and Dai, in [17], established norm inflation for (1) at zero initial data in $H^s(\mathbb{T})$ for $s < 0$. We note that Theorem 1 also holds for the corresponding homogeneous $\dot{X}_s^{p,q}(\mathcal{M})$ spaces; see Remark 1. The particular case of Theorem 1 strengthens these results by establishing the infinite loss of regularity at every initial datum in $H^s(\mathcal{M})$ for $s < 0$. In [18] (Theorem 1.7), Banquet and Villamizar-Roa proved that (1) is locally well-posed in $M_s^{2,1}(\mathbb{R})$ for $s \geq 0$. Thus, the particular case of Theorem 1 complements this result by establishing sharp, strong ill-posedness in $M_s^{2,1}(\mathbb{R})$ for $s < 0$. To the best of the authors' knowledge, there is no well-posedness result for (1) in Fourier amalgam $\widehat{w}_s^{p,q}$ ($p \neq 2$) (except in $\mathcal{F}L^1(\mathcal{M})$; see Corollary 1) or in $W^{p,q}$ (except in H^s) spaces. The infinite loss of regularity for (1) is initiated in the present paper and thus Theorem 1 is new.

We use a Fourier analytic approach to prove Theorem 1. This approach dates back to Bejenaru and Tao [19] to obtain ill-posedness for quadratic NLS and further developed by Iwabuchi in [20]. Later, Kishimoto [21] established norm inflation (NI) for NLS on a special domain (special domain: $\mathbb{R}^{d_1} \times \mathbb{T}^{d_2}, d = d_1 + d_2$ and with non-linearity: $\sum_{j=1}^n v_j u^{\rho_j}(\bar{u})^{\sigma_j - \rho_j}$ where $v_j \in \mathbb{C}, \sigma_j \in \mathbb{N}, \rho_j \in \mathbb{N} \cup \{0\}$ with $\sigma_j \geq \max(\rho_j, 2)$) and Oh [22] established NI at general initial data for cubic NLS. Recently, this approach has been used to obtain strong ill-posedness for NLW in [15,23]. We refer to [21] (Section 2) for a detailed discussion of this approach.

We now briefly comment on and outline the proof of Theorem 1. We first justify the convergence of a series of Picard terms, the smooth solutions to (1), in Wiener algebra $\mathcal{F}L^1$ (see Corollary 1). This is possible since the linear BBM propagator is unitary on $\mathcal{F}L^1$ and the bilinear operator for the nonlinearity in (2) is bounded (see Lemma 1). Then, (1) experiences NI at general initial data because (with appropriately chosen initial data close to the given data) one Picard term dominates, in $X_s^{p,q}$–norm, the rest of the Picard iterate terms in the series for $s < 0$ and also this term becomes arbitrarily large (see (16)–(18)). To this end, we perturb general initial data u_0 by $\phi_{0,N}$. Here, $\phi_{0,N}$ is defined on the Fourier side by a scalar (depends on N) multiplication of the characteristic function on the union of two intervals obtained by translation of $[-1,1]$ by $\pm N$ and so the size of support of $\phi_{0,N}$ remains uniform. Specifically, we set

$$\mathcal{F}\phi_{0,N} = R\chi_{I_N},$$

where $I_N = [-N-1, -N+1] \cup [N-1, N+1]$ with $N \gg 1$, $R = R(N) \gg 1$ (to be chosen later) and

$$u_{0,N} = u_0 + \phi_{0,N}.$$

Eventually, this $u_{0,N}$ will play the role of $u_{0,\epsilon}$ in Theorem 1. Similarly, $\phi_{0,N}$ was used by Bona and Tzvetkov to establish that the solution map fails to become C^2 in [3] and also by Panthee [16] to conclude that, in fact, the solution map is discontinuous. In [3], the size of the support of $\phi_{0,N}$ on the Fourier side was allowed to vary as $N \to \infty$ with a normalizing constant to ensure that $\|\phi_{0,N}\|_{H^s} \sim 1$, whereas in [16], $\mathcal{F}\phi_{0,N}$ is taken as χ_{I_N}, which implies $\|\phi_{0,N}\|_{H^s} \to 0$ as $N \to \infty$. To establish NI with infinite loss of regularity, we multiply $R = R(N) \gg 1$ with Panthee's choice of $\phi_{0,N}$ to ensure that the second Picard iterates $U_2(t)[u_{0,N}]$ have the desired property (as mentioned above) and reduce the analysis when considering a single term on the ℓ^q–norm:

$$\|\langle n \rangle^\theta f(n)\|_{\ell_n^q(n=1)} = 2^{(s-\theta)/2} \|\langle n \rangle^s f(n)\|_{\ell_n^q(n=1)} \quad \text{for all } \theta \in \mathbb{R}.$$

as done in NLW case in [23]. We note that finite loss of regularity of NLW was initiated by Lebeau in [24] and infinite loss of regularity for NLS, via a geometric optics approach, by Carles et al. in [25].

The rest of the paper is organized as follows. In Section 2, we recall the definitions of the time–frequency spaces. In Section 3, we establish power series expansion of the solution in $\mathcal{F}L^1$, by establishing $\widehat{w}_s^{p,q}$-estimates of the Picard terms for general data. In Section 4, we first prove various estimates of the Picard terms with particular choices of data, and this enables us to conclude the proof of Theorem 1.

2. Function Spaces

The notation $A \lesssim B$ means $A \leq cB$ for some constant $c > 0$, whereas $A \asymp B$ means $c^{-1}A \leq B \leq cA$ for some $c \geq 1$. Let $\mathcal{F}$ denote the Fourier transform and $\langle \cdot \rangle^s = (1+|\cdot|^2)^{s/2}$, $s \in \mathbb{R}$. Here, $\widehat{\mathcal{M}}$ denotes the Pontryagin dual of $\mathcal{M}$, i.e., $\widehat{\mathcal{M}} = \mathbb{R}$ if $\mathcal{M} = \mathbb{R}$ and $\widehat{\mathcal{M}} = \mathbb{Z}$ if $\mathcal{M} = \mathbb{T}$. $\mathcal{S}'(\mathcal{M})$ denotes the space of tempered distributions; see, e.g., [26] (Part II) for details. The **Fourier–Lebesgue space** $\mathcal{F}L_s^q(\mathcal{M})$ ($1 \leq q \leq \infty, s \in \mathbb{R}$) is defined by

$$\mathcal{F}L_s^q(\mathcal{M}) = \left\{ f \in \mathcal{S}'(\mathcal{M}) : \mathcal{F}f \langle \cdot \rangle^s \in L^q(\widehat{\mathcal{M}}) \right\}.$$

In the 1980s, Feichtinger [27] introduced the **modulation spaces** $M_s^{p,q}(\mathcal{M})$ and **Wiener amalgam spaces** $W_s^{p,q}(\mathcal{M})$ using shrot-time Fourier transform (STFT) (STFT is also known as windowed Fourier transform and is closely related to Fourier–Wigner and Bargmann transform. See, e.g., [28] (Lemma 3.1.1) and [28] (Proposition 3.4.1)). The STFT of a $f \in \mathcal{S}'(\mathcal{M})$ with respect to a window function $0 \neq g \in \mathcal{S}(\mathcal{M})$ is defined by

$$V_g f(x,y) = \int_\mathcal{M} f(t)\overline{T_x g(t)} e^{-2\pi i y \cdot t} dt, \quad (x,y) \in \mathcal{M} \times \widehat{\mathcal{M}}$$

27

whenever the integral exists. Here, $T_x g(t) = g(tx^{-1})$ is the translation operator on $\mathcal{M}$. We define modulation $M_s^{p,q}(\mathcal{M})$ and Wiener amalgam spaces $W_s^{p,q}(\mathcal{M})$, for $1 \leq p, q \leq \infty, s \in \mathbb{R}$, by the norms:

$$\|f\|_{M_s^{p,q}} = \left\| \|V_g f(x,y)\|_{L^p(\mathcal{M})} \langle y \rangle^s \right\|_{L^q(\widehat{\mathcal{M}})} \quad \text{and} \quad \|f\|_{W_s^{p,q}(\mathcal{M})} = \left\| \|V_g f(x,y) \langle y \rangle^s\|_{L^q(\widehat{\mathcal{M}})} \right\|_{L^p(\mathcal{M})}.$$

The definition of the modulation space is independent of the choice of the particular window function; see [28] (Proposition 11.3.2(c)). There is also equivalent characterization of these spaces via frequency uniform decomposition (which is quite similar to Besov spaces—where decomposition is dyadic). To do this, let $\rho \in \mathcal{S}(\mathbb{R})$, $\rho : \mathbb{R} \to [0,1]$ be a smooth function satisfying $\rho(\xi) = 1$ if $|\xi| \leq \frac{1}{2}$ and $\rho(\xi) = 0$ if $|\xi| \geq 1$. Set $\rho_n(\xi) = \rho(\xi - n)$ and $\sigma_n(\xi) = \frac{\rho_n(\xi)}{\sum_{\ell \in \mathbb{Z}^d} \rho_\ell(\xi)}, n \in \mathbb{Z}$. Then, define the frequency-uniform decomposition operators by

$$\Box_n = \mathcal{F}^{-1} \sigma_n \mathcal{F}.$$

It is known [7] (Proposition 2.1), [27] that

$$\|f\|_{M_s^{p,q}(\mathcal{M})} \asymp \left\| \|\Box_n f\|_{L_x^p(\mathcal{M})} \langle n \rangle^s \right\|_{\ell_n^q(\mathbb{Z})} \quad \text{and} \quad \|f\|_{W_s^{p,q}(\mathcal{M})} \asymp \left\| \|\Box_n f \cdot \langle n \rangle^s \|_{\ell_n^q(\mathbb{Z})} \right\|_{L_x^p(\mathcal{M})}.$$

Recently, in [29], Oh and Forlano introduced **Fourier amalgam spaces** $\widehat{w}_s^{p,q}(\mathcal{M})$ ($1 \leq p, q \leq \infty, s \in \mathbb{R}$):

$$\widehat{w}_s^{p,q}(\mathcal{M}) = \left\{ f \in \mathcal{S}'(\mathcal{M}) : \|f\|_{\widehat{w}_s^{p,q}} = \left\| \|\chi_{n+Q_1}(\xi) \mathcal{F} f(\xi)\|_{L_\xi^p(\widehat{\mathcal{M}})} \langle n \rangle^s \right\|_{\ell_n^q(\mathbb{Z})} < \infty \right\},$$

where $Q_1 = (-\frac{1}{2}, \frac{1}{2}]$. The **homogeneous spaces** $\dot{X}_s^{p,q}(\mathcal{M})$ corresponding to the above spaces can be defined by replacing the Japanese brackets $\langle \cdot \rangle^s$ with $|\cdot|^s$ in their definitions.

3. Local Well-Posedness in Wiener Algebra $\mathcal{F}L^1$

The integral version of (2) is given by

$$u(t) = U(t)u_0 - \frac{i}{2} \int_0^t U(t-\tau) \varphi(D_x) u^2(\tau) d\tau \tag{3}$$

where $\mathcal{F}U(t)\varphi(D_x)u(\xi) = e^{it\varphi(\xi)} \varphi(\xi) \mathcal{F}u(\xi)$ and $U(t)u_0(x) = \mathcal{F}^{-1}(e^{it\varphi(\xi)} \mathcal{F}u_0(\xi))(x)$ is the unique solution to the linear problem

$$iu_t = \varphi(D_x)u, \quad u(x,0) = u_0(x); \quad (x,t) \in \mathcal{M} \times \mathbb{R}.$$

Let us define the operator $\mathcal{N}$ given by

$$\mathcal{N}(u,v)(t) = \int_0^t U(t-\tau)\varphi(D_x)(uv)(\tau) d\tau.$$

Definition 1 (Picard iteration). *For $u_0 \in L^2(\mathbb{R}^d)$, define $U_1[u_0](t) = U(t)u_0$ and for $k \geq 2$*

$$U_k[u_0](t) = -\frac{i}{2} \sum_{\substack{k_1, k_2 \geq 1 \\ k_1 + k_2 = k}} \mathcal{N}(U_{k_1}[u_0], U_{k_2}[u_0])(t).$$

Lemma 1. *Let $1 \leq p, q \leq \infty, s, t \in \mathbb{R}$. Then, we have*
(1) $\|U(t)u_0\|_{\widehat{w}_s^{p,q}} = \|u_0\|_{\widehat{w}_s^{p,q}}$
(2) $\|\mathcal{N}(u,v)(t)\|_{\widehat{w}_s^{p,q}} \lesssim \int_0^t \|u(\tau)\|_{\mathcal{F}L^1} \|v(\tau)\|_{\widehat{w}_s^{p,q}} d\tau \leq t\|u\|_{L^\infty((0,t),\mathcal{F}L^1)} \|v\|_{L^\infty((0,t),\widehat{w}_s^{p,q})}.$

Proof. Note that

$$\|U(t)u_0\|_{\widehat{w}_s^{p,q}} = \left\| \left\| \chi_{n+Q_1}(\xi) e^{it\varphi(\xi)} \mathcal{F} u_0(\xi) \right\|_{L_\xi^p(\widehat{\mathcal{M}})} (1+|n|^2)^{s/2} \right\|_{\ell_n^q(\mathbb{Z})} = \|u_0\|_{\widehat{w}_s^{p,q}}.$$

Using the fact that $|\varphi| \leqslant 1$, we have

$$\|\mathcal{N}(u,v)(t)\|_{\widehat{w}_s^{p,q}} = \left\| \left\| \chi_{n+Q_1}(\xi) \int_0^t e^{i(t-\tau)\varphi(\xi)} \varphi(\xi)(\mathcal{F}u * \mathcal{F}v)(\xi)(\tau) d\tau \right\|_{L_\xi^p(\widehat{\mathcal{M}})} \langle n \rangle^s \right\|_{\ell_n^q(\mathbb{Z})}$$

$$\leqslant \left\| \int_0^t \left\| \chi_{n+Q_1}(\xi) e^{i(t-\tau)\varphi(\xi)} \varphi(\xi)(\mathcal{F}u * \mathcal{F}v)(\xi)(\tau) \right\|_{L_\xi^p(\widehat{\mathcal{M}})} d\tau \langle n \rangle^s \right\|_{\ell_n^q(\mathbb{Z})}$$

$$\leqslant \left\| \int_0^t \left\| \chi_{n+Q_1}(\xi)(\mathcal{F}u * \mathcal{F}v)(\xi)(\tau) \right\|_{L_\xi^p(\widehat{\mathcal{M}})} d\tau \langle n \rangle^s \right\|_{\ell_n^q(\mathbb{Z})}$$

$$\leqslant \int_0^t \left\| \|\mathcal{F}u(\xi)(\tau)\|_{L_\xi^1(\widehat{\mathcal{M}})} \|\chi_{n+Q_1}(\xi) \mathcal{F}v(\xi)(\tau)\|_{L_\xi^p(\widehat{\mathcal{M}})} \langle n \rangle^s \right\|_{\ell_n^q(\mathbb{Z})} d\tau$$

$$= \int_0^t \|u(\tau)\|_{\mathcal{F}L^1} \|v(\tau)\|_{\widehat{w}_s^{p,q}} d\tau.$$

□

Lemma 2 (See [21]). *Let $\{b_k\}_{k=1}^\infty$ be a sequence of nonnegative real numbers such that*

$$b_k \leqslant C \sum_{\substack{k_1,k_2 \geqslant 1 \\ k_1+k_2=k}} b_{k_1} b_{k_2} \quad \forall k \geqslant 2.$$

Then, we have $b_k \leqslant b_1 C_0^{k-1}$, for all $k \geqslant 1$, where $C_0 = \frac{2\pi^2}{3} C b_1$.

Lemma 3. *There exists $c > 0$ such that for all $t > 0$ and $k \geqslant 2$, we have*

$$\|U_k[u_0](t)\|_{\widehat{w}_s^{p,q}} \leqslant (ct)^{k-1} \|u_0\|_{\mathcal{F}L^1}^{k-1} \|u_0\|_{\widehat{w}_s^{p,q}}.$$

Proof. Let $\{b_k\}$ be a sequence of nonnegative real numbers such that

$$b_1 = 1 \quad \text{and} \quad b_k = \frac{1}{k-1} \sum_{\substack{k_1,k_2 \geqslant 1 \\ k_1+k_2=k}} b_{k_1} b_{k_2} \quad \forall k \geqslant 2.$$

By Lemma 2, we have $b_k \leqslant c_0^{k-1}$ for some $c_0 > 0$. In view of this, it is enough to prove the following claim:

$$\|U_k[u_0](t)\|_{\widehat{w}_s^{p,q}} \leqslant b_k t^{k-1} \|u_0\|_{\mathcal{F}L^1}^{k-1} \|u_0\|_{\widehat{w}_s^{p,q}}.$$

By Definition 1, Lemma 1 and using the fact that $\frac{|\xi|}{1+\xi^2} \leqslant 1$, we have

$$\|U_k[u_0](t)\|_{\widehat{w}_s^{p,q}} \leqslant \sum_{\substack{k_1,k_2 \geqslant 1 \\ k_1+k_2=k}} \int_0^t \|U_{k_1}[u_0](\tau)\|_{\mathcal{F}L^1} \|U_{k_2}[u_0](\tau)\|_{\widehat{w}_s^{p,q}} d\tau \qquad (4)$$

Thus, we have

$$\|U_2[u_0](t)\|_{\widehat{w}_s^{p,q}} \leqslant t \|U[u_0]\|_{L^\infty((0,t),\mathcal{F}L^1)} \|U[u_0]\|_{L^\infty((0,t),\widehat{w}_s^{p,q})} = t \|u_0\|_{\mathcal{F}L^1} \|u_0\|_{\widehat{w}_s^{p,q}}$$

Hence, the claim is true for $k = 2$ as $b_2 = 1$. Assume that the result is true up to the label $(k-1)$. Then, from (4), we obtain

$$\|U_k[u_0](t)\|_{\widehat{w}_s^{p,q}} \leqslant \sum_{\substack{k_1,k_2 \geqslant 1 \\ k_1+k_2=k}} b_{k_1} b_{k_2} \int_0^t \tau^{k_1-1} \|u_0\|_{\mathcal{F}L^1}^{k_1} \times \tau^{k_2-1} \|u_0\|_{\mathcal{F}L^1}^{k_2-1} \|u_0\|_{\widehat{w}_s^{p,q}} d\tau$$

$$= b_k t^{k-1} \|u_0\|_{\mathcal{F}L^1}^{k-1} \|u_0\|_{\widehat{w}_s^{p,q}}.$$

Thus, the claim is true at the level k. This completes the proof. □

Corollary 1. *If $0 < T \ll M^{-1}$, then for any $u_0 \in \mathcal{F}L^1$ with $\|u_0\|_{\mathcal{F}L^1} \leqslant M$, there exists a unique solution $u \in C([0, T], \mathcal{F}L^1(\mathcal{M}))$ to the integral equation (3) associated with (2), given by*

$$u = \sum_{k=1}^{\infty} U_k[u_0] \tag{5}$$

which converges absolutely in $C([0, T], \mathcal{F}L^1(\mathcal{M}))$.

Proof. Define

$$\Psi(u)(t) = U(t)u_0 - \frac{i}{2}\mathcal{N}(u,u)(t).$$

By Lemma 1, we have

$$\|\Psi(u)\|_{C([0,T],\mathcal{F}L^1)} \leqslant \|u_0\|_{\mathcal{F}L^1} + T\|u\|_{C([0,T],\mathcal{F}L^1)}^2,$$

$$\|\Psi(u) - \Psi(v)\|_{C([0,T],\mathcal{F}L^1)} \lesssim T \max\left(\|u\|_{C([0,T],\mathcal{F}L^1)}, \|v\|_{C([0,T],\mathcal{F}L^1)}\right) \|u - v\|_{C([0,T],\mathcal{F}L^1)}.$$

Then, considering the ball

$$B_{2M}^T = \left\{\phi \in C([0,T], \mathcal{F}L^1) : \|\phi\|_{C([0,T],\mathcal{F}L^1)} \leqslant 2M\right\}$$

with $TM \ll 1$, we find a fixed point of Ψ in B_{2M}^T and hence a solution to (3). This completes the proof of the first part of the lemma. For the second part, we note that in view of Lemma 3, the series (5) converges absolutely if $0 < T \ll M^{-1}$. Then, for $\epsilon > 0$, there exists j_1 such that for all $j \geqslant j_1$, one has

$$\|u - u_j\|_{C([0,T],\mathcal{F}L^1)} < \epsilon \tag{6}$$

where

$$u = \sum_{k=1}^{\infty} U_k[u_0], \quad \text{and} \quad u_j = \sum_{k=1}^{j} U_k[u_0].$$

Note that $u, u_j \in B_{2M}^T$ for all j as $0 < T \ll M^{-1}$. Using the continuity of Ψ on B_{2M}^T, we find j_2 such that for all $j \geqslant j_2$

$$\|\Psi(u) - \Psi(u_j)\|_{C([0,T],\mathcal{F}L^1)} < \epsilon. \tag{7}$$

Note that

$$u_j - \Psi(u_j) = \sum_{k=1}^{j} U_k[u_0] - U(t)u_0 + \frac{i}{2}\mathcal{N}(u_j, u_j)$$

$$= \sum_{k=2}^{j} U_k[u_0] + \frac{i}{2} \sum_{1 \leq k_1, k_2 \leq j} \mathcal{N}(U_{k_1}[u_0], U_{k_2}[u_0])$$

$$= \frac{i}{2} \sum_{k=j+1}^{2j} \sum_{\substack{1 \leq k_1, k_2 \leq j \\ k_1 + k_2 = k}} \mathcal{N}(U_{k_1}[u_0], U_{k_2}[u_0]) = -\sum_{k=j+1}^{2j} U_{k,j}[u_0]$$

where we set

$$U_{k,j}[u_0] = -\frac{i}{2} \sum_{\substack{1 \leq k_1, k_2 \leq j \\ k_1 + k_2 = k}} \mathcal{N}(U_{k_1}[u_0], U_{k_2}[u_0]).$$

Note that $U_{k,j}$ has a lower number of terms in the sum above compared to that of U_k. Hence, proceeding as in the proof of Lemma 3, one achieves the same estimates for $U_{k,j}$. Thus, using $0 < T \ll M^{-1}$,

$$\|u_j - \Psi(u_j)\|_{C([0,T],\mathcal{F}L^1)} \leq \sum_{k=j+1}^{2j} \|U_{k,j}[u_0]\|_{C([0,T],\mathcal{F}L^1)}$$

$$\leq \sum_{k=j+1}^{2j} c^{k-1} T^{k-1} \|u_0\|_{\mathcal{F}L^1}^k$$

$$\leq M \sum_{k=j+1}^{\infty} (cTM)^{k-1} \leq 2M(cMT)^j.$$

Then, there exists j_3 such that for $j \geq j_3$, one has

$$\|u_j - \Psi(u_j)\|_{C([0,T],\mathcal{F}L^1)} < \epsilon. \tag{8}$$

Therefore, from (6)–(8), one has

$$\|u - \Psi(u)\|_{C([0,T],\mathcal{F}L^1)} < 3\epsilon.$$

Thus, u is the required fixed point for Ψ. □

4. Proof of Theorem 1

We first prove NI with infinite loss of regularity at general data in $\mathcal{F}L^1(\mathcal{M}) \cap X_s^{p,q}(\mathcal{M})$. Subsequently, for general data in $X_s^{p,q}(\mathcal{M})$, we use the density of $\mathcal{F}L^1(\mathcal{M}) \cap X_s^{p,q}(\mathcal{M})$ in $X_s^{p,q}(\mathcal{M})$ ($s < 0$). Thus, let us begin with $u_0 \in \mathcal{F}L^1(\mathcal{M}) \cap X_s^{p,q}(\mathcal{M})$. Now, define $\phi_{0,N}$ on $\mathcal{M}$ via the following relation

$$\mathcal{F}\phi_{0,N}(\xi) = R\chi_{I_N}(\xi) \quad (\xi \in \widehat{\mathcal{M}}) \tag{9}$$

where $I_N = [-N-1, -N+1] \cup [N-1, N+1]$ and $N \gg 1, R \gg 1$ to be chosen later. Note that

$$\|\phi_{0,N}\|_{\widehat{w}_s^{p,q}} \sim RN^s. \tag{10}$$

Let us set

$$u_{0,N} = u_0 + \phi_{0,N} \tag{11}$$

Lemma 4 (See Lemma 3.6. in [21]). *There exists $C > 0$ such that for u_0 satisfying (9) and $k \geqslant 1$, we have*
$$|\operatorname{supp} \mathcal{F} U_k[\phi_{0,N}](t)| \leqslant C^k, \quad \forall t \geqslant 0.$$

4.1. Estimates in $\widehat{w}_s^{p,q}(\mathcal{M})$

Lemma 5. *Let u_0 be given by (9), $s \leqslant 0$ and $1 \leqslant p, q \leqslant \infty$. Then, there exists C such that*

(1) $\|u_{0,N} - u_0\|_{\widehat{w}_s^{p,q}} \lesssim RN^s$

(2) $\|U_1[u_{0,N}](t)\|_{\widehat{w}_s^{p,q}} \lesssim 1 + RN^s$

(3) $\|U_2[u_{0,N}](t) - U_2[\phi_{0,N}](t)\|_{\widehat{w}_s^{p,q}} \lesssim tR$

(4) $\|U_k[\vec{u}_{0,N}](t)\|_{\widehat{w}_s^{p,q}} \lesssim C^k R^k t^{k-1}$.

Proof. (1) follows from (10). By Lemma 1 and (10), we have $\|U_1[\phi_{0,N}](t)\|_{\widehat{w}_s^{p,q}} = \|\phi_{0,N}\|_{\widehat{w}_s^{p,q}} \sim RN^s$. Then, (2) follows by using triangle inequality. By Lemma 3 and (10), we obtain

$$\|U_k[\phi_{0,N}](t)\|_{\widehat{w}_s^{p,q}} \leqslant \sup_{\zeta \in \widehat{\mathcal{M}}} |\mathcal{F} U_k[\phi_{0,N}](t, \zeta)| \mu_{\widehat{\mathcal{M}}}(\operatorname{supp} \mathcal{F} U_k[\phi_{0,N}](t))^{1/p} \|\langle n \rangle^s\|_{\ell^q(n \in \operatorname{supp} \mathcal{F} U_k[\phi_{0,N}](t))}$$

$$\lesssim (ct)^{k-1} R^k \|\langle n \rangle^s\|_{\ell^q(n \in \operatorname{supp} \mathcal{F} U_k[\phi_{0,N}](t))}$$

where $\mu_{\widehat{\mathcal{M}}}(A)$ denotes the $\widehat{\mathcal{M}}$-measure of the set A. Since $s \leqslant 0$, for any bounded set $D \subset \mathbb{R}$, we have

$$\|\langle n \rangle^s\|_{\ell^q(n \in D)} \leqslant \|\langle n \rangle^s\|_{\ell^q(n \in B_D)}$$

where $B_D \subset \mathbb{R}$ is the interval centered at the origin with $|D| = |B_D|$. In view of this and Lemma 4, we obtain

$$\|\langle n \rangle^s\|_{\ell^q(\operatorname{supp} \widehat{U}_k[\phi_{0,N}](t))} \leqslant \|\langle n \rangle^s\|_{\ell^q(\{|n| \leqslant C^{k/d}\})} \lesssim C^{k/q}.$$

Therefore,

$$\|U_k[\phi_{0,N}](t)\|_{\widehat{w}_s^{p,q}} \leqslant C^k t^{k-1} R^k. \tag{12}$$

Now, observe that

$$I_k(t) := U_k[u_{0,N}](t) - U_k[\phi_{0,N}](t)$$
$$= \sum_{\substack{k_1, k_2 \geqslant 1 \\ k_1 + k_2 = k}} \mathcal{N}(U_{k_1}[u_0 + \phi_{0,N}], U_{k_2}[u_0 + \phi_{0,N}]) - \mathcal{N}(U_{k_1}[\phi_{0,N}], U_{k_2}[\phi_{0,N}])$$
$$= \sum_{\substack{k_1, k_2 \geqslant 1 \\ k_1 + k_2 = k}} \sum_{(\psi_1, \psi_2) \in \mathcal{C}} \mathcal{N}(U_{k_1}[\psi_1], U_{k_2}[\psi_{2\sigma+1}])$$

where $\mathcal{C} = \{u_0, \phi_{0,N}\}^2 \setminus \{(\phi_{0,N}, \phi_{0,N})\}$. Observe that $\mathcal{C}$ has atleast one coordinate as $\vec{u}_0$. Using Lemma 1 and the proof of Lemma 3, it follows that

$$\|I_k(t)\|_{\widehat{w}_s^{p,q}} \lesssim \sum_{\substack{k_1, k_2 \geqslant 1 \\ k_1 + k_2 = k}} \sum_{(v_1, v_2) \in \mathcal{C}} \int_0^t \|U_{k_1}[v_1](\tau)\|_{\widehat{w}_s^{p,q}} \|U_{k_2}[v_2](\tau)\|_{\mathcal{F}L^1} d\tau$$

$$\leqslant (2^2 - 1) 2 \|u_0\|_{\widehat{w}_s^{p,q}} (\|u_0\|_{\mathcal{F}L^1}^{k-1} + \|\phi_{0,N}\|_{\mathcal{F}L^1}^{k-1}) \int_0^t \tau^{k-2} d\tau \sum_{\substack{k_1, k_2 \geqslant 1 \\ k_1 + k_2 = k}} b_{k_1} b_{k_2}$$

$$\leqslant 12 b_k t^{k-1} R^{k-1} \|u_0\|_{\widehat{w}_s^{p,q}} \leqslant C^k t^{k-1} R^{k-1} \|u_0\|_{\widehat{w}_s^{p,q}}$$

as $R \gg 1$. Note that (3) is the particular case $k = 2$ and (4) follows using the above and (12). □

Lemma 6. *Let u_0 be given by (9), $1 \leqslant p \leqslant \infty$, $s \in \mathbb{R}$ and $0 < T \ll 1$, and then we have*

$$\|U_2[\phi_{0,N}](T)\|_{\widehat{w}_s^{p,q}} \gtrsim \left\| \|\chi_{n+Q_1}(\xi)\mathcal{F}U_2[\phi_{0,N}](T)(\xi)\|_{L_\xi^p} \langle n \rangle^s \right\|_{\ell^q(n=1)} \gtrsim R^2 T.$$

Proof. For notational convenience, we write

$$\Gamma_\xi = \{(\xi_1,\xi_2) : \xi_1 + \xi_2 = \xi\} \quad \text{and} \quad \Phi = c(-\varphi(\xi) + \varphi(\xi_1) + \varphi(\xi_2)).$$

Using the symmetry of set Γ_ξ, we have

$$\begin{aligned}
\mathcal{F}U_2[u_0](T)(\xi) &= \int_0^T e^{ic(T-t)\varphi(\xi)} \varphi(\xi) (\mathcal{F}U_1(t)u_0 * \mathcal{F}U_1(t)u_0) dt \\
&= \int_0^T e^{ic(T-t)\varphi(\xi)} \varphi(\xi) \left[e^{ict\varphi} \mathcal{F}u_0 * e^{ict\varphi} \mathcal{F}u_0 \right](\xi) dt \qquad (13)\\
&= e^{icT\varphi(\xi)} \varphi(\xi) R^2 \int_0^T \int_{\Gamma_\xi} e^{it\Phi} \chi_{I_N}(\xi_1) \chi_{I_N}(\xi_2) d\Gamma_\xi dt.
\end{aligned}$$

Note that, with $\xi_1 + \xi_2 = \xi$, one has

$$\Phi(\xi,\xi_1,\xi_2) = c \frac{\xi \xi_1 \xi_2 (\xi^2 - \xi_1 \xi_2 + 3)}{(1+\xi_1^2)(1+\xi_2^2)(1+\xi^2)}$$

and so for $\xi \in [\frac{1}{2},1]$ and $\xi_1, \xi_2 \in I_N$, we have $|\Phi| \sim 1$. Hence, $|t\Phi| \ll 1$ for $0 < t \ll 1$. Thus,

$$\operatorname{Re} \int_0^T e^{it\Phi} dt \geqslant \frac{T}{2}.$$

Moreover, note that $|\varphi(\xi)| \gtrsim 1$ for $\xi \in [\frac{1}{2},1]$. Thus, we have for $\xi \in [\frac{1}{2},1] \subset I_N + I_N$

$$|\mathcal{F}U_2[u_0](T)(\xi)| \gtrsim R^2 T \int_{\Gamma_\xi} \chi_{I_N}(\xi_1) \chi_{I_N}(\xi_2) d\Gamma_\xi = R^2 T \chi_{I_N} * \chi_{I_N}(\xi) \gtrsim R^2 T \chi_{[-1,1]} \qquad (14)$$

as $\chi_{a+[-1,1]} * \chi_{b+[-1,1]} \gtrsim \chi_{a+b+[-1,1]}$. The above pointwise estimate immediately gives the desired estimate:

$$\|U_2[\vec{\phi}_{0,N}](T)\|_{\widehat{w}_s^{p,q}} \gtrsim \left\| \|\chi_{n+Q_1}(\xi)\mathcal{F}U_2[\vec{\phi}_{0,N}](T)(\xi)\|_{L_\xi^p([\frac{1}{2},1] \cap \widehat{\mathcal{M}})} \langle n \rangle^s \right\|_{\ell^q(n=1)} \gtrsim TR^2$$

provided $0 < T \ll 1$. □

4.2. Estimates in $W_s^{2,q}(\mathbb{R})$

Lemma 7 (inclusion). *Let $p, q, q_1, q_2 \in [1,\infty]$ and $s \in \mathbb{R}$. Then,*

(1) $\|f\|_{W_s^{2,q}} \lesssim \|f\|_{\widehat{w}_s^{2,q}}$ if $q \leqslant 2$

(2) $\|f\|_{W_s^{p,q_1}} \lesssim \|f\|_{W_s^{p,q_2}}$ if $q_1 \geqslant q_2$

Proof. (1) is a consequence of Minkowski inequality and Plancherel theorem, whereas (2) follows from the fact that $\ell^{q_2} \hookrightarrow \ell^{q_1}$ if $q_1 \geqslant q_2$. □

Lemma 8. *Let u_0 be given by (9), $s \leqslant 0$ and $1 \leqslant p \leqslant \infty$. Then, there exists C such that*

(1) $\|u_{0,N} - u_0\|_{W_s^{2,q}} \lesssim RN^s$

(2) $\|U_1[u_{0,N}](t)\|_{W_s^{2,q}} \lesssim 1 + RN^s$

(3) $\|U_2[u_{0,N}](t) - U_2[\phi_{0,N}](t)\|_{W_s^{2,q}} \lesssim tR$

(4) $\|U_k[\vec{u}_{0,N}](t)\|_{W_s^{2,q}} \lesssim C^k R^k t^{k-1}$

Proof. By Lemma 7, we have

$$\|\vec{u}_{0,N} - \vec{u}_0\|_{W_s^{2,q}} \lesssim \begin{cases} \|\vec{u}_{0,N} - \vec{u}_0\|_{\widehat{w}_s^{2,q}} \lesssim RN^s & \text{for } q \in [1,2] \\ \|\vec{u}_{0,N} - \vec{u}_0\|_{W_s^{2,2}} \lesssim RN^s & \text{for } q \in (2,\infty] \end{cases}$$

using Lemma 5 (1). Similarly, the other estimates also follow from Lemmata 5. □

Lemma 9. *Let u_0 be given by (9), $1 \leq p \leq \infty, s \in \mathbb{R}$ and $0 < T \ll 1$, then we have*

$$\|U_2[\phi_{0,N}](T)\|_{W_s^{2,q}} \gtrsim \left\| \left\| \mathcal{F}^{-1} \sigma_n \mathcal{F} U_2[\phi_{0,N}](T)(\xi) \langle n \rangle^s \right\|_{\ell^q(n=1)} \right\|_{L_\xi^2} \gtrsim R^2 T.$$

Proof. Note that using Plancherel theorem and (14), we have

$$\|U_2[\phi_{0,N}](T)\|_{W_s^{2,q}} \gtrsim \left\| \left\| \mathcal{F}^{-1} \sigma_n \mathcal{F} U_2[\phi_{0,N}](T)(x) \langle n \rangle^s \right\|_{\ell^q(n=e_1)} \right\|_{L_x^2}$$

$$= 2^{s/2} \|\sigma_{e_1} \mathcal{F} U_2[\vec{\phi}_{0,N}](T)(\xi)\|_{L_\xi^2} \gtrsim R^2 T.$$

This completes the proof. □

Proof of Theorem 1. We first consider the case $\mathcal{X}_s^{p,q} = \widehat{w}_s^{p,q}$. If the initial data $u_{0,N}$ satisfy (11), Corollary 1 guarantees the existence of the solution to (3) and the power series expansion in $\mathcal{F}L^1$ up to time $TR \ll 1$ (as $R \gg 1$). By Lemma 5, we obtain

$$\sum_{k=3}^{\infty} \|U_k[u_{0,N}](T)\|_{\widehat{w}_s^{p,q}} \lesssim T^2 R^3 \tag{15}$$

provided $TR \ll 1$. Note that

$$\|u_N(T)\|_{\widehat{w}_\theta^{p,q}} \gtrsim \left\| \|\chi_{n+Q_1} \mathcal{F} u_N(T)\|_{L^p} \langle n \rangle^\theta \right\|_{\ell^q(n=1)} \sim_{\theta,s} \left\| \|\chi_{n+Q_1} \mathcal{F} u_N(T)\|_{L^p} \langle n \rangle^s \right\|_{\ell^q(n=1)}$$

Using Corollary 1 and triangle inequality, we have

$$\|u_N(T)\|_{\widehat{w}_\theta^{p,q}}$$

$$\gtrsim \left\| \|\chi_{n+Q_1} \mathcal{F} U_2[u_{0,N}](T)\|_{L^p} \langle n \rangle^s \right\|_{\ell^q(n=1)} - c \bigg(\left\| \|\chi_{n+Q_1} \mathcal{F} U_1[u_{0,N}](T)\|_{L^p} \langle n \rangle^s \right\|_{\ell^q(n=1)}$$

$$+ \sum_{k=3}^{\infty} \left\| \|\chi_{n+Q_1} \mathcal{F} U_k[u_{0,N}](T)\|_{L^p} \langle n \rangle^s \right\|_{\ell^q(n=1)} \bigg)$$

$$\gtrsim \left\| \|\chi_{n+Q_1} \mathcal{F} U_2[u_{0,N}](T)\|_{L^p} \langle n \rangle^s \right\|_{\ell^q(n=1)} - c \|U_1[\vec{u}_{0,N}](T)\|_{\widehat{w}_s^{p,q}} - c \sum_{k=3}^{\infty} \|U_k[\vec{u}_{0,N}](T)\|_{\widehat{w}_s^{p,q}}.$$

Let $m \in \mathbb{N}$. In order to ensure $\|u_N(T)\|_{\widehat{w}_\theta^{p,q}} \gtrsim \|U_2[\vec{u}_{0,N}](T)\|_{\widehat{w}_s^{p,q}} \gg m$, we rely on the conditions

$$\left\| \|\chi_{n+Q_1} \mathcal{F} U_2[u_{0,N}](T)\|_{L^2} \langle n \rangle^s \right\|_{\ell^q(n=1)} \gg \begin{cases} \|U_1[\vec{u}_{0,N}](T)\|_{\widehat{w}_s^{p,q}}, & (16) \\ \sum_{k=2}^{\infty} \|U_k[\vec{u}_{0,N}](T)\|_{\widehat{w}_s^{p,q}}, & (17) \\ m. & (18) \end{cases}$$

Thus, to establish NI with infinite loss of regularity at u_0 in $\widehat{w}_s^{p,q}$, we claim that it is enough to have the following:

(1) $CRN^s < 1/m$
(2) $TR \ll 1$
(3) $TR^2 \gg m$
(4) $TR^2 \gg T^2 R^3 \Leftrightarrow$ (2)
(5) $0 < T \ll 1$

as $N \to \infty$. Note that (1) ensures $\|u_0 - u_{0,N}\|_{\widehat{w}_s^{p,q}} < 1/m$, whereas (2) ensures the convergence of the infinite series in view of Lemma 5. In order to use Lemma 6, we need (4). In order to prove (17), in view of Lemma 6 and (15), we need (4). Condition (3) implies (18) using Lemma 5 (3) and Lemma 6. In order to prove (16), we need (1) and (3) by using Lemma 5 (2) and Lemma 6. Thus, it follows that

$$\|u_0 - u_{0,N}\|_{\widehat{w}_s^{p,q}} < 1/m \quad \text{and} \quad \|u_N(T)\|_{\widehat{w}_\theta^{p,q}} > m.$$

Hence, the result is established. We shall now choose R and T as follows:

$$R = N^r \quad \text{and} \quad T = N^{-\epsilon}.$$

where r, ϵ are to be chosen below. Therefore, it is enough to check

$$CRN^s = CN^{r+s} < 1/m, \quad TR = N^{-\epsilon+r} \ll 1, \quad TR^2 = N^{-\epsilon+2r} \gg m, \quad T = N^{-\epsilon} \ll 1.$$

Thus, we only need to achieve:

- $r + s < 0$
- $-\epsilon + r < 0$
- $-\epsilon + 2r > 0$
- $\epsilon > 0$

and take N large enough. Let us concentrate on the choice of $\epsilon > 0$ first. Note that the second and third conditions in the above are equivalent to

$$r < \epsilon < 2r.$$

To make room for ϵ, we must have $r > 0$. Thus, r must satisfy

$$0 < r < -s$$

where the latter condition comes from the first condition. Thus, it is enough to choose

$$r = -\frac{s}{3}, \quad \epsilon = -\frac{s}{2}$$

which will satisfy all the above four conditions. Hence, the result follows.

For the case $\mathcal{X}_s^{p,q} = W_s^{2,q}$, we use same argument as above. Note that using Lemmata 8 and 9, we have

$$\|u_N(T)\|_{W_\theta^{2,q}}$$

$$\gtrsim \left\|\|\Box_n u_N(T)\langle n\rangle^\sigma\|_{\ell^q(n\geq 1)}\right\|_{L^2} \sim_{\theta,s} \left\|\|\Box_n u_N(T)\langle n\rangle^s\|_{\ell^q(n\geq 1)}\right\|_{L^2}$$

$$\gtrsim \left\|\|\Box_n U_2[u_{0,N}](T)\langle n\rangle^s\|_{\ell^q(n\geq 1)}\right\|_{L^2} - c\|U_1[u_{0,N}](T)\|_{W_s^{2,q}} - c\sum_{k=3}^{\infty} \|U_k[\vec{u}_{0,N}](T)\|_{W_s^{2,q}}$$

$$\gtrsim \left\|\|\Box_n U_2[u_{0,N}](T)\langle n\rangle^s\|_{\ell^q(n\geq 1)}\right\|_{L^2} \gg m.$$

and $\|\vec{u}_{0,N} - \vec{u}_0\|_{W_s^{2,q}} < 1/m$ provided that we choose R, N, T as in the case of $\widehat{w}_s^{p,q}$. □

Remark 1. It is easy to check that our proof of the main results will work even if we replace the weight $\langle \cdot \rangle^s$ by $|\cdot|^s$ in the function spaces involved. Since the analysis will be similar, we omit the details. We simply note that as $\langle n \rangle^s \asymp |n|^s$ for large n, we have $\|\phi_{0,N}\|_{\dot{\hat{w}}_s^{p,q}} \asymp RN^s$, where $\phi_{0,N}$ is as in (9). Moreover, it should work with any weight $n \mapsto (\omega(n))^s (s < 0)$ that is decreasing in $|n|$ and behaves as $|n|^s$ as $n \to \infty$.

Author Contributions: Both authors D.G.B. and S.H. have equally contributed in the present paper. All authors have read and agreed to the published version of the manuscript.

Funding: This research received no external funding.

Institutional Review Board Statement: Not applicable.

Informed Consent Statement: Not applicable.

Data Availability Statement: Not applicable.

Acknowledgments: Divyang G Bhimani is thankful to DST-INSPIRE (DST/INSPIRE/04/2016/001507) for the research grant. Saikatul Haque acknowledges the Department of Atomic Energy, Govt of India, for the financial support and Harish-Chandra Research Institute for the research facilities provided.

Conflicts of Interest: The authors declare no conflict of interest.

References

1. Alazman, A.; Albert, J.; Bona, J.; Chen, M.; Wu, J. Comparisons between the BBM equation and a Boussinesq system. *Adv. Differ. Equ.* **2006**, *11*, 121–166.
2. Bona, J.; Pritchard, W.; Scott, L. An evaluation of a model equation for water waves. *Philos. Trans. R. Soc. Lond. Ser. A Math. Phys. Sci.* **1981**, *302*, 457–510.
3. Bona, J.L.; Tzvetkov, N. Sharp well-posedness results for the BBM equation. *Discret. Contin. Dyn. Syst.* **2009**, *23*, 1241–1252. [CrossRef]
4. Pava, J.A.; Banquet, C.; Scialom, M. Stability for the modified and fourth-order Benjamin-Bona-Mahony equations. *Discret. Contin. Dyn. Syst.* **2011**, *30*, 851. [CrossRef]
5. Bona, J.L.; Pritchard, W.; Scott, L.R. *A Comparison of Solutions of Two Model Equations for Long Waves*; Technical Report; Wisconsin Univ-Madison Mathematics Research Center: Madison, WI, USA, 1983. Available online: https://apps.dtic.mil/sti/pdfs/ADA128076.pdf (accessed on 3 October 2021).
6. Bona, J.L.; Cascaval, R.C. Nonlinear dispersive waves on trees. *Can. Appl. Math. Q.* **2008**, *16*, 1–18.
7. Wang, B.; Hudzik, H. The global Cauchy problem for the NLS and NLKG with small rough data. *J. Differ. Equ.* **2007**, *232*, 36–73. [CrossRef]
8. Wang, B.; Huo, Z.; Hao, C.; Guo, Z. *Harmonic Analysis Method for Nonlinear Evolution Equations. I*; World Scientific Publishing Co. Pte. Ltd.: Hackensack, NJ, USA, 2011. [CrossRef]
9. Bhimani, D.G.; Ratnakumar, P.K. Functions operating on modulation spaces and nonlinear dispersive equations. *J. Funct. Anal.* **2016**, *270*, 621–648. [CrossRef]
10. Bhimani, D.G.; Manna, R.; Nicola, F.; Thangavelu, S.; Trapasso, S.I. Phase space analysis of the Hermite semigroup and applications to nonlinear global well-posedness. *Adv. Math.* **2021**, *392*, 107995. [CrossRef]
11. Bhimani, D.G.; Carles, R. Norm inflation for nonlinear Schrödinger equations in Fourier-Lebesgue and modulation spaces of negative regularity. *J. Fourier Anal. Appl.* **2020**, *26*, 34. [CrossRef]
12. Bhimani, D.G.; Grillakis, M.; Okoudjou, K.A. The Hartree-Fock equations in modulation spaces. *Comm. Partial Differ. Equ.* **2020**, *45*, 1088–1117. [CrossRef]
13. Ruzhansky, M.; Sugimoto, M.; Wang, B. Modulation spaces and nonlinear evolution equations. In *Evolution Equations of Hyperbolic and Schrödinger Type*; Birkhäuser/Springer: Basel, Switzerland, 2012; Volume 301, pp. 267–283. [CrossRef]
14. Benyi, A.; Okoudjou, K.A. *Modulation Spaces: With Applications to Pseudodifferential Operators and Nonlinear Schrodinger Equations*; Applied and Numerical Harmonic Analysis, Birkhauser, Bassel; Springer Nature: Basingstoke, UK, 2020.
15. Forlano, J.; Okamoto, M. A remark on norm inflation for nonlinear wave equations. *Dyn. Partial Differ. Equ.* **2020**, *17*, 361–381. [CrossRef]
16. Panthee, M. On the ill-posedness result for the BBM equation. *Discrete Contin. Dyn. Syst.* **2011**, *30*, 253–259. [CrossRef]
17. Bona, J.; Dai, M. Norm-inflation results for the BBM equation. *J. Math. Anal. Appl.* **2017**, *446*, 879–885. [CrossRef]
18. Banquet, C.; Villamizar-Roa, E.J. Time-decay and Strichartz estimates for the BBM equation on modulation spaces: existence of local and global solutions. *J. Math. Anal. Appl.* **2021**, *498*, 124934. [CrossRef]
19. Bejenaru, I.; Tao, T. Sharp well-posedness and ill-posedness results for a quadratic non-linear Schrödinger equation. *J. Funct. Anal.* **2006**, *233*, 228–259. [CrossRef]

20. Iwabuchi, T.; Ogawa, T. Ill-posedness for the nonlinear Schrödinger equation with quadratic non-linearity in low dimensions. *Trans. Am. Math. Soc.* **2015**, *367*, 2613–2630. [CrossRef]
21. Kishimoto, N. A remark on norm inflation for nonlinear Schrödinger equations. *Commun. Pure Appl. Anal.* **2019**, *18*, 1375. [CrossRef]
22. Oh, T. A remark on norm inflation with general initial data for the cubic nonlinear Schrödinger equations in negative Sobolev spaces. *Funkcial. Ekvac.* **2017**, *60*, 259–277. [CrossRef]
23. Bhimani, D.G.; Haque, S. Norm inflation for nonlinear wave equations with infinite loss of regularity in Wiener amalgam spaces. *arXiv* **2021**, arXiv:2106.13635.
24. Lebeau, G. Perte de régularité pour les équations d'ondes sur-critiques. *Bull. Soc. Math. France* **2005**, *133*, 145–157. [CrossRef]
25. Carles, R.; Dumas, E.; Sparber, C. Geometric optics and instability for NLS and Davey-Stewartson models. *J. Eur. Math. Soc. (JEMS)* **2012**, *14*, 1885–1921. [CrossRef]
26. Ruzhansky, M.; Turunen, V. *Pseudo-Differential Operators and Symmetries: Background Analysis and Advanced Topics*; Springer Science & Business Media: Basel, Switzerland, 2010; Volume 2.
27. Feichtinger, H.G. *Modulation Spaces on Locally Compact Abelian Groups*; Technical Report; University of Vienna: Vienna, Austria, 1983.
28. Gröchenig, K. *Foundations of Time-Frequency Analysis*; Applied and Numerical Harmonic Analysis; Birkhäuser Boston, Inc.: Boston, MA, USA, 2001; pp. xvi+359. [CrossRef]
29. Forlano, J.; Oh, T. Normal form approach to the one-dimensional cubic nonlinear Schrödinger equation in Fourier-amalgam spaces. *arXiv* **2021**, arXiv:1811.04868.

The Pauli Problem for Gaussian Quantum States: Geometric Interpretation

Maurice A. de Gosson

Faculty of Mathematics (NuHAG), University of Vienna, 1090 Vienna, Austria; maurice.de.gosson@univie.ac.at

Abstract: We solve the Pauli tomography problem for Gaussian signals using the notion of Schur complement. We relate our results and method to a notion from convex geometry, polar duality. In our context polar duality can be seen as a sort of geometric Fourier transform and allows a geometric interpretation of the uncertainty principle and allows to apprehend the Pauli problem in a rather simple way.

Keywords: covariance matrix; polar duality; uncertainty principle; reconstruction problem

1. The Pauli Problem and Quantum Tomography

The problem goes back to Pauli's question [1]:

The mathematical problem as to whether, for given probability densities $W(p)$ and $W(x)$, wave function ψ (...) is always uniquely determined, has still not been investigated in its generality.

The answer to Pauli's question is negative [2]; there is a general nonuniqueness of the solution (for a detailed discussion of the Pauli problem and its applications, see [3]). The problem can actually be formulated as from statistical quantum mechanics as follows: can we estimate the density matrix of the said state using repeated measurements on identical quantum systems? After having obtained measurements on these identical systems, can we make a statistical inference about their probability distributions (e.g., [4])? Such a procedure is an instance of quantum state tomography, and is practically implemented using a set of measurements of a so-called quorum of observables. It can be performed using various mathematical techniques, for instance the Radon–Wigner transform that we discussed in [5]; the latter has important applications in medical imaging [6]. For details and explicit constructions, see [7–14], and [15] by Man'ko and Man'ko.

Remark 1. *Everything in this paper extends mutatis mutandis to time-frequency analysis, replacing the notion of wave function by that of a signal. In this case, one takes $\hbar = 1/2\pi$ and replaces phase-space variables (x, p) with time-frequency variables (x, ω).*

2. A Simple Example

Let us discuss the Pauli problem on the simplest possible example, that of a Gaussian wave function in one spatial dimension. Assuming for simplicity, it is centered at the origin and is given by formula

$$\psi(x) = \left(\frac{1}{2\pi\sigma_{xx}}\right)^{1/4} e^{-\frac{x^2}{4\sigma_{xx}}} e^{\frac{i\sigma_{xp}}{2\hbar\sigma_{xx}}x^2} \tag{1}$$

where σ_{xx} is the variance in the position variable, and σ_{xp} the covariance in the position and momentum variables. Fourier transform

$$\widehat{\psi}(p) = \frac{1}{\sqrt{2\pi\hbar}} \int_{-\infty}^{\infty} e^{-\frac{i}{\hbar}px} \psi(x) dx$$

of the ψ is explicitly given by

$$\widehat{\psi}(p) = \left(\frac{1}{2\pi\sigma_{pp}}\right)^{1/4} e^{-\frac{p^2}{4\sigma_{pp}}} e^{-\frac{i\sigma_{xp}}{2\hbar\sigma_{pp}}p^2} \tag{2}$$

hence, the knowledge of σ_{xx} and of σ_{pp}, that is, of moduli $|\psi(x)|^2$ and $|\widehat{\psi}(p)|^2$, determines covariance σ_{xp} up to a sign because state ψ saturates the Robertson–Schrödinger inequality; so, we have

$$\sigma_{xx}\sigma_{pp} - \sigma_{xp}^2 = \tfrac{1}{4}\hbar^2 \tag{3}$$

This identity can be solved in σ_{xp} yielding $\sigma_{xp} = \pm(\sigma_{xx}\sigma_{pp} - \tfrac{1}{4}\hbar^2)^{1/2}$. The state and its Fourier transform are given by formulas

$$\psi_\pm(x) = \left(\frac{1}{2\pi\sigma_{xx}}\right)^{1/4} e^{-\frac{x^2}{4\sigma_{xx}}} e^{\pm\frac{i\sigma_{xp}}{2\hbar\sigma_{xx}}x^2} \tag{4}$$

and

$$\widehat{\psi}_\pm(p) = \left(\frac{1}{2\pi\sigma_{pp}}\right)^{1/4} e^{-\frac{p^2}{4\sigma_{pp}}} e^{\mp\frac{i\sigma_{xp}}{2\hbar\sigma_{pp}}p^2}. \tag{5}$$

Both functions ψ_+ and $\psi_- = \psi_+^*$ and their Fourier transforms $\widehat{\psi}_+$ and $\widehat{\psi}_-$ satisfy conditions $|\psi_+(x)|^2 = |\psi_-(x)|^2$ and $|\widehat{\psi}_+(p)|^2 = |\widehat{\psi}_-(p)|^2$ showing that the Pauli problem does not have a unique solution. In Corbett's [16] terminology ψ_+ and ψ_- are "Pauli partners". Let us now have a look at these things from the perspective of the Wigner transform

$$W\psi(x,p) = \frac{1}{2\pi\hbar} \int_{-\infty}^{\infty} e^{-\frac{i}{\hbar}py} \psi(x + \tfrac{1}{2}y) \psi^*(x - \tfrac{1}{2}y) dy$$

of Gaussian ψ. A straightforward calculation involving Gaussian integrals [17] yields, setting $z = (x,p)$, normal distribution

$$W\psi_\pm(z) = \frac{1}{2\pi\sqrt{\det\Sigma_\pm}} e^{-\tfrac{1}{2}\Sigma_\pm^{-1}z\cdot z} \tag{6}$$

where covariance matrix

$$\Sigma_\pm = \begin{pmatrix} \sigma_{xx} & \pm\sigma_{xp} \\ \pm\sigma_{px} & \sigma_{pp} \end{pmatrix}$$

has determinant $\det\Sigma_\pm = \tfrac{1}{4}\hbar^2$ in view of equality (3); hence,

$$W\psi_\pm(z) = \frac{1}{\pi\hbar} e^{-\tfrac{1}{2}\Sigma_\pm^{-1}z\cdot z}. \tag{7}$$

Associated covariance matrices are thus

$$\Omega_\pm = \{z : \tfrac{1}{2}\Sigma_\pm^{-1}z\cdot z \leq 1.\}$$

3. Multivariate Case: Asking the Right Questions

We generalize the discussion to the multivariate case where the real variables x and p are replaced with real vectors $x = (x_1, ..., x_n)$, $p = (p_1, ..., p_n)$.

The Wigner function cannot be directly measured, but its marginal distributions can (they are classical probability densities). In analogy with Formula (6) we determine a (centered) Gaussian, ψ such that

$$W\psi(z) = \left(\frac{1}{2\pi}\right)^n \frac{1}{\sqrt{\det\Sigma}} e^{-\tfrac{1}{2}\Sigma^{-1}z\cdot z} \tag{8}$$

where $z = (x, p)$, and the covariance matrix is

$$\Sigma = \begin{pmatrix} \Sigma_{XX} & \Sigma_{XP} \\ \Sigma_{PX} & \Sigma_{PP} \end{pmatrix} , \quad \Sigma_{PX} = \Sigma_{XP}^T . \tag{9}$$

Here, the the n-dimensional Wigner transform $W\psi$ is defined by

$$W\psi(x, p) = \left(\frac{1}{2\pi\hbar}\right)^n \int e^{-\frac{i}{\hbar} p \cdot y} \psi(x + \tfrac{1}{2}y) \psi^*(x - \tfrac{1}{2}y) d^n y .$$

The most straightforward way to determine this state is to use the properties of the Wigner transform itself. Let us start with the marginal properties [17]:

$$\int W\psi(x, p) d^n p = |\psi(x)|^2 \tag{10}$$

$$\int W\psi(x, p) d^n x = |\widehat{\psi}(p)|^2 \tag{11}$$

where the n-dimensional Fourier transform $\widehat{\psi}$ is given by

$$\widehat{\psi}(p) = \left(\frac{1}{2\pi\hbar}\right)^{n/2} \int e^{-\frac{i}{\hbar} p x} \psi(x) d^n x .$$

These formulas hold as soon as both ψ and $\widehat{\psi}$ are in $L^1(\mathbb{R}^n) \cap L^2(\mathbb{R}^n)$ [17]. These quantities allow for determining matrices

$$\Sigma_{XX} = (\sigma_{x_j x_k})_{1 \leq j,k \leq n} \text{ and } \Sigma_{PP} = (\sigma_{p_j p_k})_{1 \leq j,k \leq n}$$

by usual formulas

$$\sigma_{x_j x_k} = \int x_j x_k |\psi(x)|^2 d^n x , \quad \sigma_{p_j p_k} = \int p_j p_k |\widehat{\psi}(p)|^2 d^n p$$

and an elementary calculation of Gaussian integrals yields the values

$$|\psi(x)| = \left(\frac{1}{2\pi}\right)^{n/4} (\det \Sigma_{XX})^{-1/4} e^{-\frac{1}{4} \Sigma_{XX}^{-1} x \cdot x} \tag{12}$$

$$|\widehat{\psi}(p)| = \left(\frac{1}{2\pi}\right)^{n/4} (\det \Sigma_{PP})^{-1/4} e^{-\frac{1}{4} \Sigma_{PP}^{-1} p \cdot p} . \tag{13}$$

Here, we are exactly in the situation discussed by Pauli: $|\psi(x)|$ and $|\widehat{\psi}(p)|$ are what we can measure, so we can determine covariance blocks Σ_{XX} and Σ_{PP}, but not covariance Σ_{XP}: knowledge of the latter (and hence of $\Sigma_{PX} = \Sigma_{XP}^T$) is necessary to entirely determine state ψ. In the previous section, the problem was solved: in case $n = 1$, blocks Σ_{XX}, Σ_{PP}, and Σ_{XP} were scalars σ_{xx}, σ_{pp}, and σ_{xp}, and these are related by the uncertainty principle in the form of $\sigma_{xx}\sigma_{pp} - \sigma_{xp}^2 = \tfrac{1}{4}\hbar^2$ yielding two possible values $\sigma_{xp} = \pm(\sigma_{xx}\sigma_{pp} - \tfrac{1}{4}\hbar^2)^{1/2}$, and hence the two states (5). In the multidimensional, case we also have a simple (but not immediately obvious) formula connecting the blocks of the covariance matrix. The way out of this problem consists in using a general formula [17–19], which was initially proved by Bastiaans [20] in connection with first-order optics. Let X and Y be real $n \times n$ matrices, such that $X = X^T > 0$ and $Y = Y^T$, and set

$$\psi_{X,Y}(x) = \left(\frac{1}{\pi\hbar}\right)^{n/4} (\det X)^{1/4} e^{-\frac{1}{2\hbar}(X+iY)x \cdot x} . \tag{14}$$

This function is normalized to unity: $\|\psi_{X,Y}\|_{L^2} = 1$, and its Wigner transform is given by

$$W\psi_{X,Y}(z) = \left(\frac{1}{\pi\hbar}\right)^n e^{-\frac{1}{\hbar} G z \cdot z} \tag{15}$$

where G is the symmetric matrix

$$G = \begin{pmatrix} X + YX^{-1}Y & YX^{-1} \\ X^{-1}Y & X^{-1} \end{pmatrix}. \tag{16}$$

A fundamental fact, which is related to the uncertainty principle, is that G is a symplectic matrix, i.e., it belongs to symplectic group $\mathrm{Sp}(n)$. Equivalently, since $G = G^T$,

$$G^T J G = G J G = J$$

where

$$J = \begin{pmatrix} 0_{n \times n} & I_{n \times n} \\ -I_{n \times n} & 0_{n \times n} \end{pmatrix}$$

the standard symplectic matrix. We have $G = S^T S$, where

$$S = \begin{pmatrix} X^{1/2} & 0 \\ X^{-1/2}Y & X^{-1/2} \end{pmatrix} \tag{17}$$

is clearly symplectic. Assuming that function ψ for which we are looking is a Gaussian, comparing Formulas (8) and (15) leads to identification

$$\Sigma = \frac{\hbar}{2} G^{-1}.$$

Since $GJG = J$ the inverse G^{-1} is $-JGJ$, explicit formula

$$G^{-1} = \begin{pmatrix} X^{-1} & -X^{-1}Y \\ -YX^{-1} & X + YX^{-1}Y, \end{pmatrix}$$

so that there remains to solve matrix equation

$$\begin{pmatrix} \Sigma_{XX} & \Sigma_{XP} \\ \Sigma_{PX} & \Sigma_{PP} \end{pmatrix} = \frac{\hbar}{2} \begin{pmatrix} X^{-1} & -X^{-1}Y \\ -YX^{-1} & X + YX^{-1}Y \end{pmatrix}. \tag{18}$$

It immediately follows that we have $X = \frac{\hbar}{2} \Sigma_{XX}^{-1}$ and $Y = -\frac{2}{\hbar} \Sigma_{XP} \Sigma_{XX}^{-1}$, so the unknown Gaussian for which we were looking is

$$\psi(x) = \left(\frac{1}{2\pi}\right)^{n/4} (\det \Sigma_{XX})^{-1/4} \exp\left[-\left(\frac{1}{4}\Sigma_{XX}^{-1} + \frac{i}{2\hbar}\Sigma_{XP}\Sigma_{XX}^{-1}\right)x \cdot x\right], \tag{19}$$

which is the n-dimensional variant of (1), replacing σ_{xx} with Σ_{XX} and σ_{xp} with Σ_{XP}. This does not solve completely our problem, however, because we do not know matrix Σ_{XP}. The crucial step is to notice that, as a bonus, we obtained from (18) the matrix form of the saturated Robertson–Schrödinger equality, namely,

$$\Sigma_{PP}\Sigma_{XX} - \Sigma_{XP}^2 = \frac{1}{4}\hbar^2 I_{n \times n}. \tag{20}$$

From this formula we can deduce Σ_{XP}^2, and one finds two Pauli partners

$$\psi_{\pm}(x) = \left(\frac{1}{2\pi}\right)^{n/4} (\det \Sigma_{XX})^{-1/4} \exp\left[-\left(\frac{1}{4}\Sigma_{XX}^{-1} \pm \frac{i}{2\hbar}\Sigma_{XP}\Sigma_{XX}^{-1}\right)x \cdot x\right] \tag{21}$$

once a value of Σ_{XP} is determined (even if $\Sigma_{XP}^2 = 0$, we can have $\Sigma_{XP} \neq 0$). Here, we solved a so-called "phase retrieval problem" (see Klibanov et al. [21] for a good review of the topic): in view of Formula (12), we know that

$$\psi(x) = e^{i\Phi(x)} \left(\frac{1}{2\pi}\right)^{n/4} (\det \Sigma_{XX})^{-1/4} e^{-\frac{1}{4}\Sigma_{XX}^{-1} x \cdot x} \tag{22}$$

where Φ is an unknown real function of the position variable. We identified this phase here as being function

$$\Phi(x) = -\left(\frac{1}{2\hbar}\Sigma_{XP}\Sigma_{XX}^{-1}\right)x \cdot x\,.$$

4. Geometric Interlude

We introduce the notion of $\hbar$-polarity and duality; we see in the next section that this notion from convex geometry is quite unexpectedly related to the Pauli problem, of which it gives a limpid geometric interpretation. For a very detailed study of polarity, see Charalambos and Aliprantis [22]. In both sources, alternative competing definitions are also described; the one we use here is the most common and the best fitted to our needs.

Let X be a nonempty subset of n-dimensional configuration space $\mathbb{R}_x^n$; this may be, for instance, a set of position measurements performed on some physical system with n degrees of freedom. One defines the polar set of X as the set X^o of all points $p = (p_1, ..., p_n)$ in the momentum space $\mathbb{R}_p^n$, such that

$$px = p_1 x_1 + \cdots + p_n x_n \leq 1$$

for all points $x = (x_1, ..., x_n)$ in X. Similarly, if P is a subset of $\mathbb{R}_p^n$, one defines its polar P^o as the set of all x in $\mathbb{R}_x^n$, such that $px \leq 1$ for all p in P. We use a rescaled variant of the notion of polarity here, which we call $\hbar$ polarity. By definition, the $\hbar$-polar $X^\hbar$ of X is the set of all p, such that

$$px = p_1 x_1 + \cdots + p_n x_n \leq \hbar$$

for all points x in X. We have $X^\hbar = \hbar X^o$ and $P^\hbar = \hbar P^o$ likewise.

From now on, we assume for simplicity that X and P are convex bodies, i.e., they are convex, compact, and with a nonempty interior; we also assume that they are symmetric (i.e., $X = -X$), which implies, by convexity, that they contain 0 in their interior. Simple examples of such sets are balls and ellipsoids centered at the origin. Polar duals have the following remarkable properties:

- *Biduality*: $(X^\hbar)^\hbar = X$
- *Antimonotonicity*: $X \subset Y \implies Y^\hbar \subset X^\hbar$
- *Scaling property*: $L \in GL(n, \mathbb{R}) \implies (LX)^\hbar = (L^T)^{-1} X^\hbar$.

Let $\mathcal{B}_X^n(R)$ (resp. $\mathcal{B}_P^n(R)$) be the ball $\{x : |x| \leq R\}$ in $\mathbb{R}_x^n$ (resp. $\{p : |p| \leq R\}$ in $\mathbb{R}_p^n$). We have

$$\mathcal{B}_X^n(\sqrt{\hbar})^\hbar = \mathcal{B}_P^n(\sqrt{\hbar}) \tag{23}$$

and one can show that $\mathcal{B}_X^n(\sqrt{\hbar})$ is the only self $\hbar$-dual set in $\mathbb{R}_x^n$. Let us extend this to the case of ellipsoids. An ellipsoid in $\mathbb{R}_x^n$ centered at the origin (which is just an ordinary plane ellipse when $n = 1$) can always be viewed as the image of ball $\mathcal{B}_X^n(\sqrt{\hbar})$ by some invertible linear transformation L, in which case, it is given by inequality

$$L^{-1}x \cdot L^{-1}x = (LL^T)^{-1}x \cdot x \leq \hbar\,.$$

Conversely, if A is a positive definite symmetric matrix, inequality $Ax \cdot x \leq \hbar$ always defines an ellipsoid, since it is equivalent to the above inequality, taking for L inverse square root $A^{-1/2}$ of A. It immediately follows from the scaling property that the $\hbar$-polar of the ellipsoid is obtained by inverting the matrix of the ellipsoid:

$$X : Ax^2 \leq \hbar \iff X^\hbar : A^{-1}p \cdot p \leq \hbar \tag{24}$$

(that we have an equivalence follows from biduality property $(X^\hbar)^\hbar = X$).

5. The Pauli Problem and Polar Duality

Let us return to the Wigner transform of Gaussian states; using Formula (15), we can explicitly calculate $W\psi_\pm$, and one finds

$$W\psi_\pm(z) = (\pi\hbar)^{-n} e^{-\frac{1}{2}\Sigma_\pm^{-1} z \cdot z}$$

where covariance matrices $\Sigma_\pm$ are given by

$$\Sigma_\pm = \begin{pmatrix} \Sigma_{XX} & \pm\Sigma_{XP} \\ \pm\Sigma_{PX} & \Sigma_{PP} \end{pmatrix},$$

with $\Sigma_{PX} = \Sigma_{XP}^T$. Two ellipsoids $\Omega_\pm$ centered at the origin correspond to $\Sigma_\pm$. Let us determine orthogonal projections $\Omega_{X,\pm}$ and $\Omega_{P\pm}$ of $\Omega_\pm$ on the position and momentum spaces $\mathbb{R}_x^n$ and $\mathbb{R}_p^n$.

5.1. Case $n = 1$

We begin with case $n = 1$, and projections are line segments. Here, $\Sigma_{XX} = \sigma_{xx}$, $\Sigma_{PP} = \sigma_{pp}$, and $\Sigma_{XP} = \Sigma_{PX} = \sigma_{xp}$ and covariance ellipses $\Omega_\pm$ are defined by

$$\frac{\sigma_{pp}}{2D} x^2 \mp \frac{\sigma_{xp}}{D} px + \frac{\sigma_{xx}}{2D} p^2 \leq 1 \tag{25}$$

where $D = \sigma_{xx}\sigma_{pp} - \sigma_{xp}^2 = \frac{1}{4}\hbar^2$ (cf. Formula (3)). Orthogonal projections $\Omega_{X,\pm}$ and $\Omega_{P\pm}$ of $\Omega_\pm$ on the x and p axes are the same:

$$\Omega_X = [-\sqrt{2\sigma_{xx}}, \sqrt{2\sigma_{xx}}] \ , \ \Omega_P = [-\sqrt{2\sigma_{pp}}, \sqrt{2\sigma_{pp}}] . \tag{26}$$

Let $\Omega_X^\hbar$ be the polar dual of Ω_X: it is the set of all numbers p, such that $px \leq \hbar$ for $-\sqrt{2\sigma_{xx}} \leq x \leq \sqrt{2\sigma_{xx}}$ and is thus the interval

$$\Omega_X^\hbar = [-\hbar/\sqrt{2\sigma_{xx}}, \hbar/\sqrt{2\sigma_{xx}}] .$$

Since $\sigma_{xx}\sigma_{pp} \geq \frac{1}{2}\hbar$, we have inclusion

$$\Omega_X^\hbar \subset \Omega_P \tag{27}$$

and this inclusion reduces to equality $\Omega_X^\hbar = \Omega_P$ if and only if the Heisenberg inequality is saturated, i.e., $\sigma_{xx}\sigma_{pp} = \frac{1}{4}\hbar^2$, which is equivalent to $\sigma_{xp} = 0$.

5.2. General Case

We have similar properties in arbitrary dimension n. To study this case, we first must find the orthogonal projections of covariance ellipsoid Ω on the position and momentum spaces. Ellipsoid Ω is given by equation $Mz \cdot z \leq \hbar$ where $M = \frac{\hbar}{2}\Sigma^{-1}$ is symmetric and positive definite ($M > 0$). Writing M in block form

$$M = \begin{pmatrix} M_{XX} & M_{XP} \\ M_{PX} & M_{PP} \end{pmatrix}$$

where $M_{XX} = M_{XX}^T$, $M_{PP} = M_{PP}^T$, and $M_{XP} = M_{XP}^T$ are $n \times n$ matrices; since $M > 0$, we also have $M_{XX} > 0$ and $M_{PP} > 0$. Then, the projections of Ω on $\mathbb{R}_x^n$ and $\mathbb{R}_p^n$ are ellipsoids given by, respectively [23],

$$\Omega_X : (M/M_{PP})x \cdot x \leq \hbar\} \ , \ \Omega_P = (M/M_{XX})p \cdot p \leq \hbar \tag{28}$$

where symmetric matrices

$$M/M_{PP} = M_{XX} - M_{XP}M_{PP}^{-1}M_{PX} \tag{29}$$

$$M/M_{XX} = M_{PP} - M_{PX}M_{XX}^{-1}M_{XP} \tag{30}$$

are Schur complements in M of M_{PP} and M_{XX}; we have $M/M_{PP} > 0$ and $M/M_{XX} > 0$ so that Ω_X and Ω_P are nondegenerate (see Zhang's treatise [24] for a detailed study of the Schur complement). To prove that inclusion $\Omega_X^\hbar \subset \Omega_P$ holds, we must show that cf. implication (24)) that

$$(M/M_{PP})(M/M_{XX}) \leq I_{n\times n}, \tag{31}$$

that is, that the eigenvalues of $(M/M_{PP})(M/M_{XX})$ must be smaller than 1. To prove this, we use the following essential remark: we showed above that matrix $M = \frac{\hbar}{2}\Sigma^{-1}$ is symplectic; therefore, its entries obey some constraints. Considering that M is also symmetric, these constraints are

$$M_{XX}M_{PP} - M_{XP}^2 = I_{n\times n} \tag{32}$$

$$M_{XX}M_{PX} = M_{XP}M_{XX} \tag{33}$$

$$M_{PX}M_{PP} = M_{PP}M_{XP}. \tag{34}$$

Using Identities (33) and (34), it follows that Schur complements (29) and (30) can be rewritten as

$$\begin{aligned} M/M_{PP} &= M_{XX} - M_{PP}^{-1}M_{PX}^2 \\ &= M_{PP}^{-1}(M_{PP}M_{XX} - M_{PX}^2) \\ &= M_{PP}^{-1} \end{aligned}$$

the last equality by using the transpose of Identity (32). Similarly,

$$M/M_{XX} = M_{PP} - M_{XX}^{-1}M_{XP}^2 = M_{XX}^{-1}$$

So, summarizing, Schur complements are given by

$$M/M_{PP} = M_{PP}^{-1}, \; M/M_{XX} = M_{XX}^{-1}. \tag{35}$$

It follows that

$$(M/M_{PP})(M/M_{XX}) = M_{PP}^{-1}M_{XX}^{-1} = (M_{XX}M_{PP})^{-1}.$$

We show that $(M/M_{PP})(M/M_{XX}) \leq I_{n\times n}$; equivalently, $M_{XX}M_{PP} \geq I_{n\times n}$. Now, since $M = \frac{\hbar}{2}\Sigma^{-1}$ is symplectic, so is matrix

$$M^{-1} = \frac{2}{\hbar}\Sigma = \begin{pmatrix} \frac{2}{\hbar}\Sigma_{XX} & \frac{2}{\hbar}\Sigma_{XP} \\ \frac{2}{\hbar}\Sigma_{PX} & \frac{2}{\hbar}\Sigma_{PP}; \end{pmatrix}$$

hence, reinverting,

$$M = \begin{pmatrix} \frac{2}{\hbar}\Sigma_{PP} & -\frac{2}{\hbar}\Sigma_{PX} \\ -\frac{2}{\hbar}\Sigma_{XP} & \frac{2}{\hbar}\Sigma_{XX} \end{pmatrix} \tag{36}$$

so that $M_{XX}M_{PP} = \frac{4}{\hbar^2}\Sigma_{PP}\Sigma_{XX}$. In view of the generalized RSUP (20), we have

$$\Sigma_{PP}\Sigma_{XX} - \Sigma_{XP}^2 = \frac{1}{4}\hbar^2 I_{n\times n} \tag{37}$$

hence

$$M_{XX}M_{PP} = I_{n\times n} + \frac{4}{\hbar^2}\Sigma_{XP}^2 \tag{38}$$

and we are finished, provided that we can prove that $\Sigma^2_{XP} \geq 0$ (which is obvious if $n = 1$), or, which amounts to the same $M^2_{XP} \geq 0$. For this, since $M_{XX}M_{PX} = M_{XP}M_{XX}$ (Formula (33)), we have

$$M_{XP} = M_{XX}M_{PX}M^{-1}_{XX}; \tag{39}$$

hence, M_{XP} and M_{PX} have the same eigenvalues; since $M_{PX} = M^T_{XP}$, these eigenvalues must be real, and those of M^2_{XP} must be ≥ 0.

For completeness, we still need to discuss what happens when $\Omega^\hbar_X = \Omega_P$. In view of Formulas (28) and Equivalence (24), this means that (31) reduces to equality

$$(M/M_{PP})(M/M_{XX}) = I_{n \times n}$$

that is, by (35), $M_{XX}M_{PP} = I_{n \times n}$. Taking (38) into account, we must thus have $M^2_{XP} = 0$, which does not imply that $M_{XP} = 0$. We are in the presence of states (21) in this case, saturating the Heisenberg inequalities.

6. Discussion and Outlook

Our discussion of polar duality suggests that a quantum system localized in the position representation in a set X cannot be localized in the momentum representation in a set smaller than that of its polar dual $X^\hbar$. The notion of polar duality thus appears informally as a generalization of the uncertainty principle of quantum mechanics, as expressed in terms of variances and covariances (see [23]). The idea of such generalizations is not new, and can already be found in the work of Uffink and Hilgevoord [25,26]; see Butterfield's discussion in [27]. It would certainly be interesting to explore the connection between convex geometry and quantum mechanics, but very little work has been conducted so far.

Funding: This work was financed by grant P 33447 of Austrian Research Agency FWF. Open Access Funding by the Austrian Science Fund (FWF).

Institutional Review Board Statement: Not applicable

Informed Consent Statement: Not applicable

Data Availability Statement: Not applicable.

Acknowledgments: This work has been financed by the Grant P 33447 of the Austrian Research Agency FWF. Open Access Funding by the Austrian Science Fund (FWF).

Conflicts of Interest: The author declares no conflict of interest.

References

1. Pauli, W. *General Principles of Quantum Mechanics*; Springer Science & Business Media: Berlin, Germany, 2012; [Original Title: *Prinzipien der Quantentheorie*, Handbuch der Physik, v.5.1, 1958].
2. Esposito, G.; Marmo, G.; Miele, G.; Sudarshan, G. *Advanced Concepts in Quantum Mechanics*; Cambridge University Press: Cambridge, UK, 2015.
3. Ibort, A.; Man'ko, V.I.; Marmo, G.; Simoni, A.; Ventriglia, F. An introduction to the tomographic picture of quantum mechanics. *Phys. Scr.* **2009**, *79*, 065013. [CrossRef]
4. Wang, Y.; Xu, C. Density matrix estimation in quantum homodyne tomography. *Stat. Sin.* **2015**, *25*, 953–973. [CrossRef]
5. de Gosson, M. Quantum Harmonic Analysis of the Density Matrix. *Quanta* **2018**, *7*, 74–110. [CrossRef]
6. Wood, J.C.; Barry, D.T. Tomographic time-frequency analysis and its application toward time-varying filtering and adaptive kernel design for multicomponent linear-FM signals. *IEEE Trans. Signal Process.* **1994**, *42*, 2094–2104. [CrossRef]
7. D'Ariano, G.M. Universal quantum observables. *Phys. Lett. A* **2002**, *300*, 1–6. [CrossRef]
8. D'Ariano, G.M.; Macchiavello, C.; Paris, M.G.A. Detection of the density matrix through optical homodyne tomography without filtered back projection. *Phys. Rev. A* **1994**, *50*, 4298–4303. [CrossRef] [PubMed]
9. Bužek, V.; Adam, G.; Drobný, G. Reconstruction of Wigner Functions on Different Observation Levels. *Ann. Phys.* **1996**, *245*, 37–97. [CrossRef]
10. Lvovsky, A.I.; Raymer, M.G. Continuous-variable optical quantum-state tomography. *Rev. Mod. Phys.* **2009**, *8*, 299–332. [CrossRef]
11. Leonhardt, U.; Paul, H. Realistic optical homodyne measurements and quasiprobability distributions. *Phys. Rev. A* **1993**, *48*, 4598. [CrossRef] [PubMed]

12. Mancini, S.; Man'ko, V.I.; Tombesi, P. Symplectic tomography as classical approach to quantum systems. *Phys. Lett. A* **1996**, *213*, 1–6. [CrossRef]
13. Thekkadath, G.S.; Giner, L.; Chalich, Y.; Horton, M.J.; Banker, J.; Lundeen, J.S. Direct Measurement of the Density Matrix of a Quantum System. *Phys. Rev. Lett.* **2016**, *117*, 120401. [CrossRef] [PubMed]
14. Vogel, K.; Risken, H. Determination of quasiprobability distributions in terms of probability distributions for the rotated quadrature phase. *Phys. Rev. A* **1989**, *40*, 2847–2849. [CrossRef] [PubMed]
15. Man'ko, O.; Man'ko, V.I. Quantum states in probability representation and tomography. *J. Russ. Laser Res.* **1997**, *18*, 407–444. [CrossRef]
16. Corbett, J.V. The Pauli problem, state reconstruction and quantum-real numbers. *Rep. Math. Phys.* **2006**, *57*, 53–68. [CrossRef]
17. de Gosson, M. *The Wigner Transform*; Series Advanced Texts in Mathematics; World Scientific: Singapore, 2017.
18. de Gosson, M. *Symplectic Geometry and Quantum Mechanics*; Birkhäuser: Basel, Switzerland, 2006.
19. Littlejohn, R.G. The semiclassical evolution of wave packets. *Phys. Reps.* **1986**, *138*, 193–291. [CrossRef]
20. Bastiaans, M.J. Wigner distribution function and its application to first-order optics. *J. Opt. Soc. Am.* **1979**, *69*, 1710. [CrossRef]
21. Klibanov, M.V.; Sacks, P.E.; Tikhonravov, A.V. The phase retrieval problem. *Inverse Probl.* **1995**, *11*, 1–28. [CrossRef]
22. Charalambos, D.; Aliprantis, B. *Infinite Dimensional Analysis: A Hitchhiker's Guide*; Springer: Berlin/Heidelberg, Germany, 2013.
23. de Gosson, M. Quantum Polar Duality and the Symplectic Camel: A New Geometric Approach to Quantization. *Found. Phys.* **2021**, *51*, 60. [CrossRef]
24. Zhang, F. *The Schur Complement and Its Applications*; Springer: Berlin, Germany, 2005.
25. Hilgevoord, J. The standard deviation is not an adequate measure of quantum uncertainty. *Am. J. Phys.* **2002**, *70*, 983. [CrossRef]
26. Hilgevoord, J.; Uffink, J.B.M. Uncertainty Principle and Uncertainty Relations. *Found. Phys.* **1985**, *15*, 925.
27. Butterfield, J. On Time in Quantum Physics. In *A Companion to the Philosophy of Time*; John Wiley and Sons: Singapore, 2013; pp. 220–241.

Article

Homogeneous Banach Spaces as Banach Convolution Modules over $M(G)$

Hans Georg Feichtinger [1,2]

[1] Faculty of Mathematics, University Vienna, Oskar-Morgenstern-Platz 1, 1090 Vienna, Austria; hans.feichtinger@univie.ac.at
[2] Acoustics Research Institute, Austrian Academy of Sciences, Wohllebengasse 12-14, 1040 Vienna, Austria

Abstract: This paper is supposed to form a keystone towards a new and alternative approach to Fourier analysis over LCA (locally compact Abelian) groups G. In an earlier paper the author has already shown that one can introduce convolution and the Fourier–Stieltjes transform on $(M(G), \|\cdot\|_M)$, the space of bounded measures (viewed as a space of linear functionals) in an elementary fashion over $\mathbb{R}^d$. Bounded uniform partitions of unity (BUPUs) are easily constructed in the Euclidean setting (by dilation). Moving on to general LCA groups, it becomes an interesting challenge to find ways to construct arbitrary *fine* BUPUs, ideally without the use of structure theory, the existence of a Haar measure and even Lebesgue integration. This article provides such a construction and demonstrates how it can be used in order to show that any so-called *homogeneous Banach space* $(B, \|\cdot\|_B)$ on G, such as $(L^p(G), \|\cdot\|_p)$, for $1 \leq p < \infty$, or the Fourier–Stieltjes algebra $\mathcal{F}M(G)$, and in particular any *Segal algebra* is a *Banach convolution module* over $(M(G), \|\cdot\|_M)$ in a natural way. Via the Haar measure we can then identify $(L^1(G), \|\cdot\|_1)$ with the closure (of the embedded version) of $C_c(G)$, the space of continuous functions with compact support, in $(M(G), \|\cdot\|_M)$, and show that these homogeneous Banach spaces are *essential* $L^1(G)$-modules. Thus, in particular, the approximate units act properly as one might expect and converge strongly to the identity operator. The approach is in the spirit of Hans Reiter, avoiding the use of structure theory for LCA groups and the usual techniques of vector-valued integration via duality. The ultimate (still distant) goal of this approach is to provide a new and elementary approach towards the (extended) Fourier transform in the setting of the so-called *Banach–Gelfand triple* $(S_0, L^2, S_0')(G)$, based on the Segal algebra $S_0(G)$. This direction will be pursued in subsequent papers.

Keywords: bounded measures; convolution; homogeneous Banach spaces; integrated group representation; Segal algebra; Wiener amalgam space; bounded uniform partition of unity; locally compact groups

Citation: Feichtinger, H.G. Homogeneous Banach Spaces as Banach Convolution Modules over $M(G)$. *Mathematics* 2022, 10, 364. https://doi.org/10.3390/math10030364

Academic Editors: Elena Cordero and S. Ivan Trapasso

Received: 20 November 2021
Accepted: 6 January 2022
Published: 25 January 2022

Publisher's Note: MDPI stays neutral with regard to jurisdictional claims in published maps and institutional affiliations.

Copyright: © 2022 by the author. Licensee MDPI, Basel, Switzerland. This article is an open access article distributed under the terms and conditions of the Creative Commons Attribution (CC BY) license (https://creativecommons.org/licenses/by/4.0/).

1. Introduction

Let us begin with the observation that the usual approach to harmonic analysis over locally compact Abelian (LCA) groups G (see for example [1–4]) starts with a description of the Lebesgue space $(L^1(G), \|\cdot\|_1)$, which turns out to be a Banach algebra with respect to convolution. Based on the description of the Fourier transform as an integral transform, the traditional approach continues with the demonstration of the fact that the Fourier transform turns convolution into pointwise multiplication (the so-called convolution theorem). This result describes one of the crucial properties of the Fourier transform, and Lebesgue space appears to be a very natural and the best possible domain, because it allows one to describe the convolution product of two functions (more precisely of equivalence classes of measurable functions) in the pointwise sense (almost everywhere), combined with the corresponding norm estimate

$$\|f * g\|_{L^1} \leq \|f\|_{L^1} \|g\|_{L^1}, \quad f, g \in L^1(G).$$

It is also plausible that $(L^1(G), \|\cdot\|_1)$ is considered the natural domain for the Fourier transform, because for any *character* $\chi \in \widehat{G}$ the integral

$$\widehat{f}(\chi) = \int_G f(x)\overline{\chi(x)}dx \tag{1}$$

exists in the Lebesgue sense (for one and then for any $\chi \in \widehat{G}$) if and only if $f \in L^1(G)$. In a similar way, it appears as a natural restriction to assume that $\widehat{f}$ belongs to $L^1(\widehat{G})$ if one wants to obtain $f(x)$ back (again via the usual integral formula describing the inverse Fourier transform) from $\widehat{f}$. The range of the Fourier transform is denoted by $(\mathcal{F}L^1(\mathbb{R}^d), \|\cdot\|_{\mathcal{F}L^1})$. It is a Banach algebra with respect to pointwise multiplication, hence called the *Fourier algebra*, with respect to the norm $\|\widehat{f}\|_{\mathcal{F}L^1} := \|f\|_{L^1}$.

Although technically demanding, this approach based on measure theory allows one to formulate and answer interesting mathematical questions (e.g., about the almost-everywhere convergence of Fourier series), but it does *not reveal the relevance of convolution for applications*. The situation is different when moving on to tempered distributions, which have become the key tool for the treatment of PDEs. However, in order to make use of these tools it is necessary to first study to some extent the Schwartz space $\mathcal{S}(\mathbb{R}^d)$, a nuclear Fréchet space with a countable system of seminorms involving differentiation. For general LCA groups one can define the Schwartz–Bruhat space via structure theory, but it is even more complicated and very difficult to use.

Recalling the fact that engineers learn about the concept of *convolution* in their introductory courses on translation-invariant linear systems (TILS), this author has so far developed an approach to convolution (for bounded measures) which is based on the isometric one-to-one correspondence between linear functionals on $(C_0(G), \|\cdot\|_\infty)$ (we call them bounded measures and use the symbol $(M(G), \|\cdot\|_M)$) and bounded linear operators commuting with translations. Obviously, the space $(C_0(G), \|\cdot\|_\infty)$ of continuous, complex-valued functions vanishing at infinity forms a Banach space (even a pointwise algebra) if endowed with the sup-norm, and $C_c(G)$ (compactly supported functions) are dense in $(C_0(G), \|\cdot\|_\infty)$. It is also invariant under translations, defined as usual by

$$[T_z f](y) = f(y - z), \quad y, z \in G. \tag{2}$$

Any such TILS can be identified with a moving average resp. a convolution operator by a uniquely determined bounded measure $\mu \in (M(G), \|\cdot\|_M) = (C'_0(G), \|\cdot\|_{C'_0})$. This isometric identification allows us to transfer the *composition structure of linear operators* to the corresponding bounded measures, and call it *convolution*. Of course, this viewpoint is compatible with the usual approach (see [2], p.46). It turns out that it is the unique w^*-continuous extension of the identification of translation operators T_x with the corresponding Dirac measures $\delta_x \in M(G)$. In this way $(C_0(G), \|\cdot\|_\infty)$ is a Banach module over $(M(G), \|\cdot\|_M)$ with respect to convolution. Details are given in [5] (and in the Lecture Notes for the ETH course, see www.nuhag.eu/ETH20, accessed on 3 January 2021).

The realization of this correspondence makes use of so-called BUPUs, i.e., bounded uniform partitions of unity. They allow one to decompose every $\mu \in M(G)$ into an absolutely convergent sum of well-localized measures, which, among other approaches, allows the extension of the action of $\mu \in C'_0(G)$ to all of $C_b(G)$, the continuous, bounded functions on G (also endowed with the sup-norm). In this way it is possible to define the Fourier–Stieltjes transform of bounded measures and derive the convolution theorem before even discussing the existence of a Haar measure or the necessary Lebesgue integration theory required in order to study everything in the L^1-context.

The goal of the present manuscript is to provide an important step towards a description of the (generalized) Fourier transform over LCA groups along the lines of the approach described above. This author is convinced that the appropriate setting is that of the Banach–Gelfand triple $(S_0, L^2, S'_0)(G)$, consisting of the Segal algebra $S_0(G)$, which can be defined on arbitrary LCA groups, its dual space $S'_0(G)$, the space of so-called mild distributions, and in the middle the Hilbert space $L^2(G)$ (defined as the completion of $S_0(G)$ with respect to the usual scalar product).

Although such an approach can be realized easily in the context of $G = \mathbb{R}^d$, the Euclidean setting, making use of the special ingredients available in this context, notably the existence of a Fourier-invariant Gaussian function and dilation operators, which among other uses, allow one to create arbitrary fine BUPUs in a natural fashion, it is not so obvious whether and how one can obtain such BUPUs in the context of an abstract LCA group. Moreover, many important convolution relations make use of the fact that convolution operators induced by bounded measures act also boundedly on a large variety of Banach spaces of functions over the group G, e.g., on the usual spaces $(L^p(G), \|\cdot\|_p)$, or the Fourier algebra $\mathcal{F}L^1(G)$ and (hence) on $(S_0(G), \|\cdot\|_{S_0})$. We will provide a relatively simple construction of such arbitrary fine BUPUs, avoiding the use of structure theory of LCA groups, and derive similar results making use of these BUPUs.

The natural setting for the realization of such a general statement is the setting of *homogeneous Banach spaces* (HBS) (in the sense of Y. Katznelson), which are isometrically translation invariant by assumption. The family of *Segal algebras* (in the sense of H. Reiter) is an interesting subfamily of this class of Banach spaces of locally integrable functions over G. The second main result of this paper will deal with such Banach spaces and will demonstrate that any such HBS $(B, \|\cdot\|_B)$ is actually a Banach module over $(M(G), \|\cdot\|_M)$ (hence over $(L^1(G), \|\cdot\|_1)$) with respect to convolution.

The paper is organized in the following way. First we discuss several variations of the concept of a *bounded uniform partition of unity* (BUPU) in Section 2, and explain their mutual relationship. We also provide a few historical comments on their use in the literature.

In Section 3 the existence of arbitrary fine BUPUs is established as our first main result. Instead of the Haar measure, we use a kind of coarse measurement of the size of sets, called a *capacity* (with respect to a sufficiently small reference set). This provides the basis for our key results, without making use of the structure theory for LCA groups. Subsequently it is shown in Section 4 how to make use of such BUPUs. In Section 5 we also discuss various characterizations of the *Wiener algebra* $W = W(C_0, \ell^1)(G)$ and its dual via BUPUs.

In Section 6 our second main result is shown: any homogeneous Banach space (in the sense of Y. Katznelson) is a Banach module over $(M(G), \|\cdot\|_M)$ with respect to convolution. In fact, we formulate an even more general abstract approach based on isometric, strongly continuous representations of the group G on an arbitrary Banach space $(B, \|\cdot\|_B)$. This approach is based on the methods developed in [5] and makes use of a constructive way of approximating bounded measures by discrete measures in the w^*- sense. The technical realization of this second main result is based on the completeness of Banach spaces, which also implies that (bounded) *Cauchy nets* are actually convergent in any Banach space. The necessary background is described in Section 7. This approach also permits us to demonstrate that the w^*-convergence of bounded and tight nets leads to strong operator convergence of the corresponding convolution operators (Theorem 5).

Only then is the existence of the Haar measure invoked in order to define $(L^1(G), \|\cdot\|_1)$ as a subspace of $(M(G), \|\cdot\|_M)$, namely, as a closure of $C_c(G)$. In this sense, Section 6 characterizes the usual *integrated group representation* as the restriction of the established module structure over $M(G)$. In particular it is shown that any homogeneous Banach space is also an *essential* Banach module over $(L^1(G), \|\cdot\|_1)$.

2. Different Types of Uniform Partitions

It is the purpose of this section to compare various notions of uniform partitions of unity in the context of harmonic analysis over LCA groups. It is easy to construct arbitrary fine BUPUs of a given degree of smoothness on $\mathbb{R}$ merely by applying appropriate dilations to the basis of B-splines of sufficiently high order (or even infinitely differentiable) which are obtained as translations along the integer lattice $\mathbb{Z}$ of the convolution powers of the indicator function $\mathbf{1}_{[-1/2,1/2]}$. For B-splines of order 3 (four-fold convolution power) one obtains a Riesz basis for the cubic spline function in $\left(L^2(\mathbb{R}), \|\cdot\|_2\right)$. Via tensor products, the same can be achieved on $\mathbb{R}^d$ for $d \geq 2$.

In contrast, it is not at all clear how to provide similar families of functions in a situation where there is a lack of fine lattices (and corresponding fundamental domains) and without having an appropriate automorphism group on the underlying group (replacing dilations).

It is our main goal in this section to demonstrate that the existence of such BUPUs (using a suitable version of the BUPU concept) can be guaranteed, using relatively elementary arguments. Thus, we will *not rely on the existence of a Haar measure* on such a group G, although that would make the proof a little bit shorter.

The notion of *uniform partitions of unity* appears in different papers, which are usually similar in spirit and which mostly refer to the *uniform size of the constituents of the partition of unity*. In order to compare the different possible concepts, let us recall the corresponding definitions. The concept of choice for *this article* is that of BUPUs as introduced in [6] (i.e., Definition 2 below). It has been used regularly since then (e.g., in [7], Section 3.2.2 and in many other papers by the author).

The following situation will be the most simple and still the most useful for our purpose. It is a simplification of the concept of BUPUs as introduced in [6] (given below). Since it is natural to formulate these results in the context of locally compact groups G, we formulate the next definition by writing the group operation in a multiplicative way.

Definition 1. *Given some neighborhood $U \in \mathcal{U}(e)$ of the identity of a locally compact group G, a non-negative U-BUPU, a so-called (left) bounded uniform partition of unity of size U is a family $\Psi = (\psi_i)_{i \in I}$ of continuous, non-negative functions on G satisfying the following conditions (we write the group law multiplicatively here):*

1. *For some family $(x_i)_{i \in I}$ in G one has: $\mathrm{supp}(\psi_i) \subseteq x_i U$ for all $i \in I$;*
2. *The family $(x_i U)_{i \in I}$ satisfies the bounded overlap property (BOP); the number of intersecting neighbors is uniformly bounded (with respect to $i \in I$):*

$$\sup_{i \in I} \#\{j \mid x_i U \cap x_j U \neq \emptyset\} \leq B_0 < \infty;$$

3. $\sum_{i \in I} \psi_i(x) \equiv 1$ *on G.*

Remark 1. *The continuity of the constituents ψ_i of the BUPU requires some overlap of their supports, which is illustrated in Figure 1. On the other hand, we can apply bounded measures (i.e., linear functionals on $\left(C_0(G), \|\cdot\|_\infty\right)$) only on continuous functions with compact support, and not on the indicator functions of compact sets. Although one might think of a fine partition of the group (e.g., translates of a fundamental domain), we do not want to make use of this more measure-theoretic setting.*

Remark 2. *Observe that the bounded overlap property implies that the sum in (3) is a finite sum (with at most B_0 non-zero terms for each $x \in G$). We call B_0 the "overlap bound" of the family $(x_i U)$.*

The non-negativity of the functions ψ_i implies by (3) that $\sup_{i \in I} \|\psi_i\|_\infty \leq 1$, i.e., the family Ψ is bounded in $\left(C_0(G), \|\cdot\|_\infty\right)$ (the space of continuous complex-valued functions vanishing at infinity, endowed with the sup-norm).

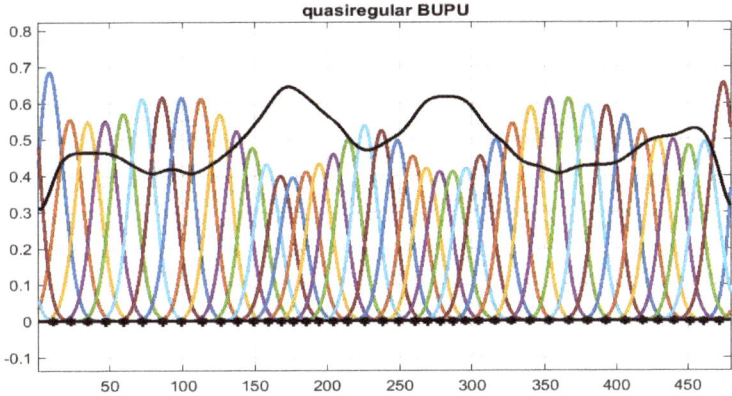

Figure 1. A typical BUPU, illustrating Definition 1, obtained by positioning shifted bump functions at well-spread locations (marked with ∗) on the line, followed by a division through the sum of those bump functions, displayed in black.

For the characterization of general Wiener amalgam spaces of the form $W(B, \ell^q)$, for example, (with a *local component* $(B, \|\cdot\|_B)$, which are more general than being just another L^p-space, but something like $(B, \|\cdot\|_B) = (\mathcal{F}L^1(\mathbb{R}^d), \|\cdot\|_{\mathcal{F}L^1})$ or $\mathcal{F}L^p$), it is important to assume the boundedness of the family Ψ in some Banach algebra (with respect to pointwise multiplication), contained in the multiplier algebra of $(B, \|\cdot\|_B)$. We assume in that case that $(A, \|\cdot\|_A) \hookrightarrow (C_0(G), \|\cdot\|_\infty)$ (continuous embedding). On the other hand, non-negativity is not required in this case. The subsequent definition of BUPUs goes back to [6].

Definition 2. *Given $U \in \mathcal{U}(e)$, a family $\Psi = (\psi_i)_{i \in I}$ is a BUPU, a bounded uniform partition of unity (of size U) in the Banach algebra $(A, \|\cdot\|_A)$ if one has:*

1. *There exists a family $(x_i)_{i \in I}$ in G such that $\mathrm{supp}(\psi_i) \subseteq x_i U$ for all $i \in I$;*
2. *The family Ψ is bounded in $(A, \|\cdot\|_A)$, i.e., $\sup_{i \in I} \|\psi_i\|_A \leq C_\Psi < \infty$;*
3. *There exists $B_0 > 0$ such that $\#\{j \mid x_i U \cap x_j U \neq \emptyset\} \leq B_0$;*
4. *$\sum_{i \in I} \psi_i(x) \equiv 1$ on G.*

The constant $C_\Psi = C(\Psi, A)$ is called the norm of the family Ψ in $(A, \|\cdot\|_A)$, and B_0 is the *overlapping constant* of the family. The family $X = (x_i)_{i \in I}$ is called the *family of centers of the BUPU* $\Psi = (\psi_i)_{i \in I}$.

For the case of a metric group G we can use balls of radius $\delta > 0$ as a basis of neighborhoods and thus it is natural to write $|\Psi| \leq \delta$ if one has $\mathrm{supp}(\psi_i) \subseteq B_\delta(x_i)$ for $i \in I$. In this case we call Ψ a $\delta - BUPU$, or a BUPU of size δ.

Remark 3. *The usefulness of BUPUs with different specific properties arises in various contexts. Let us mention only a few of them here.*

Sometimes it is enough to have some BUPUs, which may be bounded in a suitable Banach algebra $(A, \|\cdot\|_A)$, e.g., for the construction of Wiener amalgam spaces, such as $(W(\mathcal{F}L^1, \ell^1)(\mathbb{R}^d), \|\cdot\|_{W(\mathcal{F}L^1, \ell^1)})$. In fact, for such spaces one can show that different BUPUs define the same Wiener amalgam spaces with equivalent norms. However, BUPUs are not only helpful in defining new function spaces, they also play an important role in the alternative approach to convolution for the measure algebra $(M(G), \|\cdot\|_M)$, as presented in [5]. The decomposition of $\mu \in M(G)$ as an absolutely convergent sum of measures with small support allows us to take a crucial step in the isometric isomorphism between $(M(G), \|\cdot\|_M)$ and the Banach algebra (under composition) of bounded linear operators on $\left(C_0(G), \|\cdot\|_\infty\right)$ which commute with translation, the so-called TILS (translation-invariant linear systems, as they are called in engineering books).

For the work on coorbit theory developed jointly with K. Gröchenig, as well as the closely related work on irregular sampling, it is important to be able to have BUPUs which are centered at a given δ-dense subset of $\mathbb{R}^d$ (or a LCA group); see [8] or [9]; see also [10–12].

For the current paper the existence of arbitrary fine BUPUs over general LC groups will be crucial. Currently it is not clear whether one can find UPUs (in the sense of [13]) of size U (meaning with $\text{supp}(\varphi) \subseteq U$, for a given neighborhood of the identity) in the case of general groups. Fortunately, the concept of BUPUs is more flexible, and it will be the first main result of this paper to demonstrate that one can derive the existence of arbitrary fine non-negative BUPUs over any given locally compact group G using elementary considerations (reminding perhaps some readers of the construction of a Haar measure on G, see [14]).

For most applications, so-called *regular BUPUs* will be sufficient (and in fact easier to handle), and these are obtained as translates of a (smooth) function with compact support along some lattice $\Lambda \triangleleft G$. Especially over $G = \mathbb{R}^d$ it would be natural to make use of smooth BUPUs with respect to some lattice of the form $\Lambda = A\mathbb{Z}^d$, for some non-singular $d \times d$ matrix A. Note that in the Euclidean case (or, for example, also for stratified Lie groups) one can obtain "arbitrary fine BUPUs" by applying a simple dilation (or rather compression) routine to a given BUPU. If one only needs *some BUPU* over $\mathbb{R}^d$ it is quite natural to obtain BUPUs as translates of a single function:

Definition 3. *A family* $\Psi = (\psi_\lambda)_{\lambda \in \Lambda} = (T_\lambda \psi_0)_{\lambda \in \Lambda}$ *is called a regular (smooth) uniform partition of unity on* $\mathbb{R}^d$ *in* $\left(\mathcal{F}L^1(\mathbb{R}^d), \|\cdot\|_{\mathcal{F}L^1}\right)$ *if it satisfies:*

1. ψ_0 *is compactly supported and* $\widehat{\psi_0} \in L^1(\mathbb{R}^d)$, *(resp.* $\psi_0 \in \mathcal{D}(\mathbb{R}^d)$*);*
2. $\sum_{\lambda \in \Lambda} \psi_\lambda(x) = \sum_{\lambda \in \Lambda} \psi_0(x - \lambda) \equiv 1$ *on* $\mathbb{R}^d$.

Note that the finite overlap condition of support easily follows from the properties of a lattice, and that furthermore the boundedness of the family Ψ is an easy consequence of the isometric translation invariance of the algebra $(A, \|\cdot\|_A)$ under consideration (here $\left(\mathcal{F}L^1(\mathbb{R}^d), \|\cdot\|_{\mathcal{F}L^1}\right)$).

Historical note: BUPUs were introduced (although not first used) by this name by the author in [6] for the "discrete" characterization of Wiener amalgam spaces.

A slightly different approach has been taken in [13], based on earlier work of [15].

Definition 4. *Let G be a locally compact group. A family* Ψ *in* $C_c(G)$ *is called a UPU (a uniform partition of unity) if there exists some function* $\varphi \in C_c(G)$ *(i.e., continuous and compactly supported, perhaps satisfying some smoothness conditions) such that, for a suitable family* $(y_i)_{i \in I}$ *in G one has*

$$\sum_{i \in I} T_{y_i}\varphi(x) = \sum_{i \in I} \varphi(y_i^{-1}x) \equiv 1 \text{ on } G. \tag{3}$$

Although formally there is no BOP property required in this case it is shown in [13] that the family of shift parameters $(y_i)_{i \in I}$ is relatively separated, or equivalently, that such an UPU is in fact a BUPU of size $\text{supp}(\varphi)$.

We can give the following characterization of *relatively separated families* $(x_i)_{i \in I}$ as they appear in the above definitions. For details see e.g., Theorem 22 in [12].

Lemma 1. *For a discrete family* $(x_i)_{i \in I}$ *in G the following properties are equivalent:*

1. *The family is relatively separated, i.e., a finite union of separated sets, i.e., of subfamilies* $(x_j)_{j \in J}$ *with the property that* $x_j V \cap x_l V = \emptyset$ *for* $j \neq l \in J$, *for some open set* V *in G;*
2. *For any relatively compact set W the family* $(x_i W)_{i \in I}$ *has the uniformly controlled neighbors property;*

3. For any compact set $Q \subset G$ the number of points in zQ is controlled as follows:
$$\sup_{z \in G} \#\{i \mid x_i \in zQ\} = B(Q) < \infty.$$

Remark 4. *The latter property can be equivalently described as the property that the (irregular) Dirac comb $\sqcup\!\sqcup_X := \sum_{i \in I} \delta_{x_i}$ belongs to the Wiener amalgam space $W(M, \ell^\infty)$, which is the dual of the Wiener algebra $\left(W(C_0, \ell^1)(G), \|\cdot\|_W\right)$. We will not pursue this connection any further as it might confuse readers who are not familiar with the theory of Wiener amalgam spaces.*

Let us next recall that the main result of [13] describes (making use of the structure theory of locally compact groups) the existence of UPUs for arbitrary LC groups G. However, it is not claimed that one can find arbitrary fine UPUs in that paper. Still, for further reference, let us formulate their main result as follows:

Proposition 1 (Leptin/Müller). *For any locally compact group G there exist UPUs.*

Remark 5. *Using a simple compactness argument one can even rewrite the function φ as a finite sum $\varphi = \sum_{k=1}^{K} \varphi_k$ of functions with arbitrary small support and thus derive the existence of BUPUs by translating each of them using the same family of shift-parameters (y_j). However, the disadvantage (from our perspective) of this approach is the fact that it is heavily based on structure theory.*

Remark 6. *Note that of course one even can obtain a situation where the indicator function of a relatively compact set covers the group by translates along a discrete family $(y_j)_{j \in J}$, without having any group structure, i.e., not using a lattice (discrete subgroup) as the parameter set of the shift operators. Such a situation is known from wavelet theory, where one obtains such coverings on the "ax + b"-group. Although the translation parameters (taken from $\mathbb{Z}$) and the dilation parameters of the form 2^k, $k \in \mathbb{Z}$ form discrete subgroups of Abelian subgroups; the combined "geometric lattice" is not a discrete subgroup of the affine group.*

Historical Notes

There are several situations in which BUPUs have played an important role in the past. The first of these was the paper which introduced the general *Wiener amalgams* (originally called *Wiener-type spaces*) [6].

Of course, various forms of smooth BUPUs, such as B-spline systems had already been used early on, e.g., in the theory of numerical integration. In fact, any BUPU allows one to define a so-called *quasi-interpolation operator* of the form $\mathrm{Sp}_\Psi f(x) := \sum_{i \in I} f(x_i) \psi_i$. Sometimes (e.g., for the BUPU obtained by B-splines of order one, which are triangular functions), these operators interpolate the function f at the node points, but in most other cases they just approximate a given smooth function. Integration formulas thus allow us to calculate the integral of Sp_Ψ in a closed form, based on the knowledge of the sampling values $(f(x_i))$ only.

BUPUs over LC groups play a prominent role in the development of *coorbit theory*, which was put in place by the author together with K. Gröchenig (see [16]).

At the heart of coorbit theory are reconstruction methods which allow us to reconstruct an abstract wavelet transform $V_g f$ defined over a locally compact group G (such as the Heisenberg group, the "ax + b"-group, or the shearlet group, to mention concrete examples) from samples, taken over a sufficiently dense, discrete family $(x_i)_{i \in I}$ in G. The first step here is to establish a quasi-interpolation for $V_g f$, using the given sampling values only. However, one then observes that the resulting function may not belong to the range of the transform $f \mapsto V_g f$, and thus one has to project back to the range, which can be realized by means of a convolution with $V_g g$. The details are found in [8] and related papers. Of course, one has to estimate the guaranteed approximation quality for this kind of approximation, in order to have a basis for an iterative method of reconstruction (at a geometric rate).

The intuitive similarity of the properties of those wavelet transforms $V_g f$ with band-limited functions of two variables (as well as the existence of a reproducing convolution relation in both cases) then inspired the authors to deal with the "irregular sampling problem", i.e., the problem of reconstructing a band-limited function from irregular samples. Recall that the regular case, i.e., the reconstruction of a band-limited function in $L^2(\mathbb{R}^d)$ (with compact support $\operatorname{supp}(\hat{f}) \subseteq B_R(0)$) from samples along some lattice Λ can be guaranteed if the lattice Λ is fine enough, essentially making use of Poisson's formula. In the irregular case the first generation of iterative algorithms was based on the use of BUPUs, which are fine enough and are centered at the given sampling points (see [10,12]).

3. Arbitrary Fine BUPUs over LC Groups

In this section we establish our first main result, in the context of general locally compact groups. Since this includes many non-commutative groups, we choose the usual multiplicative notation for the group law.

Definition 5. *For any fixed and relatively compact subset $S \subset G$ the mapping $M \mapsto \operatorname{cap}_S(M)$ is defined on the collection of (relatively) compact sets M according to the following rule*

$$\operatorname{cap}_S(M) := \min\{\#F \mid M \subseteq \bigcup_{i \in F} x_i S\} \tag{4}$$

where the minimum is taken over all finite subsets of possible translation parameters.

Note that, based on the fact that the interior of S is non-empty and M is supposed to be compact, the minimum is taken over a non-empty subset of $\mathbb{N}$.

Remark 7. *The term "capacity" originates from a similar construction, where one measures the size of an indicator function by minimizing over all the (typically non-negative) functions in a given function's spaces, typically a Sobolev space $\mathcal{H}_s(\mathbb{R}^d)$, which dominate the indicator function $\mathbf{1}_M$ of the set M.*

Such an interpretation is in fact also possible here: Given a set S, $\operatorname{cap}_S(M)$ can be interpreted as the infimum over all norms in $W(L^\infty, \ell^1)(G)$ of functions, dominating the indicator function $\mathbf{1}_M$. We leave it to the interested reader to check the details.

Lemma 2. *For any fixed and relatively compact subset $S \subset G$ the mapping $M \mapsto \operatorname{cap}_S(M)$, defined on the collection of compact sets M, has the following properties:*

1. $\operatorname{cap}_S(S) = 1$
2. $\operatorname{cap}_S(zM) = \operatorname{cap}_S(M), \ \forall z \in G$
3. *The mapping $M \mapsto \operatorname{cap}_S(M)$ is subadditive in the sense that we have for finite unions of compact sets:*

$$\operatorname{cap}_S\left(\bigcup_{k=1}^K M_k\right) \leq \sum_{k=1}^K \operatorname{cap}_S(M_k)$$

4. *Given any finite collection of compact sets $M_k, k = 1, \ldots, K$ which are S-separated, i.e., satisfying the condition that $M_k S \cap M_j S = \emptyset$ for $k \neq j$, one has*

$$\operatorname{cap}_S\left(\bigcup_{k=1}^K M_k\right) = \sum_{k=1}^K \operatorname{cap}_S(M_k).$$

Proof. Claim (1) is obvious, and the translation invariance (2) follows from

$$M \subseteq \bigcup_{i \in F} x_i S \quad \Leftrightarrow \quad zM \subseteq \bigcup_{i \in F} (zx_i) S, \quad \forall z \in G.$$

Thus, any covering of M has a corresponding covering of equal cardinality for zM.

The subadditivity property (3) is easy to check, since the combination of all the translates needed to cover all the sets $M_i, i \in F$, obviously constitutes a covering of their union.

Finally, we check for the additivity property (4). Given a minimal covering of $\bigcup_{k=1}^{K} M_k$, using a set of translates of the form $y_i S, i = 1,...L$, we argue that each of the translates will be relevant for exactly one of the constituting sets M_k, $1 \leq k \leq K$, since due to the minimality we can limit our consideration to translates of the form zS which intersect at least one of the sets M_k.

Using an indirect argument we assume that zS has non-trivial intersection with, for instance, $x_1 S$ and $x_2 S$. Then we have $zs = x_1 s_1 = x_2 s_2$ for some elements $s, s_1, s_2 \in S$. However, we then have $z \in M_1 S \cap M_2 S = \emptyset$, in contradiction to the assumption. Thus, for every index k the collection of sets $s_i S$ with $i \in I_k$ given by

$$I_k := \{i \in F \mid M_k \cap s_i S \neq \emptyset\}$$

describes a covering of the set M_k.

This is a minimal covering, because if there was another covering of the set M_k with fewer terms, it could be used to obtain an even better covering of their union (by simply leaving the other contributions fixed), in contradiction to the assumed minimality of the covering and property (3) in Lemma 2. □

Remark 8. *Note that up to this point we have only used a few topological properties of locally compact groups G. The use of the simple expression of a capacity (which should be seen as a simplified or coarse form of a measure) will allow us to derive the existence of arbitrary fine BUPUs on any locally compact group G.*

Note that similar expressions appear in the construction of the Haar measure on a given locally compact group. We leave it to the reader to check this similarity. For us it is only important to mention that the use of this "coarse form of a measure" precedes the construction of a Haar measure and thus allows us to derive the validity of the integrated group action (as described in Section 3.2 of [2]) without any measure theory, as it does not make use of Lebesgue integration theory nor the existence of the Haar measure.

Theorem 1. *Let G be any locally compact group and $U \in \mathcal{U}(e)$ be any neighborhood of the neutral element $e \in G$. Then there exist (plenty of) BUPUs $\Psi = (\psi_i)_{i \in I}$ of non-negative functions of size U, meaning that*

$$\mathrm{supp}(\psi_i) \subseteq x_i U, \quad \forall i \in I, \tag{5}$$

for a suitable discrete (in fact uniformly separated) family $X = (x_i)_{i \in I}$ in G, and

$$\sum_{i \in I} \psi_i(x) \equiv 1. \tag{6}$$

Proof. Given U we choose some compact neighborhood $V \in \mathcal{U}(e)$ such that $V^3 \subseteq U$, and an even smaller neighborhood $S \in \mathcal{U}(e)$ with $S^2 \subseteq V$. Without the loss of generality, we will assume that all these neighborhoods are symmetric (with respect to the group action), i.e., that $z \in U$ if and only if $z^{-1} \in U$ (and the same for the other neighborhoods).

We then select a maximal family $(x_i)_{i \in I}$ with respect to the property that $\{x_i V \mid i \in I\}$ forms a *pavement* in G, i.e., such that the sets $x_i V$ do not intersect in a non-trivial way, but that there is no $z \in G$ such that zV could be added to the family without destroying this property. Consequently, any translate zV intersects at least one of the sets $x_i V$, or $zV \cap x_i V \neq \emptyset$ for some index $i \in I$. Due to the symmetry assumption, this implies that the family $(x_i V^2)$ covers the group G.

Due to the regularity of a locally compact group there exists $\varphi \in C_c(G)$ with $\varphi(y) = 1$ on V^2, $\mathrm{supp}(\varphi) \subseteq V^3$ and $\|\varphi\|_\infty = 1$. Thus (by setting $L_x \varphi(y) = \varphi(x^{-1} y)$) the sum

$$\Phi(x) := \sum_{i \in I} L_{x_i} \varphi(x) = \sum_{i \in I} \varphi(x_i^{-1} x)$$

is well defined and satisfies $\Phi(x) \geq 1$ for all $x \in G$. In order to show that the sum is finite (in a uniform sense) for each $x \in G$, let us fix $i \in I$ and consider $I_i := \{j \mid \psi_i \psi_j \neq 0\}$. Since $I_i \subseteq \{j \mid x_i V^3 \cap x_j V^3 \neq \emptyset\}$ we have to count the indices $j \in I$ with $x_j \in x_i V^6$, or

$$x_j S \subseteq x_i V^6 S \subset x_i V^7.$$

Since the family of sets $x_j S, i \in I$ is an S-separated family of translates of S, thanks to the assumption $S^2 \subseteq V$ and the pavement conditions stated at the beginning of the proof we can apply property (4) of Lemma 2 in order to finish our proof.

Hence for any fixed $i \in I$ the number of possible indices such that $\psi_i \cdot \psi_j \neq 0$ is at most $\mathrm{cap}_S(V^7)$ (because we have $\mathrm{cap}_S(x_j S) = \mathrm{cap}_S(S) = 1$, using properties (1) and (2) from Lemma 2 above).

Overall, we have established that the sum defining $\Phi(x)$ is pointwise a finite sum and the resulting function Φ satisfies

$$1 \leq \Phi(x) \leq \mathrm{cap}_S(V^7), \quad x \in G. \tag{7}$$

Consequently, we observe that the family defined by

$$\psi_i(x) := L_{x_i} \varphi(x) / \Phi(x), \; i \in I,$$

defines a partition of unity of size U, since $V^3 \subseteq U$ and

$$\mathrm{supp}(\psi_i) = \mathrm{supp}(L_{x_i} \varphi) = x_i \, \mathrm{supp}(\varphi) \subset x_i V^3 \subset x_i U.$$

□

4. Towards Integrated Group Representations

To some extent the usefulness of BUPUs is based on the fact that they allow us to define natural operators. Any non-negative BUPU $\Psi = (\psi_i)_{i \in I}$ induces two operators, namely, the *spline quasi-interpolation operator* Sp_Ψ on $(C_0(G), \|\cdot\|_\infty)$, given by

$$\mathrm{Sp}_\Psi f := \sum_{i \in I} f(x_i) \psi_i, \tag{8}$$

and its adjoint operator, the so-called *discretization operator* D_Ψ on $(M(G), \|\cdot\|_M) = (C_0'(G), \|\cdot\|_{C_0'})$, which takes the form

$$D_\Psi \mu = \sum_{i \in I} \mu(\psi_i) \delta_{x_i}. \tag{9}$$

Since any Sp_Ψ is obviously a nonexpansive operator on $(C_0(G), \|\cdot\|_\infty)$ it is also clear that its adjoint is nonexpansive on $(M(G), \|\cdot\|_M)$ as well.

Let us first recall a few facts concerning the discretized measures for the case of $G = \mathbb{R}^d$.

In [5] the following facts were derived:

Proposition 2. *Given $\mu \in M(\mathbb{R}^d)$ the net (the reader is definitely familiar with such a concept, recalling the concept of convergence of Riemann sums, which approach the limit $\int_a^b f(x) dx$, given that $f \in C([a,b])$.) $(D_\Psi \mu)_{|\Psi| \to 0}$ is w^*-convergent:*

$$D_\Psi \mu(f) \to \mu(f), \quad \forall f \in C_0, |\Psi| \to 0. \tag{10}$$

In fact, we have for any BUPU Ψ:

$$\|D_\Psi \mu\|_M \leq \|\mu\|_M, \quad \mu \in M(\mathbb{R}^d). \tag{11}$$

Moreover, the family $(D_\Psi \mu)_{|\Psi| \leq 1}$ is uniformly tight in $(M(\mathbb{R}^d), \|\cdot\|_M)$ (a bounded set $S \subset M(\mathbb{R}^d)$ is called tight if for every $\varepsilon > 0$ there exists $p \in C_c(G)$ such that $\|p\mu - \mu\|_M \leq \varepsilon, \forall \mu \in S$).

We do not go into a discussion of tightness combined with w^*-convergence, but recall that we have established strong operator norm convergence for the corresponding convolution operators (by [5]), given pointwise by $\mu * f(x) = \mu(T_x f^\vee)$, $x \in \mathbb{R}^d$:

$$\lim_{|\Psi| \to 0} \|D_\Psi \mu * f - \mu * f\|_\infty = 0, \quad f \in C_0(\mathbb{R}^d). \tag{12}$$

Our next goal is to verify that a corresponding behaviour remains valid for general (isometric) group representations on Banach spaces. In a sense, this shows that the Banach algebra $(M(G), \|\cdot\|_M)$, with the composition rule being internal convolution), provides a universal algebra which can be embedded into the Banach algebra of all operators on a variety of Banach spaces. Note that in addition to the crucial estimate (controlling the operator norm of the convolution operator $f \mapsto \mu * f$ by $\|\mu\|_M$) we have to ensure the validity of the associative law, i.e., that we have for $\mu_1, \mu_2 \in M(G)$:

$$(\mu_1 \star \mu_2) * f = \mu_1 * (\mu_2 * f), \quad f \in B. \tag{13}$$

This is non-trivial and authors often neglect to mention it, but it is obvious for Dirac measures, and hence for discrete measures, and thus can be obtained by taking limits.

Since our goal is mostly application for LCA groups, we have formulated the next definition for the Abelian setting, thus making use of additive notation for the group law.

Definition 6. *A mapping $\rho : G \to \mathcal{L}(B)$, the bounded, linear operators on a Banach spaces $(B, \|\cdot\|_B)$, is called an isometric representation of a group G on the Banach space $(B, \|\cdot\|_B)$ if the mapping ρ is a group homomorphism, i.e., satisfies*

$$\rho(x+y) = \rho(x) \circ \rho(y), \quad x, y \in G,$$

and if each of the operators are isometric on $(B, \|\cdot\|_B)$, i.e., if one has

$$\|\rho(x)f\|_B = \|f\|_B, \quad f \in B, x \in G. \tag{14}$$

Moreover, if the mapping $x \mapsto \rho(x)f$ is continuous from G to $(B, \|\cdot\|_B)$, i.e.,

$$\lim_{x \to 0} \|\rho(x)f - f\|_B = 0, \quad f \in B. \tag{15}$$

we say that the representation ρ is strongly continuous.

An important family of examples arises from the so-called *regular representation* of G, i.e., the action of the group by (left or right) translation on functions or distributions over G, i.e., $\rho(x) = T_x$ the integrated action corresponds to the *usual convolution* (see [2], p. 73). In this case the notation of *homogeneous Banach spaces* is used, which suggests calling Banach spaces endowed with an isometric, strongly continuous group representation of an LC group G an *abstract homogeneous Banach space* (cf. [17], Chap. 9).

The main result of this paper is the observation that we can establish the fact that every strongly continuous, isometric representation of $\mathbb{R}^d$ on a Banach space $(B, \|\cdot\|_B)$ gives rise to an extended representation (the so-called *integrated group representation*) of the Banach convolution algebra $(M(\mathbb{R}^d), \|\cdot\|_M)$. In fact, this extension is unique among all those who respect tight, w^*-convergence of nets (or just sequences), with the understanding that $\rho(x)$ is of course identified with $\rho(\delta_x)$ (we avoid the use of a different symbol for the integrated representation).

Remark 9. *Usually, in the standard literature on the subject, the integrated group representation describes the action of $f \in L^1(G)$ on $f \in B$, and is thus not immediately visible as a natural extension of the group representation. Aside from technical arguments (and there are many such considerations, involving abstract measure theory and a lot of functional analysis) the focus on $L^1(G)$ appears to come from a similar situation, where the group representation of a discrete group G can be extended naturally to $\ell^1(G)$, which has the "unit vectors" $\delta_x, x \in G$ as a natural (unconditional) basis. In other words, in this case any $f \in \ell^1(G)$ can be written (uniquely) as*

$$f = \sum_{x \in G} f(x)\delta_x \quad \text{with} \quad \|f\|_1 := \sum_{x \in G} |f(x)| < \infty. \tag{16}$$

However, for a discrete group we have of course $\ell^1(G) = M(G)$ and the finite, discrete measures are dense in $(M(G), \|\cdot\|_M)$ (see [18], Example 6.1.7). In contrast, for non-discrete groups the subspace $M_d(G)$ of discrete measures (of the form $\mu = \sum_{k=1}^{\infty} c_k \delta_{x_k}$ with $\sum_{k=1}^{\infty} |c_k| < \infty$) forms a proper closed subalgebra of $(M(G), \|\cdot\|_M)$. However, fortunately $M_d(G)$ is w^*–dense in $M(G)$ and the constructive way of proving this fact (described in [5]) serves as the basis for the results presented in this paper.

Remark 10. *Using the terminology of Banach modules we can state that any strongly continuous, isometric representation of G on $(B, \|\cdot\|_B)$ turns $(B, \|\cdot\|_B)$ into a Banach module over the (commutative, unital) Banach convolution algebra $(M(G), \|\cdot\|_M)$ (we use the symbol $\star$ for internal convolution).*

Later (see Section 6) we will see that the restriction of the module action to $L^1(G)$ makes $(B, \|\cdot\|_B)$ an essential Banach (convolution) module over $\left(L^1(G), \|\cdot\|_1\right)$.

Next we will show that the convolution action of bounded discrete measures on a *homogenous Banach space* can be extended to all of the measures in order to generate an action of $(M(G), \|\cdot\|_M)$ on such a Banach space $(B, \|\cdot\|_B)$.

Theorem 2. *Any abstract homogeneous Banach space $(B, \|\cdot\|_B)$ with respect to a given, strongly continuous and isometric representation ρ of a locally compact group G is also a Banach module over the Banach algebra $(M(G), \|\cdot\|_M)$ (with respect to convolution). This claim includes the validity of the following associativity law:*

$$\rho(\mu_1 \star \mu_2) = \rho(\mu_1) \circ \rho(\mu_2), \quad \mu_1, \mu_2 \in M(G). \tag{17}$$

The mapping $(\mu, f) \mapsto \mu \bullet_\rho f = \rho(\mu)f$ is the natural extension of the action of discrete measure given by $\delta_x \bullet_\rho f = \rho(x)f$ and satisfies the norm estimate

$$\|\mu \bullet_\rho f\|_B \leq \|\mu\|_M \|f\|_B, \quad \mu \in M(G), f \in B. \tag{18}$$

Proof. We start from the expected action of Dirac measures via

$$\delta_x \bullet_\rho f =: \rho(x)f, \quad f \in B. \tag{19}$$

Since discrete measures are absolutely convergent sums of Dirac measures it is then clear that we have for a discrete measure $\mu = \sum_{k=1}^{\infty} c_k \delta_{x_k}$, with $\sum_{k=1}^{\infty} |c_k| = \|\mu\|_M < \infty$:

$$\mu \bullet_\rho f = \sum_{n=1}^{\infty} c_k \rho(x_k) f, \tag{20}$$

the sum being absolutely convergent for each f and $\mu \in M_d(G)$, since we have

$$\|\mu \bullet_\rho f\|_B \leq \sum_{n=1}^{\infty} |c_k| \|\rho(x_k)f\|_B \leq \|f\|_B \sum_{n=1}^{\infty} |c_k| = \|\mu\|_M \|f\|_B. \tag{21}$$

Observe also that the assumptions concerning ρ imply that this action of $M_d(G)$ is not only an individual action (given for each $\mu \in M_d(G)$) but it in fact defines a representation of the Banach convolution algebra $(M_d(G), \|\cdot\|_{M_b})$, since we have

$$(\mu_1 \star \mu_2) \bullet_\rho f = \mu_1 \bullet_\rho (\mu_2 \bullet_\rho f), \quad \mu_1, \mu_2 \in M_d(G), f \in B \tag{22}$$

as a consequence of the validity of

$$(\delta_x \star \delta_y) \bullet_\rho f = \delta_{x+y} \bullet_\rho f = \rho(x+y)f = \rho(x)(\rho(y)f) = \delta_x \bullet_\rho (\delta_y \bullet_\rho f). \tag{23}$$

Consequently, for a given $\mu \in M(G)$ and $f \in B$ we set

$$D_\Psi \mu \bullet_\rho f = \sum_{i \in I} \mu(\psi_i) \rho(x_i) f. \tag{24}$$

Based on (21) and (11) we have for any Ψ:

$$\|D_\Psi \mu \bullet_\rho f\|_B \leq \|f\|_B \sum_{i \in I} |\mu(\psi_i)| = \|f\|_B \|D_\Psi \mu\|_M \leq \|\mu\|_M \|f\|_B. \tag{25}$$

We will show next that it is convergent, as $|\Psi| \to 0$ or $\mathrm{diam}(\Psi) \to 0$. The motivation for this approach becomes plausible once one understands $D_\Psi \mu$ on f as a Riemann-type sum for the Banach-space-valued integral of $x \to \rho(x)f$, usually written as $\int_G \rho(x)f(x)d\mu(x)$.

Given two families $\Psi = (\psi_i)_{i \in I}$ and $\Phi = (\phi_j)_{j \in J}$, with their centers $(x_i)_{i \in I}$ and $(y_j)_{j \in J}$ respectively, we define their *joint refinement* $\Psi - \Phi$ as the family $(\psi_i \phi_j)_{(i,j) \in I \diamond J}$. It is natural to take $I \diamond J$, the family of all index pairs such that $\psi_i \cdot \phi_j \neq 0$ (because all the other products are trivial and should be neglected) as the new index set. In fact, if both Ψ and Φ are sufficiently "fine" BUPUs, one has: (using the fact that $\psi_i = \sum_{j \in j} \psi_i \phi_j$, hence $\sum_{(i,j) \in I \diamond J} \psi_i \phi_j \equiv 1$ and $\sum_{(i,j) \in I \diamond J} \|(\psi_i \phi_j)\mu\|_M = \|\mu\|_M$.)

$$\|D_\Psi \mu \bullet_\rho f - D_\Phi \mu \bullet_\rho f\|_B = \sum_{(i,j) \in I \diamond J} \|\rho(x_i)f - \rho(y_j)f\|_B |\mu(\psi_i \phi_j)| \leq \tag{26}$$

$$\sup_{(i,j) \in I \diamond J} \|\rho(x_i)[f - \rho(y_j - x_i)f]\|_B \sum_{(i,j) \in I \diamond J} \|(\psi_i \phi_j)\mu\|_M \leq \varepsilon \|\mu\|_M,$$

if only Ψ resp. Φ are fine enough. Due to the completeness of $(B, \|\cdot\|_B)$ one finds that there is a uniquely determined limit, which we will call $\mu \bullet_\rho f$. It is then obvious that

$$\|\mu \bullet_\rho f\|_B = \lim_{|\Psi| \to 0} \|D_\Psi \mu \bullet_\rho f\|_B \leq \limsup_{|\Psi| \to 0} \|D_\Psi \mu\|_M \|f\|_B = \|\mu\|_M \|f\|_B. \tag{27}$$

Of course, it remains to be shown that the action defined in this way is associative, i.e., that

$$(\mu_1 \star \mu_2) \bullet_\rho f = \mu_1 \bullet_\rho (\mu_2 \bullet_\rho f), \quad \forall \mu_1, \mu_2 \in M(G), f \in B, \tag{28}$$

but this follows from the associativity for the discrete measures $D_\Psi \mu$ and $D_\Phi \mu$. Note that H. S. Shapiro (cf. [17]) makes this associativity an extra axiom, apparently because he could not prove it directly for technical reasons, based on the way in which he defines the action of bounded measures on an "abstract homogeneous Banach space". H.C. Wang exhibits in [19] an example of what he calls a *semi-homogeneous Banach space* (without strong continuity of the action of G on $(B, \|\cdot\|_B)$, which does not allow the extension to all of the bounded measures. Indeed, it is a Banach space of measurable and bounded functions on $\mathbb{R}$ which is non-trivial, but which does not contain any non-zero *continuous* function. The example was suggested to him in a correspondence by the author of this note. □

Remark 11. *In the derivation above we have used the isometric property and the fact that $\rho(x_1 x_2) = \rho(x_1) \circ \rho(x_2)$. It would have been no problem if this identity was only true "up to some constant of absolute value one", i.e., if one has a projective representation of G only, such as the mapping*

$\lambda = (t, \omega) \mapsto \rho(\lambda) = M_\omega T_t$ from $\mathbb{R}^d \times \widehat{\mathbb{R}}^d$ into the unitary operators on the Hilbert space $(L^2(\mathbb{R}^d), \|\cdot\|_2)$, which is one of the key players in time-frequency analysis. This direction will also be explored further in subsequent notes.

Remark 12. *Another possible and powerful extension of the above result will involve cases where the group action is not isometric anymore, but still bounded by some weight function, i.e., the case where each $\rho(x)$ is a bounded operator and one has control over the operator norms of these operators on $(B, \|\cdot\|_B)$. In this case, one has to replace the algebra $(M(G), \|\cdot\|_M)$ by weighted versions, and $(L^1(G), \|\cdot\|_1)$ by Beurling algebras (see [3]). This direction will also be pursued elsewhere in more detail. This is a crucial starting point for the analysis of TMIBs, i.e., translation- and modulation-invariant function spaces (see e.g., [20,21]).*

5. The Wiener Algebra $W(C_0, \ell^1)$

The purpose of this section is to demonstrate that the concept of homogeneous Banach spaces over LCA groups, originally introduced in a book by Y. Katznelson [22] (see Remark 14 below), can be introduced *without* making use of the Haar integral. For this purpose we will make use of Wiener's algebra (as described in [23]), which is found already in Reiter's book [3,4] for $G = \mathbb{R}^d$, as a prototypical example of a Segal algebra. It was the model case for many characterizations of minimal spaces (a pointwise $C_0(\mathbb{R}^d)$-module in this case); see [23] and the subsequent papers [24,25].

Obviously, BUPUs play an important role in the description of *Wiener amalgam* spaces (such as Wiener's algebra, which is of the form $W(C_0, \ell^1)(\mathbb{R}^d)$, or the Segal algebra $S_0(\mathbb{R}^d) = W(\mathcal{F}L^1, \ell^1)(\mathbb{R}^d)$). The justification for characterizing Wiener amalgam spaces via BUPUs comes from the main results of [6]. Leaving out the details, let us summarize a few properties of Wiener's algebra on a general LCA group G:

Definition 7.

$$W(G) := W(C_0, \ell^1)(G) := \{ f \in C_0(G) \mid \|f\|_W := \sum_{i \in I} \|f \psi_i\|_\infty < \infty \}.$$

We have the following general facts, which are easily proved without making use of the existence of a Haar measure on G:

Proposition 3.
1. *$(W, \|\cdot\|_W)$ is a Banach space, for any BUPU Ψ, and continuously embedded into $(C_0(G), \|\cdot\|_\infty)$.*
2. *$(W, \|\cdot\|_W)$ is a Banach ideal in $(C_0(G), \|\cdot\|_\infty)$, i.e., pointwise products are in W; in particular, it is a Banach algebra under pointwise multiplication;*
3. *The space does not depend on the particular choice of Ψ, i.e., different BUPUs define the same space and equivalent norms;*
4. *The decomposition of $f \in W$ as $f = \sum_{i \in I} f \psi_i$ is not only valid absolutely in $(C_0(G), \|\cdot\|_\infty)$, but even in $(W, \|\cdot\|_W)$. Hence, $C_c(G)$ is dense in $(W, \|\cdot\|_W)$ and W is dense in $(C_0(G), \|\cdot\|_\infty)$;*
5. *For any open, relatively compact neighborhood Q of the identity we have the following atomic characterization of W, via the absolutely convergent series:*

$$W_{at} := \{ f \in C_0(G) \mid f = \sum_{k=1}^\infty f_k, \text{ with } \sum_{k=1}^\infty \|f_k\|_\infty < \infty, \exists x_k \in G : \mathrm{supp}(f_k) \subseteq x_k + Q \}.$$

6. *The corresponding (equivalent)* `inf`*-norm (infimum over all admissible sums) is isometrically translation-invariant, with continuous translation, i.e.,*

$$\|T_x f\|_W = \|f\|_W, x \in G, \quad \text{and} \quad \lim_{x \to e} \|T_x f - f\|_W = 0, \quad \forall f \in W. \tag{29}$$

Remark 13. *As a matter of fact, the functions in $W(\mathbb{R}^d)$ are (even absolutely Riemann) integrable and thus W is a dense subspace of $(L^1(\mathbb{R}^d), \|\cdot\|_1)$. Combined with property (29), this implies that*

$W(C_0, \ell^1)(\mathbb{R}^d)$ is in fact a Segal algebra on $\mathbb{R}^d$ (see [3,4]). Similar comments apply for general LCA groups based on Proposition 3, once the existence of a Haar measure is established (in order to characterize $(L^1(G), \|\cdot\|_1)$ as a closed ideal of $(M(G), \|\cdot\|_M)$; see Section 6).

Since $(W, \|\cdot\|_W) \hookrightarrow (C_0(G), \|\cdot\|_\infty)$ as a dense subspace, the dual space W^* (which can be characterized as the subspace $W(M, \ell^\infty)(G)$ of all Radon measures) is known in the literature as the space of *translation-bounded measures*.

First we give a characterization of W^* as a subspace of all tempered distributions (for the case $G = \mathbb{R}^d$). Note that in this case $\mathcal{S}(\mathbb{R}^d)$ is a dense subspace of W.

Lemma 3. *A tempered distribution $\sigma \in \mathcal{S}'$ extends to a bounded linear functional on $(W, \|\cdot\|_W)$ if and only if one has the following estimate:*

Fixing a compact set Q (with non-void interior) there exists a constant $B(Q)$ such that one has: For any $\varphi \in \mathcal{D}(\mathbb{R}^d) = \mathcal{S}(\mathbb{R}^d) \cap C_c(\mathbb{R}^d)$ (the space of infinitely smooth functions with compact support) with $\mathrm{supp}(\varphi) \subseteq x + Q$ for some $x \in G$:

$$|\sigma(\varphi)| \leq B(Q) \|\varphi\|_\infty. \tag{30}$$

Equivalently one has: A tempered distribution defines a translation-bounded measure if and only if for any $p \in \mathcal{D}(\mathbb{R}^d)$ the family $(T_x p \cdot \sigma)$ constitutes a bounded family in $(M(\mathbb{R}^d), \|\cdot\|_M)$.

Due to the atomic characterization of $W(G)$, we can also provide a kind of *atomic representation* of W^*, which works as follows:

Lemma 4. *Given any well-spread family $(x_i)_{i \in I}$ in G, the elements $\sigma \in W^*$ can be characterized as the w^*–convergent series of the following form (recall that $(\sigma \cdot h) := \sigma(h \cdot f)$ by definition.)*

$$\sigma = \sum_{i \in I} \mu_i \cdot T_{x_i} p, \tag{31}$$

for some fixed, non-zero $p \in C_c(G)$ and some bounded family $(\mu_i)_{i \in I}$ in $(M(G), \|\cdot\|_M)$.

Proof. The proof has two directions. First of all we fix some U-BUPU $\Psi = (\psi_i)_{i \in I}$ and some $p \in C_c(G)$ with $\|p\|_\infty = 1$, $p(x) \equiv 1$ on U, and hence $\psi_i = \psi_i \cdot T_{x_i} p$ for $i \in I$.

This allows us to decompose any linear functional $\sigma \in W^*$ in the usual way as a w^*–convergent series of the form

$$\sigma = \sum_{i \in I} \sigma \cdot \psi_i = \sum_{i \in I} (\sigma \cdot \psi_i) \cdot T_{x_i} p. \tag{32}$$

We will check that the functionals $\mu_i := \sigma \cdot \psi_i$ define a bounded family in $(M(G), \|\cdot\|_M)$. In fact, we have, thanks to the atomic characterization

$$\|\mu_i\|_M = \|\sigma \psi_i\|_M \leq \|\psi_i\|_\infty \|\sigma \cdot (T_{x_i} p)\|_M \leq C \|\sigma\|_{W^*}, \quad i \in I. \tag{33}$$

In order to prove the converse, let $(\mu_i)_{i \in I}$ be a bounded family in $(M(G), \|\cdot\|_M)$. We have to control the norm of the functional σ given by Equation (32). Due to the atomic characterization it is enough to present an estimate for the atoms, i.e., a uniform estimate (with respect to the sup-norm) for functions $f \in C_c(G)$ with $\mathrm{supp}(f) \subset z + Q$, for some $z \in G$. The assumptions concerning the family $(x_i)_{i \in I}$ then imply that one has for the compact set $K = \mathrm{supp}(p)$ the following uniform bound (*independent of z*):

$$\#F = \#\{i \in I, (x_i + I) \cap (z + K) \neq \emptyset\} \leq C(X) < \infty.$$

Using $\mathrm{supp}(T_{x_i} p \cdot f) \subseteq \mathrm{supp}(T_{x_i} p) = x_i + K$ and $\|T_{x_i} p \cdot f\|_\infty \leq \|f\|_\infty$ we conclude

$$|\sigma(f)| \leq \sum_{i \in I} |(\mu_i \cdot T_{x_i} p)(f)| = \sum_{i \in F} |\mu_i(T_{x_i} p \cdot f)| \leq C(X) \sup_{i \in I} \|\mu_i\|_M \|f\|_\infty. \tag{34}$$

Remark 14. *This definition appears to be different from the setting chosen in Katznelson's book [22], p. 127. He assumes only instead of condition (1) that one has a continuous embedding* $(B, \|\cdot\|_B) \hookrightarrow L^1_{loc}(\mathbb{R}^d)$. *However, due to the translation invariance property (2) imposed on the norm of* $(B, \|\cdot\|_B)$, *this implies immediately that one has* $(B, \|\cdot\|_B) \hookrightarrow W(L^1, \ell^\infty)$, *which is a closed subspace of* $W(M, \ell^\infty)$ *(the usual characterization of the dual of* $W(C_0, \ell^1)$ *in the context of Wiener amalgam spaces).*

Conversely, one can show that the continuous shift property implies that in the case that $(L^1(G), \|\cdot\|_1)$ *is defined in the usual way with the help of Lebesgue integration combined with the existence of a Haar measure on G, the continuous shift property (3), in conjunction with (1) and (2), actually implies that* B *is contained in the subspace* $W(L^1, \ell^\infty) \subset W(M, \ell^\infty)$.

Equipped with these spaces, which can be described now for any LCA group G without the use of the Haar measure or structure theory, we can provide a definition of a homogeneous Banach space on G (HBSG).

Definition 8. *A Banach space* $(B, \|\cdot\|_B)$ *is called a homogeneous Banach space on an LCA group G (HBSG) given that*

1. $(B, \|\cdot\|_B) \hookrightarrow W^*$;
2. *Translation is isometric on* $(B, \|\cdot\|_B)$, *i.e.,*

$$\|T_x f\|_B = \|f\|_B, \quad \forall f \in B, x \in G;$$

3. *Translation is strongly continuous on* $(B, \|\cdot\|_B)$, *i.e.,*

$$\lim_{x \to 0} \|T_x f - f\|_B = 0, \quad \forall f \in B.$$

The following lemma provides a connection between the different notions. For simplicity we formulate the result for $G = \mathbb{R}^d$, endowed with the Lebesgue integral. It is valid for general LCA groups.

Lemma 5. *For any HSBG on* $G = \mathbb{R}^d$, *we have* $(B, \|\cdot\|_B) \hookrightarrow L^1_{loc}(\mathbb{R}^d)$.

Proof. In the current situation the abstract results imply that $(B, \|\cdot\|_B)$ is an essential Banach module over $L^1(\mathbb{R}^d)$ with respect to convolution. By means of the Cohen–Hewitt factorization theorem (see [26]) any $f \in B$ can be written as $f = g * h$, for some $g \in L^1(\mathbb{R}^d)$ and some $h \in B \subset W(M, \ell^\infty)(\mathbb{R}^d)$. However, the convolution relations for Wiener amalgams established in [6] imply (altogether) that

$$B = L^1(\mathbb{R}^d) * B \subset L^1(G) * W(M, \ell^\infty)(\mathbb{R}^d) \subset W(L^1, \ell^\infty)(\mathbb{R}^d) \subset L^1_{loc}(\mathbb{R}^d). \tag{35}$$

□

6. Homogeneous Banach Spaces as Essential L^1-Modules

Let us start with the comment that the so-called *regular representation of a group G*, i.e., the mapping which assigns to any $x \in C(G)$ the (left) translation operator T_x (this operator is denoted by L_x in [3]) is of course one of the most important cases for the application of the abstract principle developed in Section 6.

It is also clear that the general assumptions which allow us to invoke Theorem 2 are satisfied for any homogeneous Banach space on G. Since such Banach spaces usually contain many functions from $C_c(G)$ and since in this case it is clear that the abstract form of the convolution coincides with the pointwise action as defined via the pairing of $C_0(G)$ and $M(G)$ it is justified to still call the mapping $\mu \bullet_\rho f$ convolution in this case and simply write

$\mu * f$. In view of density considerations, it is possible to verify, in case there are different possible interpretations of the symbol "*", that the result does not depend on the context.

This *seemingly harmless*, but nevertheless highly non-trivial use of this symbol in situations which are generated by different technical considerations is well justified in all the cases which are considered here. Occasionally a strict verification of such a claim has to be undertaken. However, unlike the approach taken occasionally by experts in distribution theory, we take care in regard to the "existence of the convolution product" at an individual level (in such a situation even the associative law may fail!) and we emphasize module actions and bilinear pairings for Banach spaces, which are obtained via an extension of standard operations.

We can thus summarize our findings so far in the following theorem:

Theorem 3. *Let $(B, \|\cdot\|_B)$ be a homogeneous Banach space of an LCA group G. Then $(B, \|\cdot\|_B)$ is a Banach module over $(M(G), \|\cdot\|_M)$ with respect to convolution. In fact, the action of μ on $f \in B$ is defined as the limit of expressions of the form $D_\Psi \mu * f$, in the norm of $(B, \|\cdot\|_B)$.*

Although it is enough to know the Riemann integral (on $C_c(\mathbb{R}^d)$) for the case $G = \mathbb{R}^d$ (or similar elementary LCA groups), we have to invoke to the existence of the Haar measure on G, which is a translation-invariant linear functional on $C_c(G)$ (in fact on $W(C_0, \ell^1)(G)$). This allows us to endow $C_c(G)$ with the L^1-norm, and establish that $C_c(G)$ with this norm is a normed space. With a little bit of extra work, one then goes on to show that the bounded measure μ_k induced by $k \in C_c(G)$ via the mapping $f \mapsto \int_G f(x)k(x)dx$, or better $f \mapsto H(f \cdot k)$ (here we write H for the Haar functional, i.e., the linear functional arising in the construction of the so-called Haar measure (see e.g., [1])) is in fact an isometric embedding from $C_c(G)$ into $(M(G), \|\cdot\|_M)$. Consequently, it makes sense to define the space $(L^1(G), \|\cdot\|_1)$ simply as the closure of $C_c(G)$, more precisely of $\{\mu_k \mid k \in C_c(G)\}$ in $(M(G), \|\cdot\|_M)$.

Continuing our efforts to develop the foundations of harmonic analysis without the use of measure theory, we have to establish a few basic properties:

Lemma 6. *1. $(L^1(G), \|\cdot\|_1)$ is a Banach space;*
2. $(L^1(G), \|\cdot\|_1)$ is a homogeneous Banach space;
3. In fact, $(L^1(G), \|\cdot\|_1)$ is a closed ideal in $(M(G), \|\cdot\|_M)$.
4. $L^1(G)$ is w^*–dense in $(M(G), \|\cdot\|_M)$.

Proof. By definition $(L^1(G), \|\cdot\|_1)$ is a closed subspace subspace of $(M(G), \|\cdot\|_M)$ and hence complete, and thus a Banach space. The uniform continuity of any $k \in C_c(G)$ implies that $\|T_x k - k\|_\infty \to 0$ for $x \to 0$. Due to the(joint) compact support of all these translates (for x near 0, resp. the neutral element $e \in G$) one also has $\lim_{x \to 0} \|T_x f - f\|_1 = 0$ for $f \in L^1(G)$ by approximation. Due to the continuous embedding $(W(C_0, \ell^1)(G), \|\cdot\|_W) \hookrightarrow (C_0(G), \|\cdot\|_\infty)$ it is clear that $L^1(G)$ is contained in W^*, and thus the formal axioms for an HBSG are satisfied.

As a consequence of Theorem 3 it is also an $M(G)$-module with respect to convolution and thus a closed ideal in $(M(G), \|\cdot\|_M)$, once it is verified that the external action of $(M(G), \|\cdot\|_M)$ on $(L^1(G), \|\cdot\|_1)$ is compatible with the internal (e.g., obtained by a pointwise definition of $f * g(x)$ for $f, g \in C_c(G)$, or using Lebesgue integration). Observe that the convolution of a compactly supported measure $\mu \in (M(G), \|\cdot\|_M)$ with $k \in C_c(G)$ is a continuous function in $C_c(G)$ and thus, by taking limits, $L^1(G)$ is a closed ideal of $(M(G), \|\cdot\|_M)$. The pointwise relation $\mu * k(x) = \mu(T_x k^{\vee})$ implies

$$\mathrm{supp}(\mu * k) \subset \mathrm{supp}(\mu) + \mathrm{supp}(k). \tag{36}$$

Since any measure $\mu \in (M(G), \|\cdot\|_M)$ can be approximated by finite sums of the form $\sum_{i \in F} \mu \psi_i$ (in the norm of $M(G)$) the obvious estimate

$$\|\mu * k\|_1 = \|\mu \star \mu_k\|_M \leq \|\mu\|_M \|\mu_k\|_M = \|\mu\|_M \|k\|_1, \quad \mu \in M(G), k \in C_c(G), \quad (37)$$

we see that $(L^1(G), \|\cdot\|_1)$ is a closed ideal in $(M(G), \|\cdot\|_M)$.

In order to verify the w^*–density of $L^1(G)$ in $M(G)$ it is enough to check that it is possible to find an approximation of Dirac measures in the w^*–sense, because this implies the possibility of approximating discrete measures by elements of $L^1(G)$ (in fact by elements in $C_c(G)$) by means of transitivity.

In fact, given $h \in C_0(G)$ and $x \in G$, the uniform continuity of h implies that δ_x can be approximated well by non-negative functions $k \in C_c(G)$ with small support U centered around x. In fact, assuming $\int_G k(x)dx = 1$ (just a normalization) it is easy to estimate the difference

$$|\delta_x(f) - \mu_k(f)| = |1 \cdot f(x) - \int_G f(y)g(y)dy| \leq \int_U |f(x) - f(y)||k(x)|dx < \varepsilon. \quad (38)$$

□

Next, we can also recall the definition of a Segal algebra:

Definition 9. *A Banach space $(B, \|\cdot\|_B)$, which is continuously and densely embedded into $(L^1(G), \|\cdot\|_1)$, and which is also a homogeneous Banach space, is called a Segal algebra (in Reiter's sense; see [3,4]).*

Our knowledge so far implies immediately the following claim:

Lemma 7. *Any Segal algebra $(B, \|\cdot\|_B)$ is a so-called Banach ideal in $(L^1(G), \|\cdot\|_1)$, i.e., it is a Banach space with its own right, and an (left) ideal in $(L^1(G), \|\cdot\|_1)$, satisfying the estimate*

$$\|g * f\|_B \leq \|g\|_1 \|f\|_B, \quad g \in L^1(G), f \in B. \quad (39)$$

In order to check that any homogeneous Banach space is an *essential* Banach module over $(L^1(G), \|\cdot\|_1)$ we will prove the third main result of this article. We start from the same situation as in Theorem 2. The following theorem is inspired by the results in [27], in particular Theorem 2.2, in which such a result was shown using different arguments.

Theorem 4. *Given a HBSG and a bounded and tight net $(\mu_\alpha)_{\alpha \in I}$ in $(M(G), \|\cdot\|_M)$ with*

$$\mu_0 = w^*\text{-}\lim_{\alpha \to \infty} \mu_\alpha$$

then one has norm convergence

$$\lim_{\alpha \to \infty} \|\mu_\alpha * f - \mu_0 * f\|_B = 0, \quad f \in B.$$

The result will be realized in the abstract setting of Theorem 2. This is our third main result. It shows that in the current context for bounded and tight nets in $(M(G), \|\cdot\|_M)$, the w^*-convergence of measures results in strong operator norm convergence of the corresponding convolution operators.

Theorem 5. *Let ρ be a strongly continuous, isometric representation of the locally compact group G on the Banach space $(B, \|\cdot\|_B)$ and $(\mu_\alpha)_{\alpha \in I}$ a bounded and tight net in $(M(G), \|\cdot\|_M)$ with $\mu_0 = w^*\text{-}\lim_{\alpha \to \infty} \mu_\alpha$. Then one has*

$$\lim_{\alpha \to \infty} \|\mu_\alpha \bullet_\rho f - \mu_0 \bullet_\rho f\|_B = 0, \quad \forall f \in B. \quad (40)$$

Proof. Given $\varepsilon > 0$ and $f \in B$ we have to find α_0 such that $\alpha \succeq \alpha_0$ implies

$$\|\mu_\alpha \bullet_\rho f - \mu_0 \bullet_\rho f\|_B \leq \varepsilon. \tag{41}$$

For convenience we assume that $\|f\|_B = 1$.

According to Theorem 2 we can find $U \in \mathcal{U}(e)$ such that for any $U - BUPU$ Ψ one has

$$\|(D_\Psi \mu_\alpha - \mu_\alpha) \bullet_\rho f\|_B = \|\mu_\alpha \bullet_\rho f - D_\Psi \mu_\alpha \bullet_\rho f\|_B \leq \varepsilon/4 \quad \forall \alpha \in \{I, 0\}. \tag{42}$$

Let us now fix one such BUPU $\Psi = (\psi_i)_{i \in I}$. Based on the definition of tightness, we find that there exist compactly supported functions $p \in C_c(G)$ (one should think of plateaus as similar to functions, as they arise, e.g., as *finite* partial sums of the form $\sum_{i \in F} \psi_i$ from any BUPU Ψ on G.) such that

$$\|\mu_\alpha \cdot p - \mu_\alpha\|_M \leq \varepsilon/4, \quad \forall \alpha \in I. \tag{43}$$

By taking limits, the estimate (43) will be also valid for $\alpha = 0$ (the limit measure μ_0).

Thus, up to a controllable error we may assume that the measures $(\mu_\alpha)_{\alpha \in I}$ (and their limit μ_0) have joint compact support, and consequently there exists some finite set $F \subset I$ such that $\mu_\alpha(\psi_i) = 0$ for $i \in I \setminus F$, for all $\alpha \in I$ and $\alpha = 0$.

Based on the assumed w^*-convergence of the net $(\mu_\alpha)_{\alpha \in I}$, we can find some index α_0 with

$$\sum_{i \in F} |\mu_\alpha(\psi_i) - \mu_0(\psi_i)| \leq \varepsilon/4, \quad \forall \alpha \succeq \alpha_0, \tag{44}$$

which in turn implies that we have for $\alpha \succeq \alpha_0$:

$$\|D_\Psi \mu_\alpha \bullet_\rho f - D_\Psi \mu_0 \bullet_\rho f\|_B \leq \sum_{i \in F} |\mu_\alpha(\psi_i) - \mu_0(\psi_i)| \|\rho(x_i) f\|_B \leq \varepsilon/4. \tag{45}$$

By combining the estimates (42), (44) and (45) we have verified (41), i.e., we can estimate $\|(\mu_\alpha - \mu_0) \bullet_\rho f\|_B$ in the following way:

$$\leq \|(\mu_\alpha - D_\Psi \mu_\alpha) \bullet_\rho f\|_B + \|(D_\Psi \mu_\alpha - D_\Psi \mu_0) \bullet_\rho f\|_B + \|(D_\Psi \mu_0 - \mu_0) \bullet_\rho f\|_B \leq 3\varepsilon/4.$$

□

There are many applications of this rather strong statement, so we present only a striking one. As is well known, bounded approximate units in $(L^1(G), \|\cdot\|_1)$ are obtained by taking a sequence (or net) of non-negative (for simplicity) functions $(k_\alpha)_{\alpha \in I}$ with shrinking support and with $\int_G k_\alpha(x) = 1$ for all $\alpha \in I$. Such a sequence is often called a *Dirac sequence* in the literature, and it is obviously tight and bounded in $(L^1(G), \|\cdot\|_1)$. It is a simple exercise to verify that $\mu_\alpha := \mu_{k_\alpha}$ is then a w^*-convergent net with

$$w^*\text{-}\lim_{\alpha \to \infty} \mu_\alpha = \delta_0. \tag{46}$$

As a consequence we thus have:

Corollary 1. *Given the situation of Theorem 4, and a bounded approximate unit $(g_\alpha)_{\alpha \in I}$ in $(L^1(G), \|\cdot\|_1)$, then one has*

$$\lim_{\alpha \to \infty} \|g_\alpha \bullet_\rho f - f\|_B = 0, \quad \forall f \in B. \tag{47}$$

As pointed out in Section 5.2 of [5] the net $D_\Psi \mu$ provides a tight w^*-approximation to μ. Combining this fact with the iteration principle (see [28], p. 69) for convergent nets, we come up with a verification of the associativity law which is required for Banach modules.

Corollary 2. *In the situation of Theorem 5 let* $\mu_1, \mu_2 \in M(G)$ *be given. Then*

$$\lim_{|\Psi| \to 0} \|D_\Psi \mu_1 \bullet_\rho (D_\Psi \mu_2 \bullet_\rho f) - (\mu_1 \star \mu_2) \bullet_\rho f\|_B = 0, \quad f \in B. \tag{48}$$

Combining the observations made so far we come to the following final result, which shows that the notion of the *integrated group representation* arises as a consequence of the approach presented in this paper:

Theorem 6. *Given an isometric, strongly continuous representation of a locally compact group G on a Banach space* $(B, \|\cdot\|_B)$, *the restriction of the Banach module action of* $(M(G), \|\cdot\|_M)$ *to the closed ideal* $(L^1(G), \|\cdot\|_1)$ *turns* $(B, \|\cdot\|_B)$ *into an essential Banach module over* $(L^1(G), \|\cdot\|_1)$.

Conversely, the w^**–continuity of the action of* $M(G)$ *for bounded and tight families implies that the action of all of* $M(G)$ *is uniquely determined by the integrated group action, i.e., the* $L^1(G)$*-module properties.*

Remark 15. *We think that it is easier to obtain the integrated group representation of* $(L^1(G), \|\cdot\|_1)$ *on* $(B, \|\cdot\|_B)$ *by way of restriction, instead of going the more cumbersome way of extending the representation of* $(L^1(G), \|\cdot\|_1)$ *by taking (vague) limits.*

7. Some Basic Functional Analysis

An important tool from functional analysis is the fact that any Banach space is complete with respect to convergence of the *Cauchy net*, not just *Cauchy sequences*.

Although Cauchy nets (implicitly) appear in many places, e.g., in the definition of the Riemann integral, they are typically not discussed as such. The reader could consult Bourbaki ([29]) for details on nets, or [30] (Prop. 2.1.40), but in order to make this note more self-contained, let us collect some relevant facts.

Definition 10. *A set* $(I, \succeq)$ *is called a directed set with respect to the orientation (given by* $\succeq$*), if it satisfies the following properties:*
1. *one has transitivity, i.e., if* $\alpha \succeq \beta$ *and* $\beta \succeq \gamma$ *then* $\alpha \succeq \gamma$;
2. *Given* $\alpha, \beta \in I$ *there exists* $\gamma \in I$ *such that* $\gamma \succeq \alpha$ *and* $\gamma \succeq \beta$.

Of course, in many cases one can have a partially ordered set and choose $\gamma = \max(\alpha, \beta)$ in the above setting, but this operation need not be meaningful in the general case.

Definition 11. *A net in a set X is a mapping from a directed set* $(I, \succeq)$, *usually described as an indexed family* $(x_\alpha)_{\alpha \in I}$.

A net in a metric space (X, d) *is called convergent if there exists some* $x_0 \in X$ *such that one has: Given* $\varepsilon > 0$ *there exists* α_0 *such that*

$$\alpha \succeq \alpha_0 \Rightarrow d(x_0, x_\alpha) < \varepsilon.$$

In this case we also write: $\lim_{\alpha \to \infty} x_\alpha = x_0$.

Nets are natural generalizations of sequences (and are thus often just called *generalized sequences*). The analogue of a Cauchy sequence is of course a *Cauchy net*.

Definition 12. *A net* $(x_\alpha)_{\alpha \in I}$ *is a Cauchy net if for any* $\varepsilon > 0$ $\exists \alpha_0 \in I$ *such that*

$$\alpha, \beta \succeq \alpha_0 \quad \Rightarrow \quad d(x_\alpha, x_\beta) < \varepsilon.$$

Remark 16. *Typical nets relevant for our discussion are the nets of the form* $(\mathrm{St}_\rho g)_{\rho \to 0}$, *with* $[\mathrm{St}_\rho g](x) = \rho^{-d} g(x/\rho)$, *with* $\rho_1 \succeq \rho_2$ *if* $\rho_2 \leq \rho_1$, *which are used to generate Dirac nets (bounded approximate units) in* $(L^1(\mathbb{R}^d), \|\cdot\|_1)$.

Other nets occur naturally, such as the index set to the Riemann sums for an integral of the form $\int_a^b f(x)dx$, given by some finite decomposition of the interval $[a,b]$ and the choice of a family of points (ξ_i) in the corresponding intervals. As we all know, a Riemannian sum is considered good if the maximal length appearing in the corresponding decomposition is controlled by a positive value $\delta > 0$. Furthermore, given two decompositions, one can generate the joint refinement as a decomposition which is "better" than both of the decompositions generating it.

Theorem 7. *A normed space $(B, \|\cdot\|_B)$ is complete if and only if any Cauchy net is convergent in $(B, \|\cdot\|_B)$.*

Note: it is well known that a Banach space is complete if and only if every Cauchy sequence is convergent, or equivalently, if every absolutely convergent series is convergent in $(B, \|\cdot\|_B)$. It is also clear that any Cauchy sequence is a Cauchy net (using the index set $\mathbb{N}$ with natural ordering as index set). Thus, it is clear that we only have to verify that any Cauchy sequence $(x_\alpha)_{\alpha \in I}$ is convergent in $(B, \|\cdot\|_B)$.

Proof. First we determine a sequence ε_n, e.g., $\varepsilon = 2^{-n}$ for $n \geq 1$, and, following the definition of a Cauchy net, a sequence α_n such that $\alpha, \beta \succeq \alpha_n$

$$\alpha, \beta \succeq \alpha_n \quad \Rightarrow \quad \|x_\alpha - x_\beta\|_B < \varepsilon_n. \tag{49}$$

Without the loss of generality (due to the majorization property) we can determine the sequence α_n inductively with $\alpha_{n+1} \succeq \alpha_n$. Formally we choose $x_{\alpha_0} = 0 \in B$.

The series $\sum_{n \geq 1}(x_{\alpha_n} - x_{\alpha_{n-1}})$ is then absolutely convergent, because

$$\sum_{n \geq 1} \|x_{\alpha_n} - x_{\alpha_{n-1}}\|_B \leq \sum_{n \geq 1} \varepsilon_n \leq 1 < \infty.$$

Hence the partial sums are

$$\sum_{n=1}^{N}(x_{\alpha_n} - x_{\alpha_{n-1}}) = x_{\alpha_N} \quad (!)$$

are convergent, i.e., there exists some $x_0 \in B$ with

$$\lim_{n \to \infty} x_{\alpha_n} = x_0 \text{ in } (B, \|\cdot\|_B).$$

Invoking the initial Cauchy net condition, we complete the argument by showing (once a limit has been identified) that we indeed have

$$\lim_{\alpha \to \infty} x_\alpha = x_0 \text{ in } (B, \|\cdot\|_B).$$

□

Remark 17. *It should be noted as a delicate point that the convergent Cauchy sequence obtained in the proof does not have to be a subnet of the original Cauchy net, because the notation of a subnet (which we do not need here) is more complex than just the idea of a subsequence of a given sequence. At least, it does not just mean reducing the index set (which for sequences has a natural order) to a subset of the original index set with strictly increasing enumeration of the elements of the subsequence.*

Funding: This research received no external funding.

Institutional Review Board Statement: Not applicable.

Informed Consent Statement: Not applicable.

Data Availability Statement: Not applicable.

Acknowledgments: During the preparation of this paper the author received support from the FWF project [I 3403], the ANACRES network funded by OEAD and Open Access Funding by the University of Vienna.

Conflicts of Interest: The author declares no conflict of interest.

References

1. Deitmar, A. *A First Course in Harmonic Analysis*; Universitext Springer: New York, NY, USA, 2002.
2. Folland, G.B. *A Course in Abstract Harmonic Analysis*; Studies in Advanced Mathematics; CRC Press: Boca Raton, FL, USA, 1995.
3. Reiter, H. *Classical Harmonic Analysis and Locally Compact Groups*; Clarendon Press: Oxford, UK, 1968.
4. Reiter, H.; Stegeman, J.D. *Classical Harmonic Analysis and Locally Compact Groups*, 2nd ed.; Clarendon Press: Oxford, UK, 2000.
5. Feichtinger, H.G. A novel mathematical approach to the theory of translation invariant linear systems. In *Recent Applications of Harmonic Analysis to Function Spaces, Differential Equations, and Data Science*; Pesenson, I., Le Gia, Q., Mayeli, A., Mhaskar, H., Zhou, D., Eds.; Applied and Numerical Harmonic Analysis; Birkhäuser: Cham, Switzerland, 2017; pp. 483–516.
6. Feichtinger, H.G. Banach convolution algebras of Wiener type. In *Proceedings of the Conference on Functions, Series, Operators, Budapest*; Volume 35 of Colloquia Mathematica Societatis Janos Bolyai; Nagy, B.S., Szabados, J., Eds.; North-Holland: Amsterdam, The Netherlands, 1983; pp. 509–524.
7. Feichtinger, H.G.; Zimmermann, G. A Banach space of test functions for Gabor analysis. In *Gabor Analysis and Algorithms: Theory and Applications*; Applied and Numerical Harmonic Analysis; Feichtinger, H.G., Strohmer, T., Eds.; Birkhäuser: Boston, MA, USA, 1998; pp. 123–170.
8. Feichtinger, H.G.; Gröchenig, K. Banach spaces related to integrable group representations and their atomic decompositions, I. *J. Funct. Anal.* **1989**, *86*, 307–340. [CrossRef]
9. Feichtinger, H.G.; Gröchenig, K. Multidimensional irregular sampling of band-limited functions in L^p-spaces. In Proceedings of the Conference at the Mathematical Research Institute, Oberwolfach, Germany, 12–18 February 1989; pp. 135–142.
10. Feichtinger, H.G.; Gröchenig, K. Iterative reconstruction of multivariate band-limited functions from irregular sampling values. *SIAM J. Math. Anal.* **1992**, *23*, 244–261. [CrossRef]
11. Feichtinger, H.G. *Discretization of Convolution and Reconstruction of Band-Limited Functions from Irregular Sampling*; Academic Press: Boston, MA, USA, 1991; pp. 333–345.
12. Feichtinger, H.G. New results on regular and irregular sampling based on Wiener amalgams. In *Function Spaces*; Volume 136 of Lect. Notes Pure Appl. Math.; Jarosz, K., Ed.; Marcel Dekker: New York, NY, USA, 1992; pp. 107–121.
13. Leptin, H.; Müller, D. Uniform partitions of unity on locally compact groups. *Adv. Math.* **1991**, *90*, 1–14. [CrossRef]
14. Weil, A. *L'integration dans les Groupes Topologiques et ses Applications*; Hermann and Cie: Paris, France, 1940.
15. Helffer, H.; Nourrigat, J. Caracterisation des opérateurs hypoelliptiques homogènes invariants à gauche sur un groupe de Lie nilpotent gradué. *Commun. Part Diff. Equat.* **1979**, *4*, 899–958. [CrossRef]
16. Gröchenig, K. *Foundations of Time-Frequency Analysis*; Applied and Numerical Harmonic Analysis; Birkhäuser: Boston, MA, USA, 2001.
17. Shapiro, H.S. *Topics in Approximation Theory*; Volume 187 of Lecture Notes in Mathematics; Springer: Berlin, Germany, 1971.
18. Simon, B. *Operator Theory. A Comprehensive Course in Analysis*; Part 4; American Mathematical Societye: Providence, RI, USA, 2015.
19. Wang, H.C. *Homogeneous Banach Algebras*; Marcel Dekker: New York, NY, USA; Basel, Switzerland, 1977.
20. Dimovski, P.; Pilipovic, S.; Vindas, J. New distribution spaces associated to translation-invariant Banach spaces. *Monatsh. Math.* **2015**, *177*, 495–515. [CrossRef]
21. Feichtinger, H.G.; Gumber, A. Completeness of shifted dilates in invariant Banach spaces of tempered distributions. *Proc. Am. Math. Soc.* **2021**, *149*, 5195–5210. [CrossRef]
22. Katznelson, Y. *An Introduction to Harmonic Analysis*; Dover Publ. Inc.: New York, NY, USA, 1976.
23. Feichtinger, H.G. A characterization of Wiener's algebra on locally compact groups. *Arch. Math.* **1977**, *29*, 136–140. [CrossRef]
24. Feichtinger, H.G. A characterization of minimal homogeneous Banach spaces. *Proc. Am. Math. Soc.* **1981**, *81*, 55–61. [CrossRef]
25. Feichtinger, H.G. Minimal Banach spaces and atomic representations. *Publ. Math. Debr.* **1987**, *34*, 231–240.
26. Hewitt, E.; Ross, K.A. *Abstract Harmonic Analysis*; Springer: Berlin/Heidelberg, Germany; New York, NY, USA, 1970; Volume II.
27. Feichtinger, H.G. Multipliers from $L^1(G)$ to a homogeneous Banach space. *J. Math. Anal. Appl.* **1977**, *61*, 341–356. [CrossRef]
28. Kelley, J.L. *General Topology*, 2nd ed.; Springer: Berlin/Heidelberg, Germany; New York, NY, USA, 1975.
29. Bourbaki, N. *Integration. II. Chapters 7–9*; Elements of Mathematics (Berlin); Springer: Berlin, Germany, 2004.
30. Megginson, R. *An Introduction to Banach Space Theory*; Volume 183 of Graduate Texts in Mathematics; Springer: New York, NY, USA, 1998.

Article

Wavelet Energy Accumulation Method Applied on the Rio Papaloapan Bridge for Damage Identification

Jose M. Machorro-Lopez [1,*], Juan P. Amezquita-Sanchez [2], Martin Valtierra-Rodriguez [2], Francisco J. Carrion-Viramontes [3], Juan A. Quintana-Rodriguez [3] and Jesus I. Valenzuela-Delgado [3]

1. Cátedras Conacyt-Instituto Mexicano del Transporte, km 12 Carretera Estatal No. 431 "El Colorado-Galindo" San Fandila, Pedro Escobedo C.P. 76703 Querétaro, Mexico
2. ENAP-Research Group, CA-Sistemas Dinámicos, Facultad de Ingeniería, Universidad Autónoma de Querétaro (UAQ), Campus San Juan del Río, Río Moctezuma 249, Col. San Cayetano, San Juan del Río C.P. 76807 Querétaro, Mexico; jamezquita@uaq.mx (J.P.A.-S.); martin.valtierra@enap-rg.org (M.V.-R.)
3. Instituto Mexicano del Transporte, km 12 Carretera Estatal No. 431 "El Colorado-Galindo" San Fandila, Pedro Escobedo C.P. 76703 Querétaro, Mexico; carrion@imt.mx (F.J.C.-V.); jaquintana@imt.mx (J.A.Q.-R.); jesusivan12300@gmail.com (J.I.V.-D.)
* Correspondence: jmachorro@imt.mx

Abstract: Large civil structures such as bridges must be permanently monitored to ensure integrity and avoid collapses due to damage resulting in devastating human fatalities and economic losses. In this article, a wavelet-based method called the Wavelet Energy Accumulation Method (WEAM) is developed in order to detect, locate and quantify damage in vehicular bridges. The WEAM consists of measuring the vibration signals on different points along the bridge while a vehicle crosses it, then those signals and the corresponding ones of the healthy bridge are subtracted and the Continuous Wavelet Transform (CWT) is applied on both, the healthy and the subtracted signals, to obtain the corresponding diagrams, which provide a clue about where the damage is located; then, the border effects must be eliminated. Finally, the Wavelet Energy (WE) is obtained by calculating the area under the curve along the selected range of scale for each point of the bridge deck. The energy of a healthy bridge is low and flat, whereas for a damaged bridge there is a WE accumulation at the damage location. The Rio Papaloapan Bridge (RPB) is considered for this research and the results obtained numerically and experimentally are very promissory to apply this method and avoid accidents.

Keywords: Rio Papaloapan Bridge; vibration signals; damage identification; wavelet energy accumulation method

Citation: Machorro-Lopez, J.M.; Amezquita-Sanchez, J.P.; Valtierra-Rodriguez, M.; Carrion-Viramontes, F.J.; Quintana-Rodriguez, J.A.; Valenzuela-Delgado, J.I. Wavelet Energy Accumulation Method Applied on the Rio Papaloapan Bridge for Damage Identification. *Mathematics* 2021, 9, 422. https://doi.org/10.3390/math9040422

Academic Editor: Elena Cordero

Received: 29 December 2020
Accepted: 16 February 2021
Published: 21 February 2021

Publisher's Note: MDPI stays neutral with regard to jurisdictional claims in published maps and institutional affiliations.

Copyright: © 2021 by the authors. Licensee MDPI, Basel, Switzerland. This article is an open access article distributed under the terms and conditions of the Creative Commons Attribution (CC BY) license (https://creativecommons.org/licenses/by/4.0/).

1. Introduction

The structural evaluation to determine damage, deterioration and/or abnormal operating conditions in complex civil structures is essential to determine the operational reliability and residual life of them [1]. Traditionally, most of the damage detection programs are based on visual inspections, which are expensive and limited in access to all parts of the structure. Additionally, the internal damage is not detectable with a visual inspection and it is not possible to obtain a quantitative estimation of the damage or the remaining structural capacity. Recent health monitoring systems for structures include different non-destructive tests, but in all cases the evaluation is localized and do not allow global evaluations of the structures [2].

So far, it has been recognized that vibration analysis and modal analysis are the only techniques that have the potential for global evaluation of structures [1,3]. In these cases, health monitoring is carried out by analyzing changes in the characteristic behavior of vibration through natural frequencies, damping ratios and modal shapes. Many algorithms have been developed to make such a comparison, but, in general, they are classified considering four different approaches: matrix optimization, sensitivity methods, techniques for assigning characteristic values, and minimum range disturbance methods [4]. However, for the particular case of the vehicular bridges it is still necessary to increase the efforts to provide more sophisticated and reliable methods for early damage identification, since there are many documented cases of catastrophic failures of these structures even in the most developed countries.

Two of the most recent and disastrous accidents due to vehicular bridges collapse are related with the Bridge 9340 in the United States of America in 2007 and the Morandi Bridge in Italy in 2018. The Bridge 9340 failed on 1 August 2007, collapsing into the Mississippi River in Minneapolis, Minnesota, USA during the evening rush hour. Thirteen people died and 145 were injured. The bridge transported 140,000 vehicles daily and after the collapse the government recommended the inspection of 700 bridges of similar construction in the country, since after the collapse a possible design defect was discovered on the bridge related to large steel sheets called gusset plates, which were used to connect girders together in the truss structure [5]. On the other hand, the other tragic example occurred on 14 August 2018. During a heavy storm, a 210 m section of the Morandi Bridge in Genoa, Italy collapsed, being one of the most serious collapses of bridges in Europe. As a result of the collapse, three trucks and 35 vehicles fell down from 45 m height to a mountain of rubble. Most of the vehicles and the structure fell into the Polcevera River, others collapsed on the warehouses of an electricity company and on the railway tracks. Around 43 people died according to authorities [6]. Thus, considering that many vehicular bridges around the world could have mistakes within their civil design, wrong selection of materials and even more, which could be operating beyond their useful life and/or overloaded, the probability of structural damage increases and the risk of collapsing, with the corresponding human fatalities and economic losses for not detecting a damage early enough, is high.

The use of vibration signals from the bridges are still considered the most promissory way to detect non-visible damage in this kind of civil structure in a global and online mode; however, those signals have to be post-processed in such a way that damage detection methods could be developed and implemented on the bridges with a low quantity of false alarms and ensuring the reliability of the use of them. The quantity and importance of vibration methods based on wavelets for damage detection on bridges have significantly increased in the last decade, for example, Golmohamadi et al. [7] used a wavelet-based technique to evaluate damage on bridges by using the energy of wavelet coefficients. For this, they used Continuous Wavelet Transform (CWT) in cases of numerical models of healthy and damaged bridges; subsequently they calculated the total energy of the wavelet coefficients as an index of sensitivity to damage. Likewise, McGetrick and Kim [8] investigated the feasibility of a low-cost alternative method based on wavelets for periodic monitoring of bridges, consisting of the use of an instrumented vehicle with accelerometers in their axes. They found that damage can be located more accurately for low vehicle speeds and long bridges, indicating the level of damage by the maximum Wavelet Transform (WT) coefficient from Morlet-type mother wavelets. On the other hand, there are works developed by Reddy and Swarnamani [9] and Walia et al. [10] focused on analyzing the sensitivity of wavelet coefficients to detect and quantify damage on structures. Recently, Quiñones and Montejo [11] evaluated two techniques based on wavelets to identify damage in civil structures. The first technique was based on analyzing the evolution of the structure frequencies through CWT, whereas with the second one they analyzed the singularities generated in high frequencies of the structure response through functions obtained with FWT (Fast Wavelet Transform). The conclusion of the study was that the wavelet parameters should be chosen according to the expected frequency content of the structure and carry out both analyses to ensure efficiency in the damage detection. Zhu and Sun [12] developed a new bridge damage detection index based on Wavelet Energy (WE) change. Their numerical results, using a simply supported beam model, show that with this index it is possible to detect and locate the damage in the structure in a valid way. However, in their simulations they only apply constant excitation and, in reality, the damage could be masked by the effect of environmental excitation, experimental noise and other uncertainties. Those drawbacks faced by Zhu and Sun were addressed in the research carried out by Li and Li [13], whom proposed an index based on the virtual impulse response and WT, named Energy Spectrum Anomaly Measure (ESAM), to identify the existence of damage in civil structures. This research was based on a numerical model of three Degrees of Freedom (DOFs) and they demonstrated that their index is sensitive and reliable to identify damage even in noise conditions. Chen and Oyadiji [14] presented a novel multiple mode wavelet index by using the DWT (Discrete Wavelet Transform) of the modal frequency curves to identify structural damage. With FEM (Finite Element Method)-based models and laboratory tests they demonstrated the functionality of the proposed method. The results suggest that the developed index provides an unequivocal identification of damage compared to the poor resolution offered by the typical WT diagrams to detect damage in the high frequency region when there are high frequency components. Finally, Ercolani et al. [15] showed the implementation of the CWT to detect damage in a FEM model of a bridge with a prestressed concrete slab. They included different types of damage in the structural model, obtained the vertical displacements of the structure under the action of static charges and demonstrated the usefulness of the WT for the detection of damages. Likewise, other recent studies which have had a significant contribution in the topic of damage detection on beams/bridges by using wavelet-based methods can be found in [16–28].

There are many deteriorated bridges around the world, without an adequate maintenance and without knowing if they have any kind of damage that may lead to their collapse. Additionally, taking into account that an important percentage of the bridges have been operating for decades in seismic regions, with hostile environmental conditions, and/or that mistakes may have occurred during the design and/or construction, the probability of collapse increases. Thus, countries need efficient integral monitoring systems of their main bridges to know their structural condition constantly and avoid catastrophic failures, like the ones presented previously, involving human fatalities and big economic losses. This article presents the development and results of the application (in the cable-stayed bridge RPB) of the wavelet-based method called WEAM, which is capable of detecting, locating (with great accuracy) and quantifying different types of damage on vehicular bridges by using just a few sensors and obtaining the WE. The WE is calculated from the CWT diagrams by means of the area under the curve along the selected range of scale for each point of the bridge deck. The energy of a healthy bridge is low and flat, whereas for a damaged bridge there is an accumulation of WE at the location of the damage. The adequate filtering of the signals and selection of the mother wavelet (Savitzky-Golay filter and Mexican hat mother wavelet, respectively, for the cases here studied) are essential for the success of the method, as it was reported in [29]. The WEAM is applied in detail by using a FEM model with reliable results for identifying damage with high accuracy. On the other hand, regardless of the fact that the WEAM requires a controlled test to be applied in real bridges and that the failure of the RPB took place before this method could be applied, the acquired data for the RPB when it is healthy as well as when a cable broke down are analyzed by using the most useful measurements with random traffic and damage detection is possible by calculating the WE. Thus, the WEAM is promissory to be systematically applied on main bridges to avoid accidents like the one that occurred in the RPB.

2. Proposed Methodology

The detailed step-by-step application of the WEAM for damage detection and localization consists of:

1. Instrument the bridge with vibration sensors proportionally distributed along the bridge deck.
2. Obtain the displacement and/or acceleration vibration responses for the undamaged bridge (baseline) and for the current condition of the bridge to be analyzed while a

heavy enough vehicle passes, preferably with constant and low speed and under ambient excitations (mainly wind and pedestrians).

3. Apply an adequate filter to eliminate the greatest quantity of noise (for the cases studied in this article, the best results were obtained by using a Savitzky-Golay filter).

4. Subtract the current (probably damaged) signals and the corresponding healthy signals.

5. Obtain the CWT 3-D colored diagrams for the healthy and subtracted signals. A wide range of scale, adequate mother wavelet (Mexican hat mother wavelet was the most useful for the purposes of this research) and convenient color map must be used.

6. Eliminate the border effects by extending the signals on both sides.

7. Once a clue of damage is detected in the CWT 3-D colored diagrams from the subtracted signals, by comparing with the healthy ones, select the most convenient range of scale.

8. Obtain the CWT 3-D colored diagrams for the healthy and subtracted signals without border effects and for the new convenient range of scale (area of interest).

9. Calculate and graph the area under the curve (WE) for each CWT diagram (different measurement positions for healthy and subtracted cases) along the selected range of scale and along the bridge deck (see Section 2.2).

10. Obtain and graph the average WE considering all the measurement positions for the baseline case and current case (subtracted).

11. Compare the average WE for the baseline case and the current case (subtracted). If they are similar, the current case is also healthy; otherwise, if there is a sudden increment of WE, the current case would be damaged and the position of the damage will be determined by the position of the maximum value of the ridge of WE accumulation (corresponding with the position of the vehicle on the bridge).

It should be noted that, once the characterization of the bridge to be studied is done and the effect of all the possible dangerous damages are known with this method, the steps, including the selection of the most convenient filter, range of scale, and mother wavelet, would be eliminated and the diagnosis would be faster. The schematic diagram of the proposed methodology is presented in Figure 1.

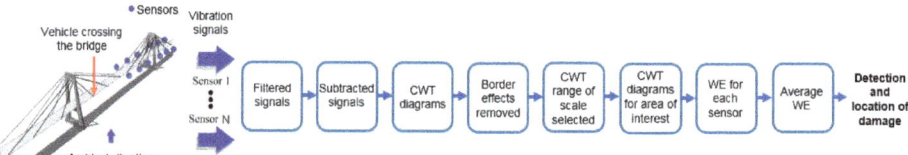

Figure 1. Proposed methodology schematic diagram.

2.1. Description of the Rio Papaloapan Bridge and Its Major Failures

The Rio Papaloapan Bridge (RPB) is a cable-stayed bridge located in the state of Veracruz in Mexico. Built in 1994, it has a main span of 203 m and a total length of 407.21 m with 112 cables distributed in 8 semi-harps (see Figures 2 and 3). The numbering of the cables for each semi-harp is from 1 to 14, the number 1 being the shortest one and 14 being the longest one. Due to the dimensions and importance of this bridge, as well as the major failures that have occurred on it, this bridge was selected for the present research.

Figure 2. The Rio Papaloapan Bridge.

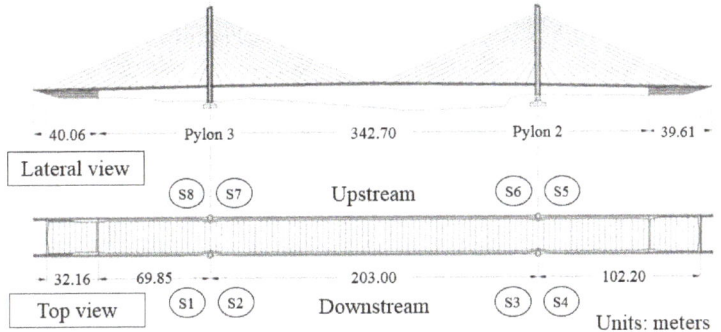

Figure 3. Bridge layout for general dimensions and semi-harps identification.

The upper anchoring system design [30] consists of one steel plate welded to the anchoring elements, which are cylindrical on one side and flat on the welded side (Figure 4). The cylindrical side is threaded to screw the collar that holds the cable in the upper side.

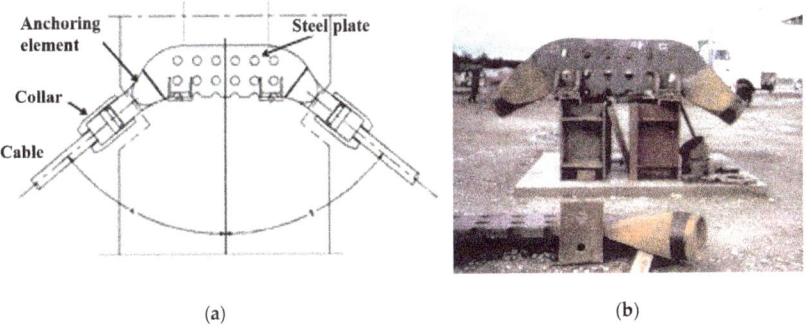

Figure 4. Assembly design of the upper anchoring system: (**a**) General design and (**b**) assembly before installation.

This bridge, until now, has had two major fractures of the anchoring elements. The first occurred in January 2000, which was due to microstructural deficiencies of the steel. Despite the excellent quality of the steel, a deficient casting process resulted in a low toughness brittle material with a microstructure with large grain size (ASTM 2) and a high content of pores and inclusions [31,32]; in this case, defects in the heat affected zone grew due to fatigue until complete fracture [33]. Unfortunately, no Structural Health Monitoring (SHM) system was implemented at the time this accident occurred.

The second failure occurred on 10 June 2015. In this case, it took place in the weld interface between the anchoring element and the steel plate of cable T1S5 (corresponding with cable 1 of the semi-harp 5). Analyses showed that an initial crack grew due to fatigue until it reached a size of almost 65% of the cross-section area. In Figure 5 clearly two different zones can be identified; the first showed oxidation on its surface after failure, which is characteristic of fatigue growth, indicating that it had sufficient time to seep water into the crack. The second corresponded to the final break due to overload, characteristic of a ductile fracture [34].

Figure 5. Failed anchoring element of cable 1 semi-harp 5 (T1S5).

After the first failure of the bridge, a full-scope SHM system was installed in 2013, which became the first cable-stayed bridge in Mexico with a full scope remote monitoring system. The system design was based on FBG (Fiber Bragg Grating) sensors and it was configured into 3 sub-systems: sensors, local monitoring and photovoltaic.

The sensor sub-system has 24 strain gages, 24 accelerometers, 1 displacement sensor, 8 tilt meters and 5 temperature sensors, all FBG; the local monitoring system includes a FO interrogator, 1 multiplexor and a computer; and the photovoltaic sub-system has 96 solar cells, 36 deep cycle batteries and their controllers. Additionally, the SHM system includes 2 video cameras, one weather station and a seismological station. The SHM system is communicated via satellite to the CMPEI in the Mexican Institute of Transportation.

The sensors were distributed to analyze the dynamics of the bridge deck and of the four towers; thus, the strain gages (which were used for the purpose of this article) are located 10 under each one of the main girders of the bridge deck, and one on the side at the half height of each tower (L1-L12 and R1-R12 in Figure 6a). On top of each one of the four towers, 2 tilt meters and 2 accelerometers are located. The other 16 accelerometers were placed on the middle of cables 4 and 11 of each semi-harp. The measurements obtained with those tilt meters and accelerometers were not used for the purpose of this article; however, their positions can be figured out by analyzing Figures 3 and 6a. Additionally, in Figure 6b two pictures of sensor R2 installed on the bridge are included.

Although the complete SHM system above described was operating on the bridge before the second failure occurred, the damage was not detected. Since the SHM system was implemented, a historical tracking of the values of the typical parameters, such as natural frequencies, modal shapes, deformations, inclinations, cables tension, etc., has been registered in detail. However, none of them had abnormal variations to warn that there was an important element damaged. Therefore, a reliable method for damage identification is here proposed to avoid bridges' failures.

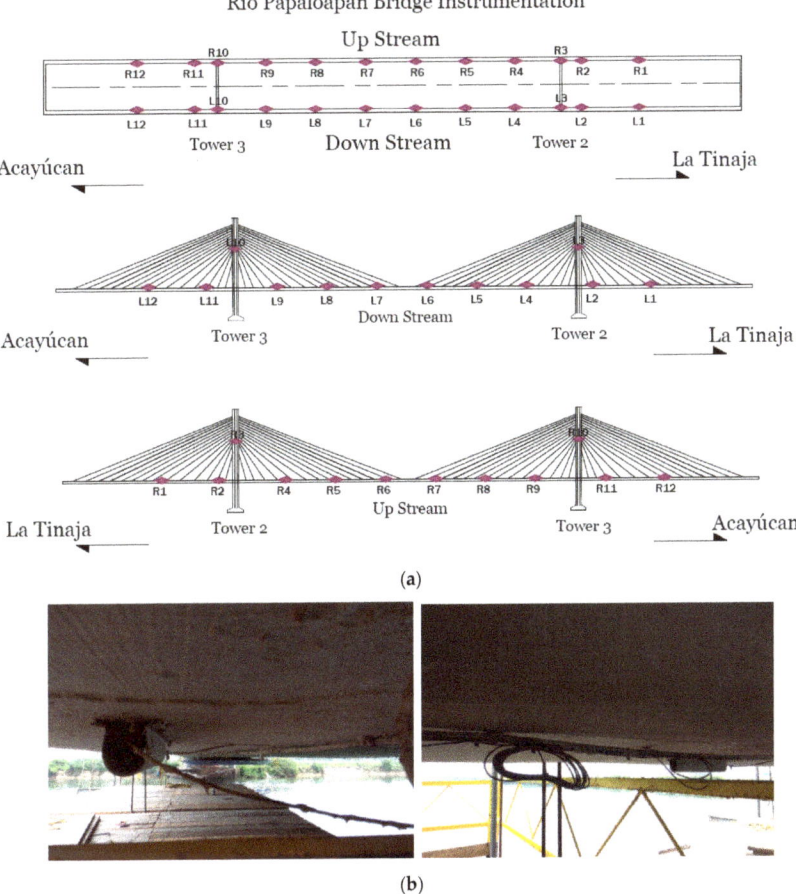

Figure 6. (a) Distribution diagram of the strain gages placed on the bridge (L1-L12 and R1-R12) and (b) pictures of sensor R2 installed on the bridge.

2.2. Continuous Wavelet Transform (CWT)

Wavelets are very useful for processing the structural vibration data and performing analyses to assess a structure, since this tool provides information that neither the Fast Fourier Transform (FFT) nor the Short Time Fourier Transform (STFT) can display.

The FFT converts a signal from its original domain (time) to a representation in the frequency domain. Transforming a signal from the time domain to the frequency domain, the time information is lost and it is impossible to determine when a particular event took place. On the other hand, the STFT is a sequence of Fourier transforms of a windowed signal. STFT provides the time-localized frequency information for situations in which frequency components of a signal vary over time, whereas the standard Fourier transform provides the frequency information averaged over the entire signal time interval. However, the major disadvantage of the STFT is the fixed width of the sliding window, which limits the resolution in frequency.

A wavelet is a wave-like oscillation with an amplitude that begins at zero, increases, and then decreases back to zero; that is, wavelets are small waves (signals) highly localized in time that descend rapidly to zero after a few oscillations, and have a null average value (like the signals recorded by a heart monitor). Generally, wavelets are intentionally crafted to have specific properties that make them useful for signal processing; as a mathematical tool, wavelets can be used to extract information from many different kinds of data.

Wavelet Transform (WT) is one of the most important techniques in signal processing to build a framework in the identification of modal properties. As a time-frequency analysis tool, WT has the advantages of dealing with non-stationary, transient and non-linear signals.

The Continuous Wavelet Transform (CWT) is one of the most-widely used forms of the WT, which provides a time-frequency representation of a signal by using a variable-size windowing technique simultaneously. The CWT decomposes the signal into a series of small waves or "wavelets"; those wavelets can be real or complex functions and there is a wavelets' family available. For each application, a certain wavelet may be more appropriate than others, but, in general, to find it, a trial and error process is required. The selected wavelet is called the "mother wavelet" and can be a function of space or time. Thus, the CWT is generated by choosing a single mother wavelet, and then forming a continuous family of wavelets by translating and dilating the mother wavelet; this is used to sequentially assess the similarity between the mother wavelet and a portion of the signal to be analyzed at all times or locations of the signal. Wavelets with finer scales are an indicator of high frequency information of the signal, while wavelets with coarser scales are appropriate to capture low frequency components. As a result, any irregularity or discontinuity in the signals that are not visible easily by visual inspections or conventional methods may exhibit high values of coefficients through CWT [35].

Thus, while the FFT decomposes a signal into infinite length sines and cosines, effectively losing all time-localization information, the CWT is used to construct a time–frequency representation of a signal that offers very good time and frequency localization. The CWT is an excellent tool for mapping the changing properties of non-stationary signals.

In this way, a mother wavelet function is defined as [36]:

$$\psi(t) \in L^2(\mathbb{R}), \tag{1}$$

which is limited in the time domain. That is, $\psi(t)$ has values in a certain range and zeros elsewhere. Another property of a mother wavelet is zero-mean; and the other property is that the mother wavelet is normalized. Mathematically, those two latest properties are represented as:

$$\int_{-\infty}^{\infty} \psi(t)dt = 0 \tag{2}$$

$$\| \psi(t) \|^2 = \int_{-\infty}^{\infty} \psi(t)\psi^*(t)dt = 1. \tag{3}$$

As the translation and dilation properties indicate, the mother wavelet can form a basis set denoted by:

$$\left\{ \psi_{s,u}(t) = \frac{1}{\sqrt{s}} \psi\left(\frac{t-u}{s}\right) \right\}\bigg|_{u \in \mathbb{R}, s \in \mathbb{R}+}, \tag{4}$$

where u is the translating parameter, indicating which region is of concern, whereas s is the scaling parameter greater than zero because negative scaling is undefined. The multiresolution property ensures the obtained set $\{\psi_{s,u}(t)\}$ is orthonormal. Thus, the CWT is the coefficient of the basis $\psi_{s,u}(t)$, that is,

$$Wf(s,u) = \langle f(t), \psi_{s,u} \rangle \tag{5}$$

$$Wf(s,u) = \int_{-\infty}^{\infty} f(t)\psi^*_{s,u}(t)dt \tag{6}$$

$$Wf(s,u) = \int_{-\infty}^{\infty} f(t)\frac{1}{\sqrt{s}}\psi^*\left(\frac{t-u}{s}\right)dt. \tag{7}$$

Through this transform, it is possible to map a one-dimensional signal $f(t)$ to a two-dimensional coefficients $Wf(s,u)$. The two variables can perform the time-frequency analysis. Then, the location of a particular frequency (parameter s) at a certain time instant (parameter u) can be indicated.

If the $f(t)$ is a $L^2(\mathbb{R})$ function. The inverse CWT is:

$$f(t) = \frac{1}{C_\psi} \int_0^\infty \int_{-\infty}^\infty Wf(s,u) \frac{1}{\sqrt{s}} \psi\left(\frac{t-u}{s}\right) du \frac{ds}{s^2}, \tag{8}$$

where C_ψ is defined as:

$$C_\psi = \int_0^\infty \frac{|\Psi(\omega)|^2}{\omega} d\omega < \infty, \tag{9}$$

where $\Psi(\omega)$ is the Fourier transform of the mother wavelet $\psi(t)$. This equation is also called the admissibility condition.

For the particular purpose of his article, all the types of mother wavelets that can be implemented with MATLAB© were tried and it was found that the Mexican hat mother wavelet was the most useful due to its satisfactory properties. The nickname, "Mexican hat," is because the shape of the function is like a typical Mexican hat. The function of this type of mother wavelet is:

$$\psi(t) = \frac{2}{\pi^{1/4}\sqrt{3\sigma}} \left(\frac{t^2}{\sigma^2} - 1\right) \exp\left(-\frac{t^2}{2\sigma^2}\right). \tag{10}$$

Finally, in order to estimate the WE, which is the parameter that indicates if there is a damage and its location by using the WEAM (as described in Section 2), the area under the curve generated by the wavelets coefficients along the selected range of scale must be calculated for each point of the bridge deck (i.e., from L_{min} to L_{max}, where L is the total length considered for the bridge deck), as it is represented in the following equation just for one point of L:

$$WE = \int_{s_{min}}^{s_{max}} f(Wf) ds \tag{11}$$

where s_{min} and s_{max} are the minimum and maximum values of scale, respectively, from the range of scale selected; whereas $f(Wf)$ represents the function of the curve of the coefficients along the selected range of scale just for one point of the total length (L) considered. In this way, after obtaining the WE for all the points of L, damage can be detected and located, because the corresponding total WE of a healthy bridge is a low and flat curve, whereas for a damaged bridge the corresponding WE curve is higher and there is a WE accumulation at the damage location, as it will be demonstrated in the next section.

3. Validation of Proposed Methodology

In this section, the proposed method explained meticulously in Section 2 is applied for its numerical validation. Thus, for this purpose, a detailed FEM model of the RPB is developed in ANSYS© in order to study different scenarios of damage included damaged deck and damage on cables (simulating the failure of a cable occurred in 2015 into the real bridge). The numerical transient responses obtained while a constant force (load) moves on different nodes along the bridge deck (simulating a vehicle passing through the bridge) as well as the experimental signals from the real bridge are post-processed with a code written in MATLAB© (R2017a), which provides the Wavelet Energy (WE) and determines if a damage exists and its location.

The numerical results obtained applying the WEAM show the great capability of this method to detect damage and locate it with high precision, even when significant percentage of noise was included in the signals. On the other hand, regardless that the WEAM is useful with a controlled test and the failure of the RPB took place before this method could be applied, the acquired data from the real bridge when it was healthy as well as when a cable broke down are analyzed by using the most useful measurements and damage detection is possible by calculating the WE. Thus, the WEAM is promissory to be systematic applied on the main bridges to avoid accidents like the one occurred in the RPB in 2015.

3.1. Numerical Simulation

3.1.1. Cable-Stayed Bridge Finite Element Model

A numerical FEM code named "BRITRANSYS" was written in ANSYS© (V 14.0) and contains two parts: (a) A detailed model based on the characteristics of the RPB with the possibility of including different types of damage like damage on deck and cables; (b) the transient solution/responses obtained while a force moves on different nodes along any section or the whole bridge deck (simulating a vehicle passing through the bridge), different speeds and weights for the "vehicle" can be considered and the dynamic responses (displacements and accelerations) can be obtained in any node of the model.

As for the FEM model, the ANSYS APDL© code was built as follows: The model geometry of the RPB was created in AutoCAD©, then became APDL© commands through an Excel© sheet in the form of keypoints coordinates; initial/final keypoints were defined for each line. The writing of commands for areas was made by using simple APDL© commands, mainly "*DO".

Three different types of elements were used to build the model: BEAM188 for towers, main girders and transverse girders; SHELL181 for slab; and LINK180 for cables. Then the material properties were defined for each structural element as well as the cross-sectional properties.

BEAM188 is a 3-D two-node beam element suitable for analyzing slender to moderately stubby/thick beam structures. The element is based on Timoshenko beam theory which includes shear-deformation effects and it has six or seven DOFs at each node. SHELL181 is a four-node structural element with six DOFs at each node: Translations in the three directions, and rotations about the three axes. It is suitable for analyzing thin to moderately-thick shell structures. LINK180 is a 3-D spar/truss element that is useful in a variety of engineering applications. This element is a uniaxial tension–compression element with three DOFs at each node: Translations in the three nodal directions. Tension-only (cable) and compression-only (gap) options are supported. Plasticity, creep, rotation, large deflection and large strain capabilities are included and no bending of the element is considered.

Every cable in the bridge has specific values of area, mass and stress (related with tension). Stresses data were load to the software in a vector array with 112 spaces, the spaces were filled by loading data with the "*VREAD" command, this command takes the data previously stored in a ".txt" extension file. Then, area and mass values were assigned to each line that correspond to a cable. Previously, for meshing the structural elements, their attributes like cross-sectional area, material and element type were assigned to each different structural elements group. Once this was done, the whole model was meshed to be composed of 7365 elements and 8053 nodes. Finally, the restrictions and the initial state that define the initial stress of every cable were defined. To finish a base bridge model, the command "SOLVE" was set.

Likewise, in order to obtain the displacement/acceleration dynamic responses, a specific lane where the moving load passes and the corresponding longitudinal section of the bridge deck were defined, then the respective nodes one after the other (in straight line shape) were created and consecutively numbered. After that, the moving load simulating a vehicle was defined with a specific weight and speed and set on each node through the ANSYS© transient solution. Finally, this part of the code defines the nodes and the responses to be obtained, then the corresponding data are saved in ".txt" format to be post-processed. Figure 7 shows the healthy FEM model which was calibrated with experimental results obtained from the RPB monitoring.

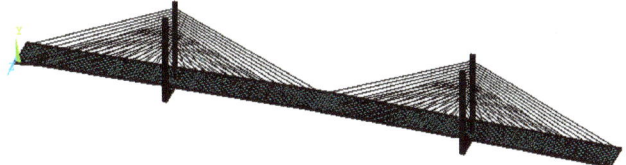

Figure 7. ANSYS© FEM model of the RPB.

On the other hand, a MATLAB© (R2017a) code called "MAT_BRITRANSYS" was developed in order to post-process the signals from the FEM model/simulations and follow the methodology (WEAM-Wavelet Energy Accumulation Method) for damage detection. This code loads two numerical simulations from the ANSYS© code (one healthy and one damaged in ".txt" format) for different measurement positions along the considered longitudinal bridge deck section (the same measurement positions for healthy and damaged cases), and provides: time-domain plots (waveforms), frequency-base plots (FFT's), spectrograms and CWT 3-D colored diagrams; all for original, noisy (Gaussian noise added) and filtered (Savitzky-Golay filter used) signals. Even more, this code also post-processes the CWT diagrams and performs subtractions (damaged signals-healthy signals), removes the border effects (by means of signal extensions) to bring the border effects to "inexistent" parts of the considered bridge deck, calculates the total wavelet energy for all the respective bridge deck for each point of measurement, and makes an average of the total wavelet energy considering the different positions of the measurements. Then, a damage can be detected and its location identified by means of the accumulation of this energy. For analyzing the real data from the RPB, the same code was used with some modifications according to the quantity, position and type of sensors.

3.1.2. Results from Numerical Simulations

Two of the most dangerous faults that can lead to the collapse of the RPB (as in any cable-stayed bridge) are a damage on the deck and a damaged cable. Both cases are studied in this section considering the FEM model and applying the WEAM, as it was described in Section 2.

All the types of mother wavelets that can be selected with MATLAB© and different types of filters were implemented; the best results to identify damage were obtained with the Mexican hat mother wavelet and a Savitzky-Golay filter.

The first case studied was a damage on the deck, simulated by reducing by 30% the cross-sectional area (0.30 h, where h is the height of the deck) in 5% of the 203 m length bridge (bridge deck between pylons). The cross-section of the deck is rectangular with a height (h) = 0.20 m and a width (w) = 23.40 m. The damage was placed at 25%, 50% and 75% of the considered length of the bridge deck (one at time) and the measurement points were established at 25%, 50% and 75% of the considered length of the bridge deck (all at the same time for each case of healthy bridge and bridge with a single damage). It is important to mention that, under the deck (slab), the bridge has a very rigid structure composed by two main girders and 117 transverse girders; therefore, that reduction of 30% of the cross-sectional area impacts in a stiffness reduction of 22% on the damaged section.

As it has been notified [8,29], low vehicle speeds allow damage identification more accurately on long bridges. However, the selection of a vehicle with low speed crossing all the RPB would impact significantly in computing time. Thus, in the interest of reducing the computing time, a moving force representing a vehicle type T3S3 (nomenclature not related with the corresponding of cables and semi-harps) fully loaded (54,000 kgf) was selected to cross just the bridge deck between pylons; that is, L = 203 m (instead of 407.21 m) with a speed of 1 m/s and sampling frequency of 64 Hz. This configuration and selecting an adequate resolution for the CWT diagrams according to the range of scale allowed having an equilibrium between computing time and accuracy of results for damage identification.

It should be noted that it does not matter if the vehicle starts its movement at the first node or later, the results for identifying damage are not affected as long as the vehicle passes at the damage location. The selected lane for the moving force was the right lane of the downstream side and the measurement points were located on the corresponding nodes of the right side of the deck (downstream side) where the moving force does not pass. It is important to notice that regardless the CWT provides pseudo frequency (scale)-time domain info, if the vehicle speed is known (as it happens in the numerical simulations) then the CWT diagrams are easier to analyze by including the length of the bridge deck (distance) instead of time, so that we can know the damage position on the bridge corresponding with the vehicle position.

In Figure 8, the CWT diagrams for a healthy bridge deck and a damaged bridge deck at 25% of L obtained from the corresponding acceleration signals at the three locations are shown. As it can be observed in this figure, for this initial wide range of scale (from 1 to 500) there is a tiny clue of damage around 0.25 L, but it is not very evident because it is partially masked. In this range of scale, the WE is amplified mainly in the zone of the influence of the first natural frequency and secondly in the regions of the border effects (around 0% and 100% of L) and damage (around 25% of L), hindering a clear damage identification. Thus, comparing the damaged diagrams (Figure 8b) with the corresponding ones of the healthy case (Figure 8a) could seem very similar each other; however, the presence of damage is there but masked.

In order to increase the evidence of damage, the signals used for obtaining the diagrams shown in Figure 8 were subtracted (damaged ones—healthy ones) and then the resultant signals were extended by using the MATLAB© command "wextend" (antisymmetric-padding) for eliminating the border effects. In Figure 9, the subtracted and extended CWT diagram is shown just for one measurement in the interest of brevity. It can be observed that the border effects were taken out of the real bridge length considered; whereas the useful subtraction effect cannot be clearly distinguished yet because the scale range is not the convenient. Therefore, just the zone inside the yellow square must be considered, in this way the real bridge length is again analyzed (but now without border effects), whereas the scale from 250 to 500 allows to focus on the damage effect and the influence of the subtraction will be appreciated. Likewise, once the step related with the subtraction of signals was applied, the cases presented in every figure as "damaged bridge" correspond with the use of the subtracted signals.

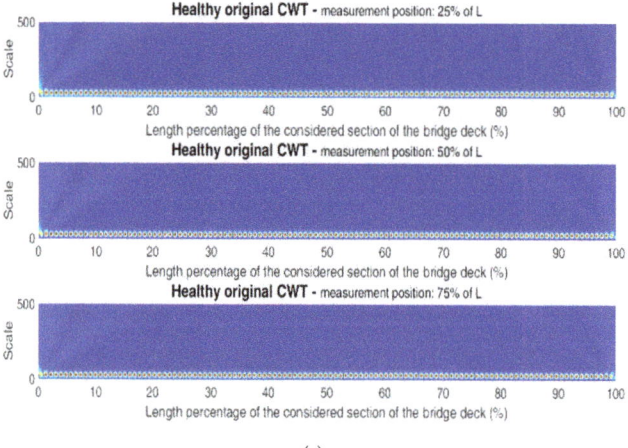

(a)

Figure 8. *Cont.*

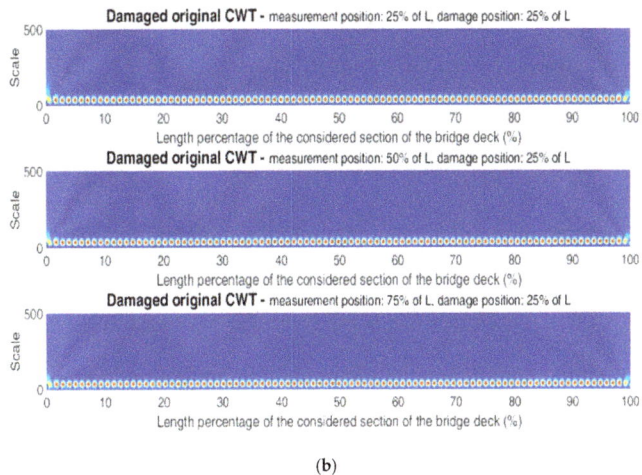

(b)

Figure 8. CWT diagrams from original acceleration signals: (**a**) Healthy bridge deck and (**b**) damaged bridge deck at 0.25 L. Three different measurement positions for each one (from top to bottom: 0.25 L, 0.50 L, and 0.75 L).

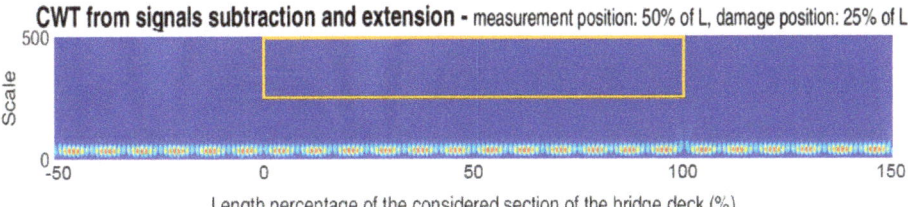

Figure 9. CWT diagram from acceleration signals subtraction and extension for measurement position at 0.50 L and damage position at 0.25 L, showing with a yellow square the important region to calculate the WE.

Thus, the CWT diagrams for the three measurement positions considering the region of the yellow square are shown in Figure 10b and the respective ones for the healthy bridge are shown in Figure 10a. Comparing those figures, the presence of damage is clear with evident indicators of high wavelets' coefficients (energy) around the damage location. It should be noted that damage identification is possible even if the measurements come far away from the damage position; however, the closer the measurement is to the position of the damage, the greater the energy, as it will be shown next.

The WE energy for a healthy and a damaged bridge deck was calculated for each point of the considered length by means of the area under the curve along the adjusted range of scale. The results for healthy and damaged cases are shown in Figure 11, where it can be observed that the WE for the healthy cases is very low and flat with tiny WE accumulation at the measurement points and at the ends because of the remaining border effects. Whereas, for the damaged cases, no matter the measurement point, the WE accumulation is always around the damage location and its magnitude is much higher compared with the healthy cases. Even for the case of measurement at 0.75 L, the percentage of error for the damage localization is very acceptable (4.1%), while for the other two measurements it is smaller due to the closeness with damage (2.8% and 1.6% for measurement at 0.50 L and 0.25 L, respectively). The advantage of this method of detecting damage using just one point of measurement far away from damage is interesting.

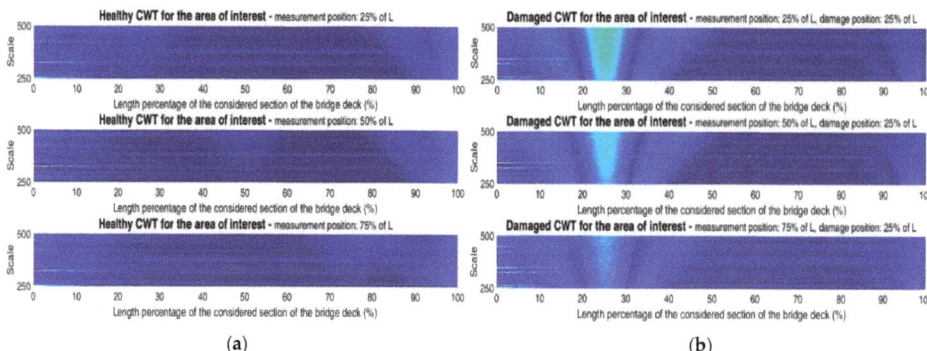

Figure 10. CWT diagrams from acceleration signals for the area of interest: (**a**) Healthy bridge deck and (**b**) damaged bridge deck at 0.25 L. Three different measurement positions for each one (from top to bottom: 0.25 L, 0.50 L, and 0.75 L).

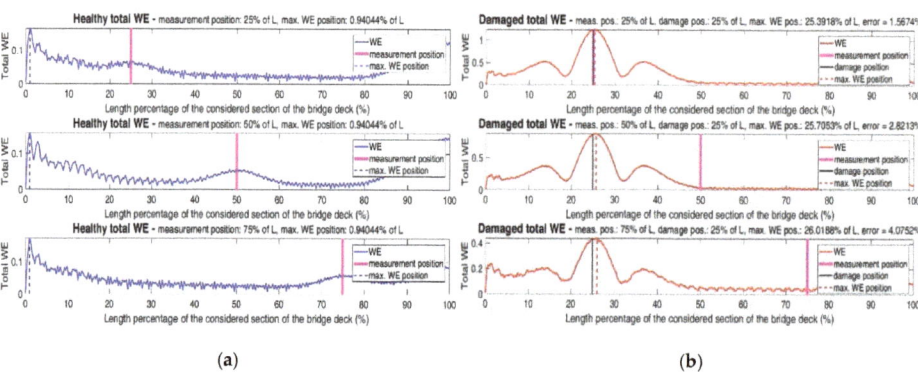

Figure 11. Total WE from acceleration signals: (**a**) Healthy bridge deck and (**b**) damaged bridge deck at 0.25 L. Three different measurement positions for each one (from top to bottom: 0.25 L, 0.50 L and 0.75 L).

In real cases, just one value of the total WE would be useful and; therefore, the average of the WE considering all the measurement points must be calculated. Moreover, it must be taken into account that the signals would contain significant percentages of noise, making the damage identification difficult and requiring a useful filter. Thus, in Figure 12, the total WE for all the measurement positions and respective averages are presented for healthy and damaged cases considering the original, noisy and filtered signals. The original signals are signals generated with the FEM simulations and no noise was added and no filters were used (like the ones used for the previous diagrams exhibited); for the noisy signals, 15% of Gaussian noise was added; and for the filtered signals a Savitzky-Golay filter (order = 2; window length = 19) was implemented for the noisy signals. It can be observed in Figure 12 that the percentage of error in damage identification for average noisy signal increased 2.6 times with respect to the original case (still acceptable considering the big percentage of noise added). Whereas, for the filtered case, the percentage of error was reduced 1.4 times with respect to the noisy case. In all the scenarios, damage detection and localization were possible and the percentage of error was less than 5.0%.

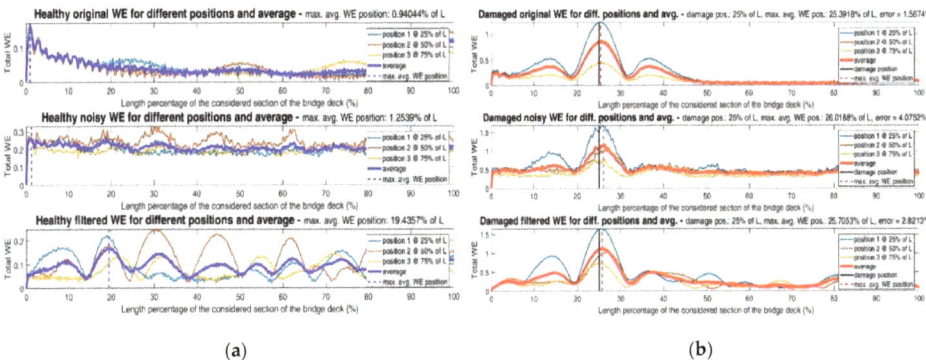

Figure 12. Total WE from acceleration signals for different measurement positions and average: (**a**) Healthy bridge deck and (**b**) damaged bridge deck at 0.25 L. Three different conditions of the signals for each one (from top to bottom: Original, noisy and filtered).

Lastly, for an easy visualization, in Figure 13 just the average WE is shown for a healthy and a damaged bridge deck and for the three scenarios of signals (original, noisy and filtered), with the respective percentage of error. It is important to notice that if the considered vehicle speed is set to 2, 3, 4 and 5 m/s, the percentage of error for the damage location considering the original signals changes to 1.85%, 2.15%, 2.49% and 2.91%, respectively. Whereas, for the speed of 1 m/s, the corresponding percentage of error is 1.57%, as it can be observed in Figure 13.

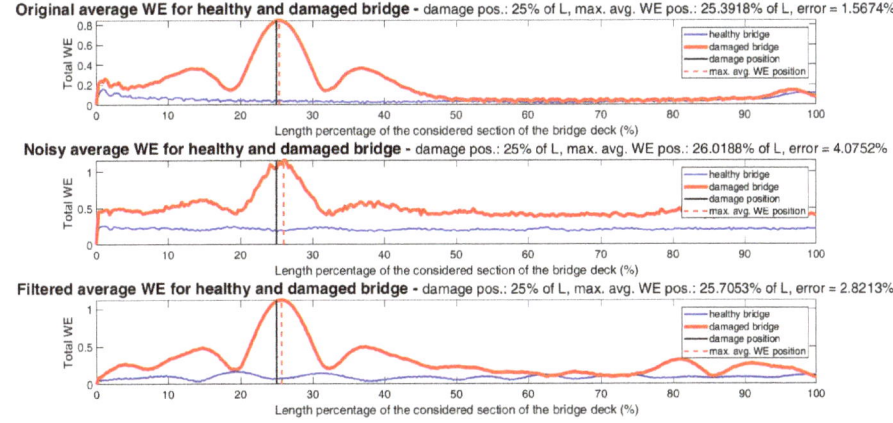

Figure 13. Total average WE from acceleration signals for a healthy bridge deck and a damaged bridge deck at 0.25 L. Three different conditions of the signals (from top to bottom: Original, noisy and filtered).

Likewise, the damage location was changed and set on the midspan between pylons (0.50 L) and at 0.75 L. The noisy and filtered CWT diagrams for the area of interest are shown in Figure 14 for damage at 0.50 L and in Figure 15 for damage at 0.75 L. Whereas, the total average WE energy from original, noisy and filtered signals are shown in Figure 16 for a healthy and a damaged bridge deck at 0.50 L and in Figure 17 for a healthy and a damaged bridge deck at 0.75 L.

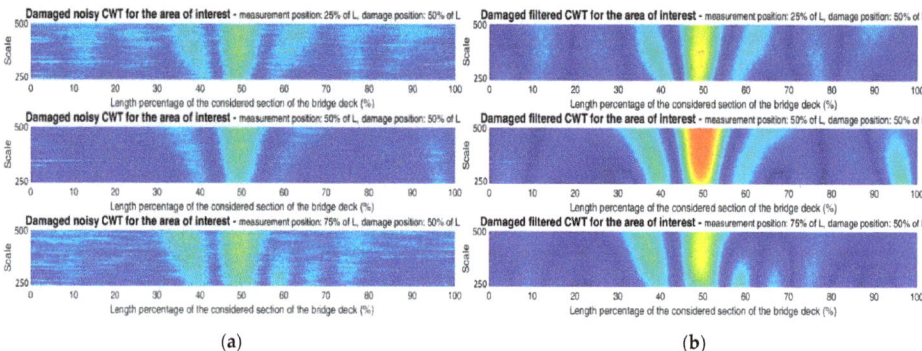

Figure 14. CWT diagrams from acceleration signals for the area of interest for damaged bridge deck at 0.50 L and different conditions of the signals: (**a**) Noisy signals and (**b**) filtered signals. Three different measurement positions for each one (from top to bottom: 0.25 L, 0.50 L, and 0.75 L).

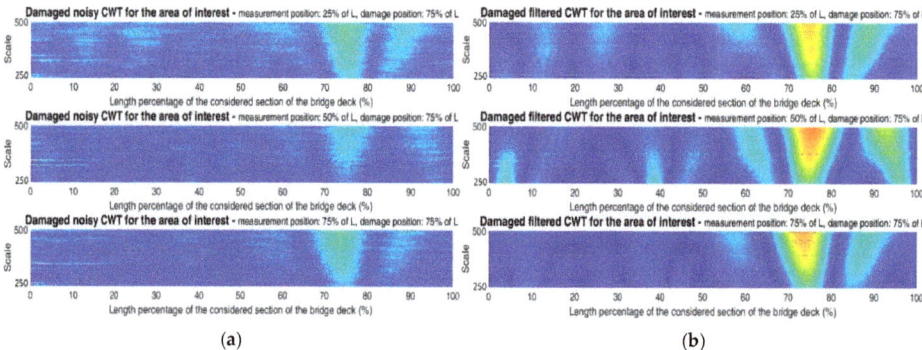

Figure 15. CWT diagrams from acceleration signals for the area of interest for damaged bridge deck at 0.75 L and different conditions of the signals: (**a**) Noisy signals and (**b**) filtered signals. Three different measurement positions for each one (from top to bottom: 0.25 L, 0.50 L, and 0.75 L).

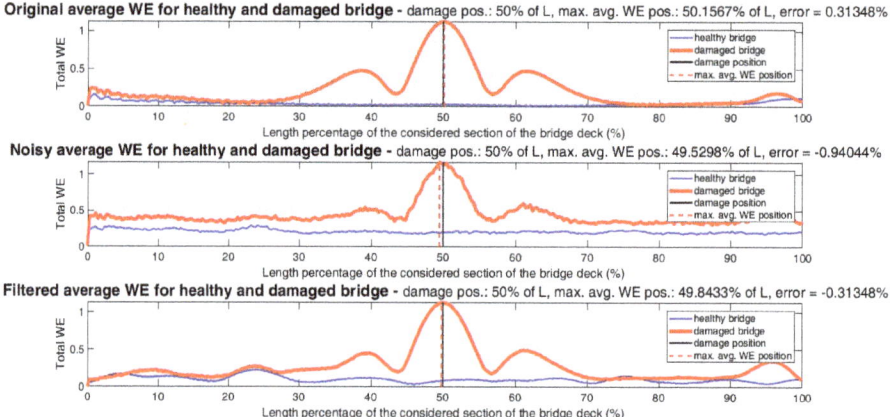

Figure 16. Total average WE from acceleration signals for a healthy bridge deck and a damaged bridge deck at 0.50 L. Three different conditions of the signals (from top to bottom: Original, noisy and filtered).

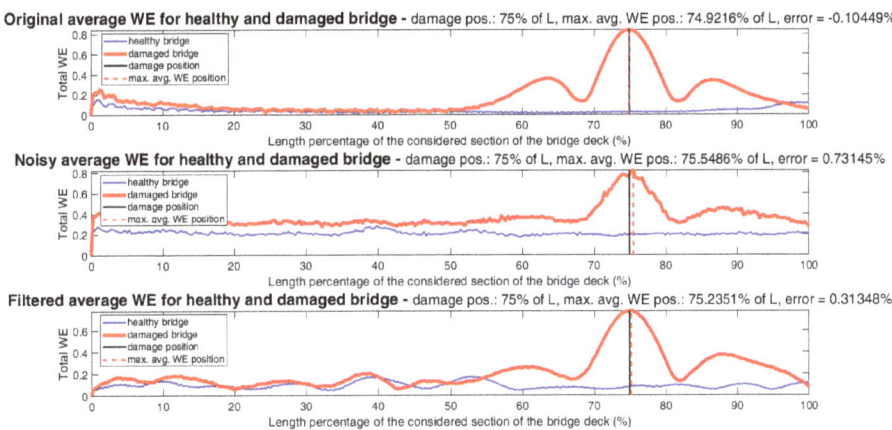

Figure 17. Total average WE from acceleration signals for a healthy bridge deck and a damaged bridge deck at 0.75 L. Three different conditions of the signals (from top to bottom: Original, noisy and filtered).

The CWT diagrams shown in Figures 14 and 15 are overwhelming for damage identification at 0.50 L and 0.75 L, respectively. By using the noisy signals, the damage identification is evident because of the change of color representing higher wavelets' coefficients. Whereas, by using the filtered signals, the CWT diagrams are clearer and the damage identification is even easier.

As for the total average WE, that WE is high for both cases of damaged bridge deck (at 0.50 L and 0.75 L) and low for the healthy corresponding cases (see Figures 16 and 17). Moreover, the WE for the damaged signals is accumulated in the vicinity of the damage position and, in this way, the differences between the positions of the maximum values of the average WE and the values of the respective damage positions are very small, whereas, for the healthy cases, there are no remarkable accumulations.

Taking into account the case of damage at 50% of L (Figure 16), the percentage of error for the damage identification by considering the maximum value of the WE accumulation was 0.31% for the original signal, then it increased three times for the noisy signal and, finally, it came back to the same original absolute value for the filtered signal (0.31%). For the original signal, damage was identified slightly to the right of the real position, whereas, for both the noisy and filtered signals, damage was identified slightly to the left of the real position.

On the other hand, considering the damage at 75% of L (Figure 17), the absolute percentages of error for the damage identification were 0.10%, 0.73% and 0.31% for original, noisy and filtered signals, respectively. For the original signal, the damage was identified slightly to the left of the real position, whereas, for noisy and filtered signals, it was identified slightly to the right of the real position.

Thus, by using the acceleration signals and following sequential steps for consolidating the WEAM, damage was detected and located with high accuracy; no matter its position on the bridge deck, the condition of the signals (original, noisy or filtered), the quantity of the measurement points (single or average of multiple points) nor the location of the measurement points (on the damage, close or far away). It is important to mention that once the area of interest is determined on the CWT diagrams, damage identification becomes easy on the very same CWT diagrams and the total average WE diagrams will confirm the existence and location of damage. Furthermore, those WE diagrams help provide a value of the maximum WE to quantify how severe the damage is.

The same case of damage analyzed above by using the acceleration signals is henceforth studied with the corresponding displacement signals from the vibration of the bridge. In Figure 18 the CWT diagrams from original displacement signals at three different positions are shown for a healthy and a damaged bridge deck at 25% of L. A huge initial scale range was used (from 1 to 10,000) in order to explore a clue of damage and again, at a glance, no clear indications of damage were found.

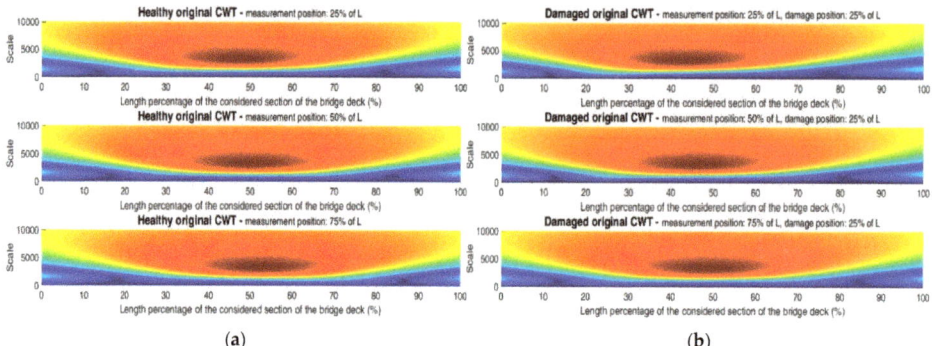

Figure 18. CWT diagrams from original displacement signals: (**a**) Healthy bridge deck and (**b**) damaged bridge deck at 0.25 L. Three different measurement positions for each one (from top to bottom: 0.25 L, 0.50 L, and 0.75 L).

After performing the signals' subtractions and extensions, as well as using the useful range of scale (from 250 to 500), the previous diagrams now look like those in Figure 19. In the new figure it is possible to see that there are no border effects. Moreover, the energy for the healthy cases (Figure 19a) is accumulated around the measurement point, as expected, but that energy is low, as it can be observed in Figure 20a.

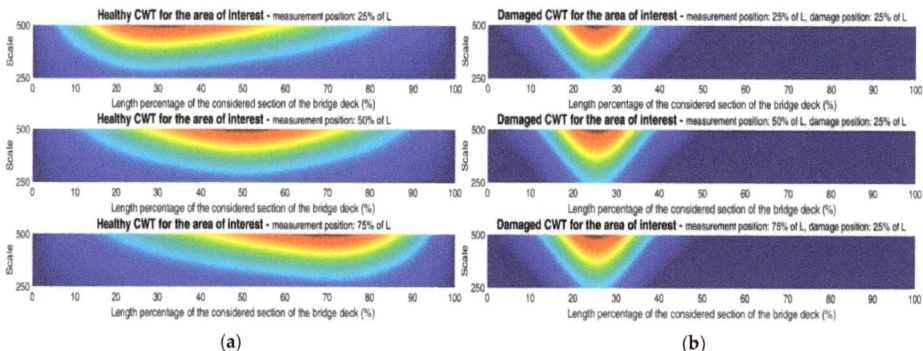

Figure 19. CWT diagrams from displacement signals for the area of interest: (**a**) Healthy bridge deck and (**b**) damaged bridge deck at 0.25 L. Three different measurement positions for each one (from top to bottom: 0.25 L, 0.50 L and 0.75 L).

On the other hand, for the damaged case, all the energy is accumulated around the damaged location no matter the measurement point. Additionally, out of the zone of damage the energy is practically zero, which was achieved by means of the signals' subtraction, which is why the shape of the energy expansion looks almost identical for all the cases of damage with different measurement positions (Figure 19b). However, the energy is higher as long as the measurement point is closer to damage, as it can be seen in Figure 20b.

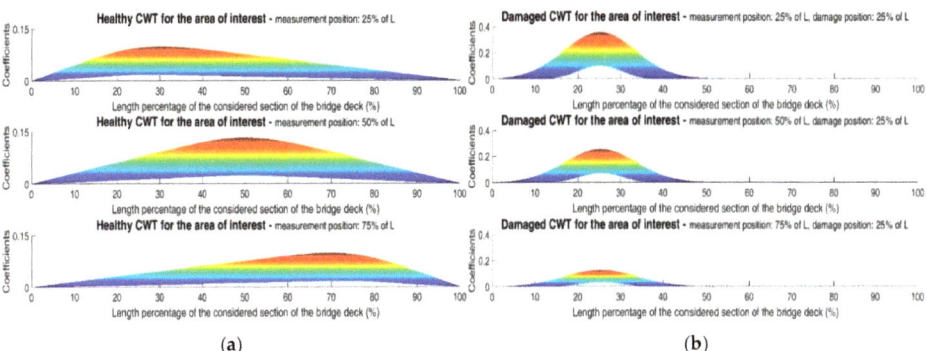

Figure 20. CWT diagrams from displacement signals for the area of interest and showing the coefficients instead of scale: (**a**) Healthy bridge deck and (**b**) damaged bridge deck at 0.25 L. Three different measurement positions for each one (from top to bottom: 0.25 L, 0.50 L and 0.75 L).

Part of the energy accumulated in the zone of damage is lost during the subtraction, but the advantage is that no energy will be displayed in the zone of the measurement when damage is not there and the plots will look clearer. Whereas the disadvantage of lost energy because of the subtraction and the far measurements can be compensated with the average of the WE.

Now, in the interest of brevity, just the filtered displacement signals were used to calculate the total average WE diagrams, because this is the most realistic scenario to deal with. That is, the signals will always contain noise and a filter has to be used to reduce that noise. Thus, in Figure 21, the corresponding total average WE diagrams for healthy and damaged bridge deck at 0.25 L, 0.50 L and 0.75 from filtered displacement signals are shown. In Figure 21 the difference of WE between healthy and damaged cases is evident; therefore, the existence and location of damage was confirmed and the percentage of error was again very low (no more than 1.60%).

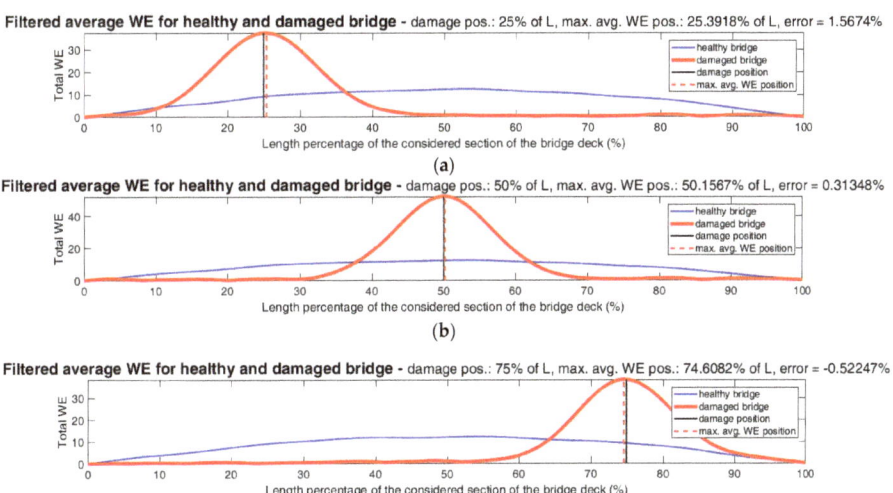

Figure 21. Total average WE from filtered displacement signals: (**a**) Healthy bridge deck vs. damaged bridge deck at 0.25 L; (**b**) healthy bridge deck vs. damaged bridge deck at 0.50 L; and (**c**) healthy bridge deck vs. damaged bridge deck at 0.75 L.

In order to quantify the severity of damage and the sensitivity of this method, four different magnitudes of this type of damage on the bridge deck, additionally to the one studied above, were simulated at 25% of L, for a total of five cases, that is: 0.10 h, 0.20 h, 0.30 h, 0.40 h, and 0.50 h of height reduction. The total average WE's for all these cases are shown in Figure 22. The signals used for those plots were the acceleration signals after being added with 15% of noise and then filtered. This was in order to analyze the most common signals available in real SHM (acceleration) and their condition (noisy and then filtered). The tiny differences of the healthy WE's for the different diagrams of Figure 22, even when the original healthy signals are obviously the same, are due to the randomness of the added noise. The code was configured to analyze one healthy case and one damaged case at the same time. Consequently, the healthy case was run for each case of damage and the noise was not the same, thus the filtered WE's were not identical.

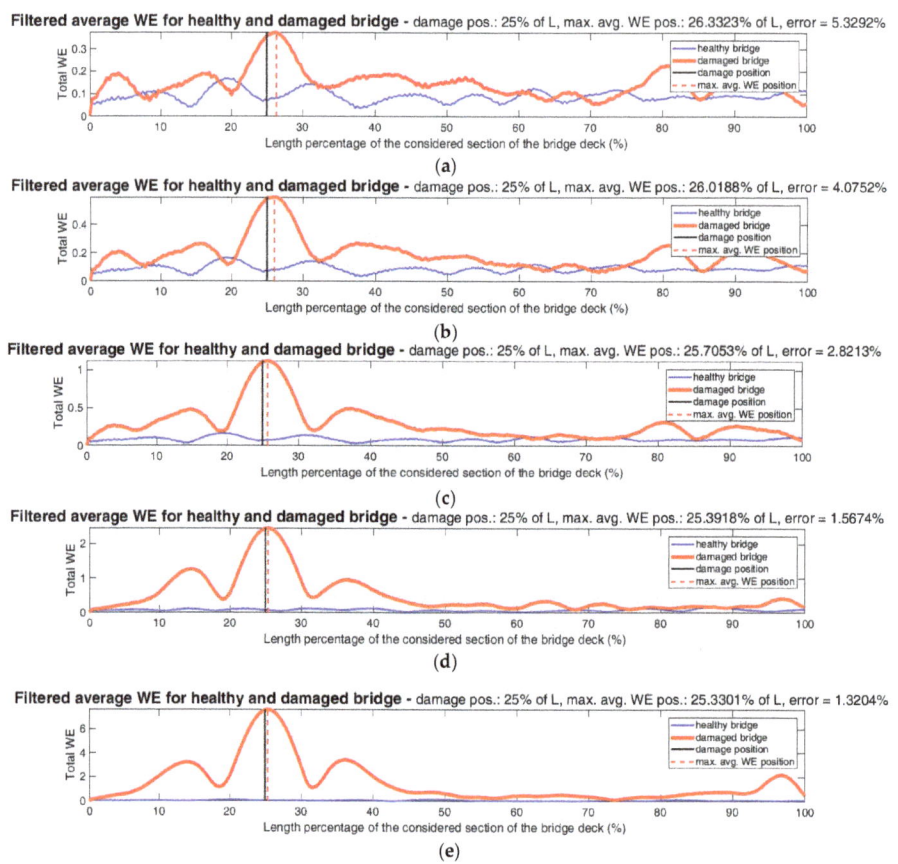

Figure 22. Total average WE from filtered acceleration signals: (**a**) Healthy bridge deck vs. damaged bridge deck with 0.10 h reduction; (**b**) healthy bridge deck vs. damaged bridge deck with 0.20 h reduction; (**c**) healthy bridge deck vs. damaged bridge deck with 0.30 h reduction; (**d**) healthy bridge deck vs. damaged bridge deck with 0.40 h reduction; and (**e**) healthy bridge deck vs. damaged bridge deck with 0.50 h reduction. All the cases of damage are at 0.25 L.

Additionally, in Figure 23 it is possible to see the healthy average WE and all the damaged average WE's together in the same plot, for an easier visualization of the impact of the magnitude of damage in the WE and the sensitivity of this method.

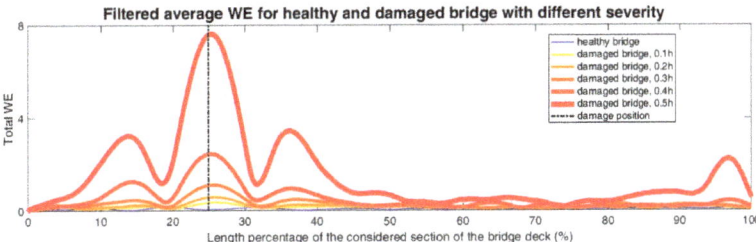

Figure 23. Total average WE from filtered acceleration signals for healthy bridge deck and damaged bridge deck at 0.25 L with different severity.

In Table 1, a summary of the results shown in Figures 22 and 23 is presented. In the table, as expected, it is clear the tendency about the increment of damaged WE and ratio of maximum average damaged WE/maximum average healthy WE as the severity of damage increases; as well as the increment of the damage localization accuracy as the magnitude of damage increases. Nevertheless, the highest percentage of error in those cases presented in Table 1 (5.33%) is still very acceptable considering the low magnitude of damage (0.10 h), high percentage of noise (15%) and the kind of signal used (acceleration instead of displacement).

Table 1. Analysis of damage severity for different magnitudes of damage on the bridge deck at 0.25 L presented in Figures 22 and 23.

	Analysis of Damage Severity on Bridge Deck at 0.25 L		
Damage Magnitude	Max. Avg. Damaged WE	Max. Avg. Damaged WE/ Max. Avg. Healthy WE	Error in Damage Localization (%)
0.10 h	0.37	2.22	5.33
0.20 h	0.60	3.55	4.08
0.30 h	1.12	6.65	2.82
0.40 h	2.46	13.32	1.57
0.50 h	7.65	41.35	1.32

The experimental validation of the quantification of damage will be performed by using a lab model in future works, since in the real bridge is not possible. Cracks of different severity will be induced on the deck of the lab model in order to correlate the different WE curves with the corresponding level of damage.

Finally, in regards to the numerical part of this article, for the other type of damage (damaged cable) just three cases were analyzed: healthy bridge, bridge with damaged cable T1S5, and bridge with damaged cable T10S7. For all those cases, the total length of the bridge had to be considered (407.21 m) and again three points of measurement were established, this time at 0.33 L, 0.50 L and 0.66 L instead of 0.25 L, 0.50 L and 0.75 L. This was because the first point and the last one would have been located practically on the pylons and it was not convenient, then the best distribution to keep just three measurement points was two points at 1 L/3 and 2 L/3 and one additional at the mid-span (1 L/2).

The case of damaged cable T1S5 corresponds with the real case analyzed in the next section, where cable 1 of the semi-harp 5 collapsed and whose failure was described previously. The anchor of this cable on the deck (according to the lateral view of Figure 3 from left to right) is found at 0.77 L, and there was no numerical point of measurement at this location (the nearest one at 0.66 L which represents 42 m of distance). The tension of this cable was reduced by 40%.

As for the damaged cable T10S7, this cable is number 10 of semi-harp 7 and is anchored at 0.42 L (practically between the first and second numerical measurement points with around 32 m of distance) and its tension was reduced by 50%. The purpose of this latest case was to analyze other locations of damaged cable and the magnitude of lost tension.

Since the considered current length of the bridge is twice the previous length taken into account for analyzing damage on the deck, in order to reduce the computing time and avoid a crash up of any of the two codes used with either ANSYS© or MATLAB©, the sampling frequency was halved (32 Hz). The moving force represented again a vehicle type T3S3 fully loaded (54,000 kgf); however, now to cross the whole bridge (L = 407.21 m) with a speed of 2 m/s. The selected lane was the right lane of the upstream side and the measurements were established on the nodes of the right side of the deck (upstream side) where the moving force does not pass. Higher vehicle speeds were simulated with excellent results for detecting and locating damage with good accuracy, but just the lowest speeds were included in this article in the interest of brevity.

As it was explained before, by the time the fault of the T1S5 occurred, the instrumentation was not planned for acquiring useful data for being used with this WEAM and, unfortunately, the acceleration sensors were not placed on the deck. Thus, considering the available instrumentation when the cable broke, the strain measurements of the deck would be the most useful ones and; therefore, for these numerical simulations, just the displacement signals were used.

In Figure 24, the original CWT diagrams are shown for the healthy case and bridge with damaged cable at 0.77 L, before and after the signals subtraction, just to show that, even when the convenient range of scale had not been selected yet, the subtraction was very useful to start providing a clue of the damage location. In Figure 25, the original CWT diagrams without border effects and for the area of interest are shown for the three cases (healthy, damaged cable at 0.77 L and damaged cable at 0.42 L), and the perspective to observe the magnitude of the coefficients for the damaged cable T1S5 is shown in Figure 26. Lastly, in Figure 27, the corresponding total filtered average WE's can be observed.

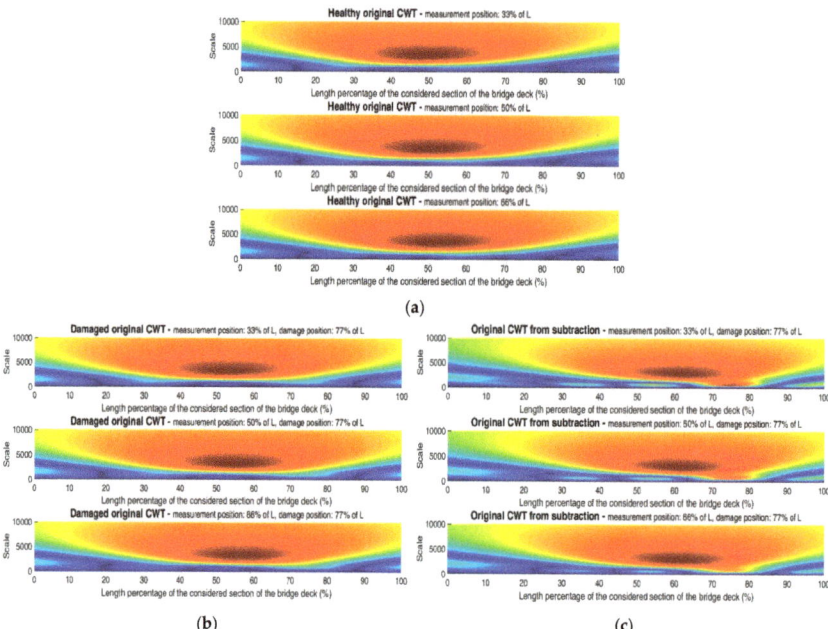

Figure 24. CWT diagrams from original displacement signals: (**a**) Healthy bridge; (**b**) bridge with damaged cable at 0.77 L before the signals subtraction; and (**c**) bridge with damaged cable at 0.77 L after the signals subtraction. Three different measurement positions for each one (from top to bottom: 0.33 L, 0.50 L, and 0.66 L).

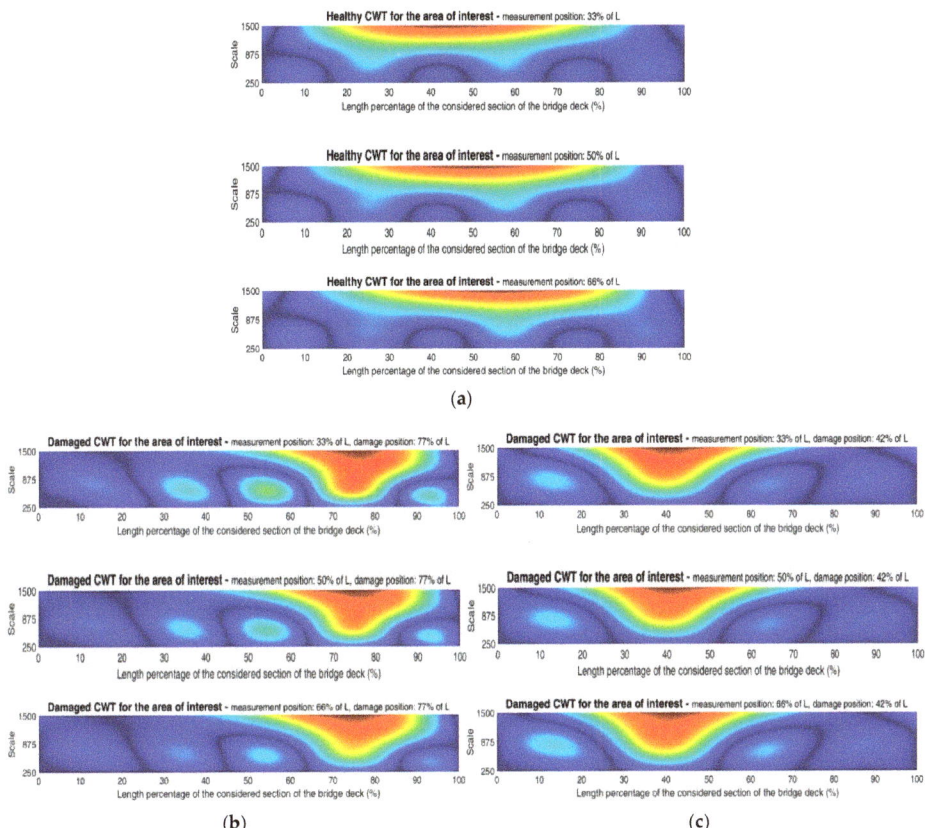

Figure 25. CWT diagrams from original displacement signals for the area of interest: (**a**) Healthy bridge; (**b**) bridge with damaged cable at 0.77 L; and (**c**) bridge with damaged cable at 0.42 L. Three different measurement positions for each one (from top to bottom: 0.33 L, 0.50 L and 0.66 L).

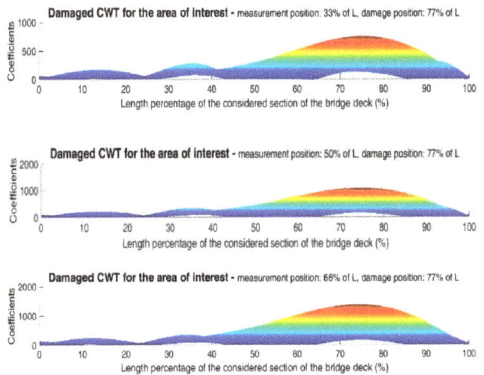

Figure 26. CWT diagrams from original displacement signals for the area of interest for bridge with damaged cable at 0.77 L and three different measurement positions (from top to bottom: 0.33 L, 0.50 L and 0.66 L), showing the magnitude of the coefficients.

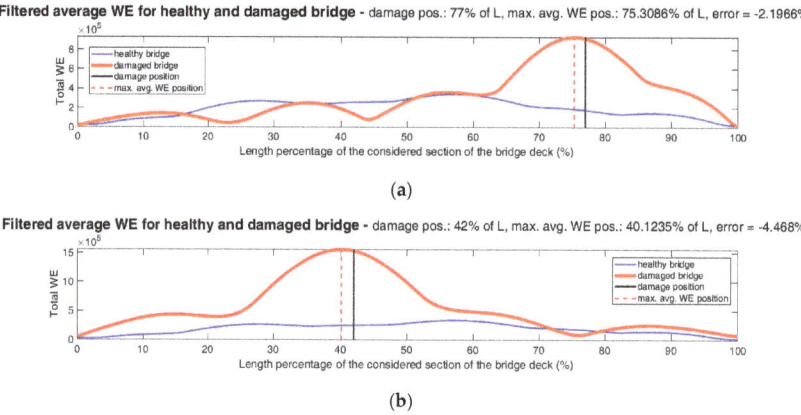

Figure 27. Total average WE from filtered displacement signals: (**a**) Healthy bridge vs. bridge with damaged cable at 0.77 L and (**b**) healthy bridge vs. bridge with damaged cable at 0.42 L.

In Figure 24, small differences between the healthy bridge case and the bridge with damaged cable at 0.77 L before the signals subtraction are observed for the original wide range of scale (1 to 10,000). However, after the signals subtraction, the corresponding CWT diagrams show evident inclinations of the highest coefficients toward the damage location for the same range of scale; this helped to provide a clue of the damage location and define the range of scale to calculate the WE.

The detection and localization of the damaged cables were possible by using the same range of scale defined as the most convenient for damage on the deck (250 to 500). However, in order to use a wider range of scale where the highest coefficients have influence around the damage locations, the convenient range of scale for these cases of damaged cables was defined from 250 to 1500 and the corresponding CWT diagrams for the area of interest are exposed in Figure 25, the evidences of damage are clear. Additionally, in Figure 26 the magnitude of the coefficients around 1000 can be appreciated for the case of damaged cable T1S5, which is useful to compare with the real case and numerical damage on deck.

Finally, in Figure 27, the total filtered average WE for each case of damaged cable compared with the healthy case are presented. For the damaged cable T1S5 (at 0.77 L), the percentage of error in the damage location was 2.20%. On the other hand, the maximum WE of the damaged curve was approximately 2.5 times the maximum WE of the healthy case and the same magnitude higher (2.5), with respect to the second bigger ridge of the same damaged curve. That is, the ridge of maximum WE accumulation indicating the damage location at 0.77 L is high enough to be distinguished to the second highest ridge of the same curve and the first highest ridge of the healthy curve. For the case of damaged cable at 0.42 L, the maximum WE increased 1.6 times with respect to the corresponding value for damaged cable at 0.77 L, which can be due to the more critical position of this cable and greater loss of tension percentage. The percentage of error for its damage location was also very acceptable (4.47%) considering that the signals were added with noise and then filtered.

The significant increments of the WE for the cases presented in Figure 27, in relation to the cases of damaged deck shown previously, are attributed to the damage nature and the consideration of a wider range of scale.

Thus, in this section it was demonstrated that, if the WEAM is applied as it was explained in Section 2, detection and location of different types of damage in a vehicular bridge is possible with high precision and by using just a few sensors. Moreover, this method also allows distinguishing among different severities of damage.

3.2. Results from the Real Failure Case

In this section, the most useful available data acquired during the monitoring of the second major failure of the RPB that occurred on 10 June 2015 (collapse of cable 1 of the semi-harp 5-T1S5) are analyzed and compared with the respective ones of the bridge when it was thought to be healthy (baseline) on 22 August 2014. These data corresponded with the measurements on the deck obtained with strain gages (125 Hz of sampling frequency), see Figure 6a.

As it was mentioned previously, a controlled test, with the adequate instrumentation to follow the steps of the WEAM, was not possible to be performed early enough to warn about the damage on cable T1S5, thus to avoid its fault. Nevertheless, the data acquired with random traffic almost a year before the incident (healthy case), and some minutes before the collapse of the cable (damaged case), are valuable to demonstrate that this method is promissory and its application could have avoided this failure and will avoid accidents in the future.

First, in Figure 28b the filtered damaged spectrogram (based on the STFT) of measurement point R2 (see Figure 6a) is shown for 840 s of monitoring. An evident mark at around 674 s can be distinguished and corresponds with the instant when the cable broke; however, before and after that event, there are no indicators about a damaged cable nor the absence of a cable, even when the signal was filtered and the measurement point is the nearest to the anchor of the damaged cable on the deck. Furthermore, comparing the first 670 s of Figure 28b (when damage existed and failure was imminent) with Figure 28a, which shows the respective spectrogram for 120 s of baseline acquisition, no clue of damage can be established and they look very similar to each other.

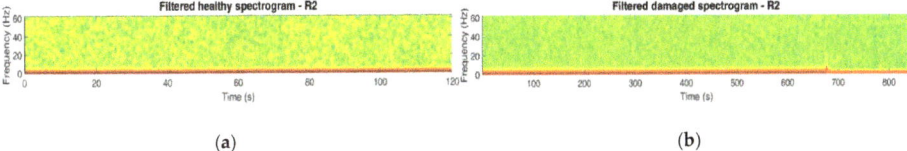

(a)   (b)

Figure 28. Spectrograms from filtered experimental signals: (**a**) Healthy bridge and (**b**) damaged cable T1S5.

On the other hand, the WE was always clearly higher for the damaged measurements instead of the healthy ones. This was observed for all measurement points by analyzing the CWT and WE diagrams for different periods of 120 s of damaged signals acquired on June 10, 2015, before the accident, and periods of 120 s of healthy signals acquired on August 22, 2014, as well as for the few months before and after that latest date. However, in the interest of brevity, just the CWT and WE diagrams from three measurement points (R1, R2 and R4) and for the same 120 s of the spectrogram of Figure 28a are shown for the healthy case and for the first 120 s of the spectrogram of Figure 28b for the damaged case.

Comparing the CWT diagrams of Figure 29 (healthy) and Figure 30 (damaged) without border effects and for the area of interest suggested in the numerical part (scale from 250 to 500), the higher wavelet activity and higher wavelets' coefficients for the damaged case with respect to the healthy case are evident. Additionally, in Figure 30 it can be seen that the highest wavelets' coefficients for the damaged case were obtained for the nearest measurement point to the damage (R2). That is, the location of this measurement was the nearest to the anchor of cable T1S5 on the deck. These results had to alert that the bridge was damaged due to the significant increment of the wavelets' coefficients in relation to the baseline case and had to suggest that damage was located around R2.

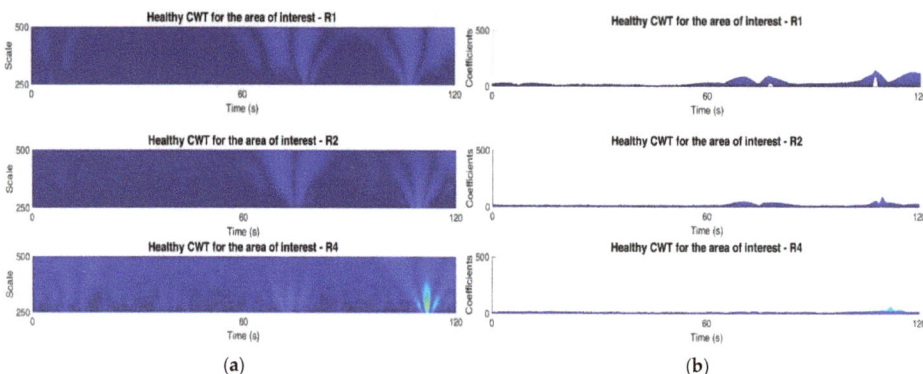

Figure 29. CWT diagrams from filtered experimental signals of healthy bridge for the area of interest: (**a**) Showing the scale in vertical axis and (**b**) showing the coefficients in vertical axis. Three different measurement positions for each one (from top to bottom: R1, R2 and R4).

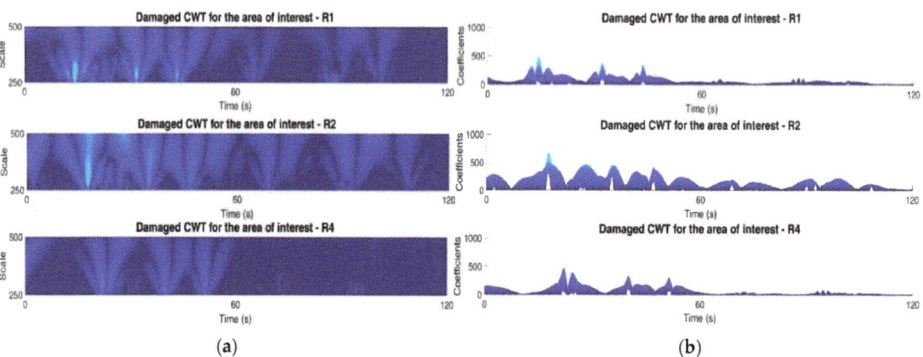

Figure 30. CWT diagrams from filtered experimental signals of damaged cable T1S5 for the area of interest: (**a**) Showing the scale in vertical axis and (**b**) showing the coefficients in vertical axis. Three different measurement positions for each one (from top to bottom: R1, R2, and R4).

As it was mentioned previously, the results of just three measurement points were displayed. However, even considering the rest of the measurements, R2 showed the highest wavelets' coefficients. Additionally, in order to know how big the increment of wavelets' coefficients was at the moment of cable T1S5 collapse, the corresponding CWT diagram is shown in Figure 31. Regardless of the fact that multiple factors included in real data cannot be represented numerically, and that the types of signals were not the same, there is a good agreement about the magnitude of the wavelets' coefficients for numerical and experimental cases of RPB with the damaged cable.

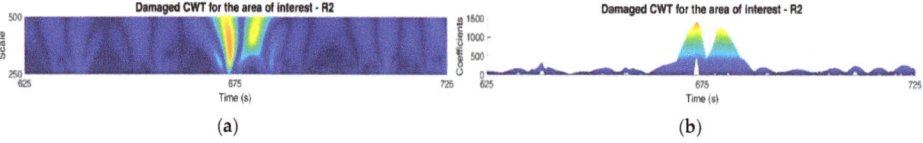

Figure 31. CWT diagram from filtered experimental signal of measurement position R2 around the moment of cable T1S5 collapse: (**a**) Showing the scale in vertical axis and (**b**) showing the coefficients in vertical axis.

Finally, the total WE's obtained from the CWT diagrams of Figures 29 and 30 are shown in Figure 32. In Figure 33, the corresponding total average WE for the healthy and damaged cases are exposed into the same plot. The WE's for single measurements are clearly higher for damaged cases (Figure 32) and the maximum total average WE is almost five times higher for the damaged case with respect to the healthy case (Figure 33). This exercise was additionally made for four different periods of 120 s of the healthy bridge and the damaged cable, and in all the cases the average WE was higher for the damaged bridge and the magnitudes of the maximum average WE's were similar to the ones shown in Figure 33. Then, regardless of the randomness of the traffic, significantly higher WE was observed for the damaged bridge and the detection and localization of the damage was possible. Nevertheless, in future works a controlled test will be performed during the maintenance programs, which involves the removal of cables for changing damaged upper anchoring systems, and, in this way, each step of the proposed method will be carried out for a precise validation.

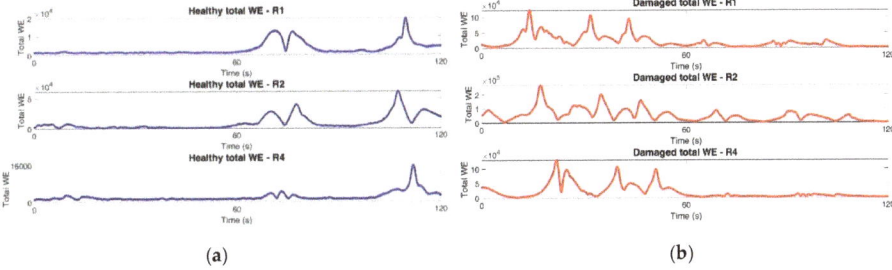

Figure 32. Total WE from filtered experimental signals: (**a**) Healthy bridge and (**b**) damaged cable T1S5. Three different measurement positions for each one (from top to bottom: R1, R2 and R4).

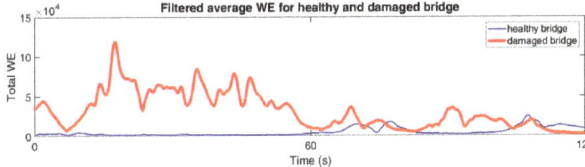

Figure 33. Total average WE from filtered experimental signals for healthy bridge vs. damaged cable T1S5.

Considering the exhaustive and interesting review of bridge monitoring using passing vehicles presented in [37], with a summary table of the most promissory methods for damage detection, the method here proposed has the advantages of detecting, locating (with great accuracy) and quantifying different types of damage on vehicular bridges by using just a few sensors. The disadvantage; however, is the need of performing controlled tests with a low speed vehicle if just a few sensors will be used. Otherwise, if the available data correspond with random traffic, the accuracy for the damage location depends on the quantity of sensors used.

3.3. Results Discussion

As it was observed, the WE was calculated and utilized as a useful tool for identifying damage for the numerical scenarios as well as for the real scenarios. As for the numerical simulations, the WEAM was applied in detail and just a few sensors were required for damage identification with high accuracy. On the other hand, for the real conditions, it was not possible to perform a controlled test in order to follow the methodology step-by-step and the measurements with random traffic were used. Nevertheless, damage identification was also possible by calculating the WE, but the accuracy depended on the number of sensors. Thus, for both cases (numerical and real scenarios), the WE allowed for damage identification; however, in order to use just a few sensors in practical cases, the WEAM must be applied by using a controlled test.

Some of the most promising and recent researches with the same aim of detecting damage (especially damaged cables) in cable-supported bridges can be found in [38–45]. Most of those studies have focused on proposing methods for identifying damage by using only numerical simulations and academic experiments, obtaining an accuracy higher than 60% [38–43]. Despite the promising results, the authors mention that a further investigation of their proposals should be performed under real conditions. On the other hand, other works [44,45] have evaluated the efficacy of their methods under real cable-stayed bridges, reaching an accuracy higher than 90%. For example, in [44] the transfer coefficients method was employed for detecting loosened cables in the Ai-Lan bridge with an accuracy of 95%. The authors mention that its accuracy for evaluating the health condition of the bridge depends on long measurements, which can be a limitation to evaluate the bridge condition in real time. On the other hand, in [45] the global search method to detect and locate a cable loss in the RPB was investigated, where an accuracy of 90% is reached. The authors mention that their work requires use of a finite element model combined with real measurements of the bridge to determinate its condition efficiently. The above mentioned methods presented significant advances in the health monitoring of cable-stayed bridges in the last years. However, the proposed method showed results leading to important advantages over the other methods, since it can be implemented at low cost, was validated with a very detailed numerical model, presented promising results in a real bridge, can detect damage efficiently and locate it with great precision (higher than the other methods), and does not require a numerical model nor a long monitoring period during different seasons of the year. Those characteristics make the method attractive to be implemented in real bridges. Therefore, the future research will be focused on determining the values of the WE for which an alarm should be triggered in the monitoring system due to the presence of damage, so that the method can be implemented in an automatic manner.

4. Conclusions

The application of the WEAM on a detailed FEM model of a cable-stayed bridge (RPB) provided promissory results to detect different kinds of damage, such as damage on deck and cables. The use of a few points of measurement distributed along a bridge to detect damage as well as the accuracy of damage localization make this method attractive to be implemented on real bridges with a low cost. Additionally, the sensitivity of this method to detect damage in early stages and the capability to differentiate diverse positions and severities of damage were demonstrated. The results obtained with real signals acquired from the healthy and damaged RPB suggested that the WEAM could avoid collapses of bridges since a damaged cable was detected and localized by the WE increment, even when the signals were acquired with random traffic and not from a recommendable controlled test (with just one vehicle crossing the bridge with constant and low speed). The future research will be focused on analyzing the effect of the road profile and making the method automatic and capable of differentiating between a damaged deck and a damaged cable.

Author Contributions: Conceptualization, J.M.M.-L., F.J.C.-V. and J.I.V.-D.; investigation, resources, and visualization, J.M.M.-L., F.J.C.-V., J.A.Q.-R. and J.P.A.-S.; funding acquisition and formal analysis, J.M.M.-L., J.P.A.-S., M.V.-R. and F.J.C.-V.; writing—original draft, review, and editing, all authors. All authors have read and agreed to the published version of the manuscript.

Funding: This research was partially funded by the National Council of Science and Technology (Consejo Nacional de Ciencia y Tecnología, CONACYT-Mexico) by project Cátedras CONACYT 34/2018 and project SEP-CONACYT 254697.

Institutional Review Board Statement: Not applicable.

Informed Consent Statement: Not applicable.

Data Availability Statement: Not applicable.

Conflicts of Interest: The authors declare no conflict of interest.

References

1. Kong, X.; Cai, C.S.; Hu, J. The state-of-the-art on framework of vibration-based structural damage identification for decision making. *Appl. Sci.* **2017**, *7*, 1–31.
2. Trimm, M. An overview of nondestructive evaluation methods. *Pract. Fail. Anal.* **2003**, *3*, 17–31. [CrossRef]
3. Chase, S.B. Developing NDT technologies for the next century. In Proceedings of the Structural Materials Technology: An NDT Conference, San Diego, CA, USA, 20–23 February 1996; pp. 13–21.
4. Doebling, S.W.; Farrar, C.R.; Prime, M.B. A summary review of vibration-based damage identification methods. *Shock Vib. Dig.* **1998**, *30*, 91–105. [CrossRef]
5. Davey, M.; Wald, M.L. Potential flaw is found in design of fallen bridge. *The New York Times*, 21 August 2007; Volume 8, 1.
6. AFP. Why the Morandi Bridge collapsed in Genoa, Italy? *El Universal*, 14 August 2018; 1.
7. Golmohamadi, M.; Badri, H.; Ebrahimi, A. Damage diagnosis in bridges using wavelet. In Proceedings of the 2012 IACSIT Coimbatore Conferences, Coimbatore, India, 18–19 February 2012; pp. 202–207.
8. McGetrick, P.J.; Kim, C.W. A parametric study of a drive by bridge inspection system based on the Morlet wavelet. *Key Eng. Mater.* **2013**, *1*, 262–269. [CrossRef]
9. Reddy, M.D.; Swarnamani, S. Structural damage identification using signal processing method. *Int. J. Adv. Struct. Eng.* **2013**, *5*, 5–16. [CrossRef]
10. Walia, S.K.; Patel, P.K.; Vinayak, H.K.; Parti, R. Joint discrepancy evaluation of an existing steel bridge using time-frequency and wavelet-based approach. *Int. J. Adv. Struct. Eng.* **2013**, *5*, 14–25. [CrossRef]
11. Quiñones, M.M.; Montejo, L.A. Experimental and numerical evaluation of wavelet based damage detection methodologies. *Int. J. Adv. Struct. Eng.* **2015**, *7*, 69–80. [CrossRef]
12. Zhu, J.; Sun, Y. Study of a novel wavelet packet energy based damage detection index for bridges. *J. Vib. Meas. Diagn.* **2015**, *35*, 7–22.
13. Li, Q.; Li, D. Structure damage identification under ambient excitation based on wavelet packet analysis. *J. Phys.* **2017**, *842*, 1–12. [CrossRef]
14. Chen, Y.; Oyadiji, S.O. Damage detection using modal frequency curve and squared residual wavelet coefficients-based damage indicator. *Mech. Syst. Sig. Process.* **2017**, *83*, 385–405.
15. Ercolani, G.D.; Félix, D.H.; Ortega, N.F. Damage detection in a bridge board of prestressed concrete by means of the wavelet transform. *Mec. Comp.* **2018**, *36*, 185–193.
16. Gökdağ, H. Wavelet-based damage detection method for a beam-type structure carrying moving mass. *Struct. Eng. Mech.* **2011**, *38*, 81–97. [CrossRef]
17. Khorram, A.; Bakhtiari-Nejad, F.; Rezaeian, M. Comparison studies between two wavelet based crack detection methods of a beam subjected to a moving load. *Int. J. Eng. Sci.* **2012**, *51*, 204–215. [CrossRef]
18. Zhang, W.W.; Geng, J.; Zhao, Z.L.; Wang, Z.H. Numerical studies on wavelet-based crack detection based on velocity response of a beam subjecting to moving load. *Key Eng. Mater.* **2013**, *569*, 854–859. [CrossRef]
19. Khorram, A.; Rezaeian, M.; Bakhtiari-Nejad, F. Multiple cracks detection in a beam subjected to a moving load using wavelet analysis combined with factorial design. *Eur. J. Mech.* **2013**, *40*, 97–113. [CrossRef]
20. McGetrick, P.; Kim, C. A wavelet based drive-by bridge inspection system. In Proceedings of the 7th International Conference on Bridge Maintenance Safety and Management, Shanghai, China, 7–11 July 2014; pp. 1–6.
21. Vaidya, T.; Chatterjee, A. Wavelet analysis of acceleration response of beam under the moving mass for damage assessment. *J. Inst. Eng.* **2016**, *97*, 209–221. [CrossRef]
22. Yu, Z.; Xia, H.; Goicolea, J.M.; Xia, C. Bridge damage identification from moving load induced deflection based on wavelet transform and Lipschitz exponent. *Int. J. Struct. Stab. Dyn.* **2016**, *16*, 1–22. [CrossRef]
23. Janeliukstis, R.; Rucevskis, S.; Wesolowski, M.; Chate, A. Multiple damage identification in beam structure based on wavelet transform. *Procedia Eng.* **2017**, *172*, 426–432. [CrossRef]
24. Ramesh, L.; Rao, P.S. Damage detection in structural beams using model strain energy method and wavelet transform approach. *Mater. Today* **2018**, *5*, 19565–19575. [CrossRef]
25. Bakry, A.; Mourad, S.; Selmy, S. Detection of damage location in beams using discrete wavelet analysis. *EIJEST* **2018**, *26*, 29–37. [CrossRef]
26. Mardasi, A.G.; Wu, N.; Wu, C. Experimental study on the crack detection with optimized spatial wavelet analysis and windowing. *Mech. Syst. Sig. Process.* **2018**, *104*, 619–630. [CrossRef]
27. Zhu, L.F.; Ke, L.L.; Zhu, X.Q.; Xiang, Y.; Wang, Y.S. Crack identification of functionally graded beams using continuous wavelet transform. *Compos. Struct.* **2019**, *210*, 473–485. [CrossRef]
28. He, W.Y.; Zhu, S.; Ren, W.X. Two-phase damage detection of beam structures under moving load using multi-scale wavelet signal processing and wavelet finite element model. *Appl. Math. Modell.* **2019**, *66*, 728–744. [CrossRef]

29. Machorro-López, J.M.; Bellino, A.; Marchesiello, S.; Garibaldi, L. Damage detection for beams subject to moving loads based on wavelet transforms. In Proceedings of the Eleventh International Conference on Computational Structures Technology, Dubrovnik, Croatia, 4–7 September 2012; pp. 1–20.
30. Astiz, M.A. Composite construction in cable-stayed bridge towers. In Proceedings of the International Conference on Composite Construction-Conventional and Innovative, Conference Report, Innsbruck, Austria, 16–18 September 1997; pp. 127–132.
31. ASTM Standard A148/A148M-15a. In *Standard Specification for Steel Castings, High Strength, for Structural Purposes*; ASTM International: West Conshohocken, PA, USA, 2015.
32. Aguirre, A.; Carbajal, J. *Failure Analysis of Cable 11 of the Papaloapan Bridge*; Report; COMIMSA: Saltillo, Mexico, 2000.
33. López, A.; Poblano, C. *Failure Analysis and Fatigue Tests of the Failed Anchoring Element of Rio Papaloapan Bridge Cable 11, Landside, Tower 3*; Report; Mexican Institute of Transportation: Queretaro, Mexico, 2000.
34. Terán, J.; Martínez, M. *Failure Analysis of the Anchoring Element of Cable 1 Semi-Harp 5*; Report; Mexican Institute of Transportation: Queretaro, Mexico, 2015.
35. Liew, K.; Wang, Q. Application of wavelet theory for crack identification in structures. *J. Eng. Mech.* **1998**, *124*, 152–157. [CrossRef]
36. Liu, C.L. *A Tutorial of the Wavelet Transform*; NTUEE: Taipei, Taiwan, 2010; pp. 25–28.
37. Malekjafarian, A.; McGetrick, P.; Obrien, E. A review of indirect bridge monitoring using passing vehicles. *J. Shock Vib.* **2014**, *2015*, 1–16. [CrossRef]
38. Ni, Y.Q.; Zhou, H.F.; Chan, K.C.; Ko, J.M. Modal flexibility analysis of cable-stayed Ting Kau bridge for damage identification. *Comput. Aided Civ. Infrastruct. Eng.* **2008**, *23*, 223–236. [CrossRef]
39. Santos, J.P.; Cremona, C.; Orcesi, A.D.; Silveira, P. Early damage detection based on pattern recognition and data fusion. *J. Struct. Eng.* **2016**, *143*, 1–11. [CrossRef]
40. Ho, H.N.; Kim, K.D.; Park, Y.S.; Lee, J.J. An efficient image-based damage detection for cable surface in cable-stayed bridges. *Nondestruct. Test. Eva.* **2013**, *58*, 18–23. [CrossRef]
41. Scarella, A.; Salamone, G.; Babanajad, S.K.; De Stefano, A.; Ansari, F. Dynamic Brillouin scattering–based condition assessment of cables in cable-stayed bridges. *J. Bridge Eng.* **2017**, *22*, 1–12. [CrossRef]
42. An, Y.; Zhong, Y.; Tan, Y.; Ou, J. Experimental and numerical studies on a test method for damage diagnosis of stay cables. *Adv. Struct. Eng.* **2016**, *20*, 1–12. [CrossRef]
43. Meng, F.; Mokrani, B.; Alaluf, D.; Yu, J.; Preumont, A. Damage detection in active suspension bridges: An experimental investigation. *Sensors* **2018**, *18*, 3002. [CrossRef] [PubMed]
44. Chen, C.C.; Wu, W.H.; Liu, C.Y.; Lai, G. Damage detection of a cable-stayed bridge based on the variation of stay cable forces eliminating environmental temperature effects. *Smart Struct. Syst.* **2016**, *17*, 859–880. [CrossRef]
45. Quintana, J.A.; Carrion, F.; Crespo, S. Damage detection on a cable stayed bridge using wave propagation analysis. In Proceedings of the 7th European Workshop on Structural Health Monitoring, Nantes, France, 8–11 July 2014; pp. 2052–2059.

Article

Local Convergence of the Continuous and Semi-Discrete Wavelet Transform in $L^p(\mathbb{R})$

Jaime Navarro-Fuentes [1], Salvador Arellano-Balderas [1] and Oscar Herrera-Alcántara [2,*]

[1] Departamento de Ciencias Básicas, Universidad Autónoma Metropolitana, Mexico City 02200, Mexico; jnfu@azc.uam.mx (J.N.-F.); sab@azc.uam.mx (S.A.-B.)
[2] Departamento de Sistemas, Universidad Autónoma Metropolitana, Mexico City 02200, Mexico
* Correspondence: oha@azc.uam.mx

Abstract: The smoothness of functions f in the space $L^p(\mathbb{R})$ with $1 < p < \infty$ is studied through the local convergence of the continuous wavelet transform of f. Additionally, we study the smoothness of functions in $L^p(\mathbb{R})$ by means of the local convergence of the semi-discrete wavelet transform.

Keywords: admissibility condition; the continuous wavelet transform; inversion formula; semi-discrete wavelet transform; tight frames

1. Introduction

In order to study the local regularity of functions in $L^2(\mathbb{R})$ by means of the local convergence of the continuous wavelet transform (CWT), we apply its inversion formula, which is usually considered in the weak sense [1]. The same concept is applied for the case of CWT with rotations in $L^2(R^n)$ [2]. Concerning distributions u with compact support, the regular points of u can be found again by using the convergence of the CWT by means of the $L^2 - machinery$, [3].

When we move to the space $L^p(\mathbb{R}^n)$, the inversion formula for the CWT is obtained with norm convergence in $L^p(\mathbb{R}^n)$, where $1 \leq p < \infty$, [4,5]. For a.e. convergence in $L^p(\mathbb{R}^n), 1 < p < \infty$, see [6]. For the convergence at every Lebesgue point x for functions in $L^p(\mathbb{R}^n), 1 \leq p < \infty$, see [7], and for the convergence on the entire Lebesgue set of $f \in L^p(\mathbb{R}), 1 \leq p < \infty$, see [8]. Moreover, in [9,10], the continuous wavelet transform $L_h : L^p(\mathbb{R}) \to L^p(\mathbb{R}, L^2((0, \infty), \frac{da}{a})) := W^p, 1 < p < \infty$ with respect to a *wavelet* $h \in L^1(\mathbb{R}) \cap L^2(\mathbb{R})$ is a bounded linear operator and

$$\|L_h f\|_{W^p} := \left(\int_{\mathbb{R}} \left[\int_0^\infty |(L_h f)(a,b)|^2 \frac{da}{a} \right]^{\frac{p}{2}} db \right)^{\frac{1}{p}} \leq A_p \|f\|_p,$$

where A_p depends on p and h.

For the discrete wavelet transform, wavelets become an unconditional bases for $L^p(\mathbb{R})$, $1 < p < \infty$. Thus, there is a characterization for functions in $L^p(\mathbb{R})$ using only absolute values of the wavelet coefficients of f, [11].

In this paper, we extend the results of local regularity of functions $f \in L^2(\mathbb{R})$ to the space $L^p(\mathbb{R})$, $1 < p < \infty$, by means of the local convergence of the CWT. To study the regularity of functions in $L^p(\mathbb{R})$, $1 < p < \infty$ via the CWT, we give the necessary conditions to define the CWT for f in $L^p(\mathbb{R})$ with respect to an *admissible* function h in $L^1(\mathbb{R}) \cap L^2(\mathbb{R})$.

Finally, we introduce the semi-discrete wavelet transform (SDWT) to show that there is a relationship between the local regularity of functions in $L^p(\mathbb{R})$ and the local convergence of the SDWT. That is, if the dilation parameter takes only discrete values, namely $a := a^m$, where a is fixed and $a > 1$ with $m \in \mathbb{Z}$, and the translation parameter b is any value in $\mathbb{R}$, we get the SDWT. With respect to the reconstruction formula in the semi-discrete case, we will consider two functions, h_1 and h_2, instead of one h, one for the decomposition and the

other one for the inversion formula, in such a way that the admissibility condition will depend on h_1 and h_2 [12,13].

This research led us to establish a relationship between the local existence of the limit of derivatives for the CWT and SDWT, and the derivatives of functions in $L^p(\mathbb{R})$.

Some experiments are included to illustrate our results. In particular, we study the sigmoidal function, widely used in artificial neural networks, since its derivatives can be expressed in terms of itself and Stirling numbers of second order, that allow us to implement computer experiments to show graphical representations of the wavelet transform behaviour.

The reported results become relevant in research areas such as analytical chemistry, where wavelet functions can be used for derivative calculation through CWT [14,15], neural networks with wavelets to extract features from data [16], and to propose novel architectures [17], image processing with wavelets, where all their derivatives are admissible functions, such as the Beta function [18], computer vision via Shearlet Networks that take advantage of sparse representations of shearlets in biometric applications [19], and its convergence properties [20,21], as well as differential equations for numerical solutions [22], among other areas. Indeed, one of the projections of the results shown in this paper can be applied, for example, to study the regularity of weak solutions under elliptic partial differential operators.

2. Notations and Definitions

In this section, we give the definition for an admissible function. We also define the continuous wavelet transform for functions in $L^p(\mathbb{R})$, where $1 < p < \infty$ with respect to an admissible function, and we give the inversion formula for the continuous wavelet transform.

Definition 1. *For h in $L^1(\mathbb{R}) \cap L^2(\mathbb{R})$, the dilation operator J_a and the translation operator T_b are defined respectively, as:*

(1) $(J_a h)(x) = a^{-1} h(a^{-1} x)$, where $a > 0$ and $x \in \mathbb{R}$,
(2) $(T_b h)(x) = h(x - b)$, where $x, b \in \mathbb{R}$.

Notice that $J_a h$ and $T_b h$ are also in $L^1(\mathbb{R}) \cap L^2(\mathbb{R})$. In fact, $\|J_a h\|_1 = \|h\|_1$. The admissibility condition is now given.

Definition 2. *The function h in $L^1(\mathbb{R}) \cap L^2(\mathbb{R})$ is admissible (wavelet) if*

$$0 < C_h := \int_{\mathbb{R}^+} \frac{|\widehat{h}(w)|^2}{w} dw < \infty, \tag{1}$$

where $\widehat{h}$ is the Fourier transform of h, and where $\mathbb{R}^+ = (0, \infty)$.

Remark 1. *Following (1), note that if $h \in C_0^\infty(\mathbb{R})$, then $h^{(n)}$ is admissible if and only if*

$$C_{h^{(n)}} = (2\pi)^{2n} \int_{\mathbb{R}^+} w^{2n-1} |\widehat{h}(w)|^2 dw < \infty. \tag{2}$$

Given the admissibility condition, we extend the continuous wavelet transform on $L^2(\mathbb{R}, dx)$ to $L^p(\mathbb{R}, dx)$, where $1 < p < \infty$, and interpret its images as elements of the space W^p, as above. For this, we give the following definition.

Definition 3. *Consider a measurable set X with measure μ and a Banach space B with norm $\|\cdot\|_B$. The space $L^p((X, d\mu); (B, \|\cdot\|_B))$ consists of those elements, $F : X \to B$, F is strongly measurable and such that*

$$\int_X \|F(x)\|_B^p d\mu(x) < \infty.$$

According to Definition 3, if $X = \mathbb{R}$ is a measurable space with measure db and $B = L^2(\mathbb{R}^+, \frac{da}{a})$ is a normed space with norm $\|\cdot\|_2$, then

$$W^p := L^p\left((\mathbb{R}, db); L^2(\mathbb{R}^+, \frac{da}{a})\right)$$

consists of those elements $F(\cdot, b) \in L^2(\mathbb{R}^+, \frac{da}{a})$ such that

$$\int_{\mathbb{R}} \|F(\cdot, b)\|_{L^2(\mathbb{R}^+, \frac{da}{a})}^p db < \infty.$$

In this case,

$$\|F\|_{W^p} := \left(\int_{\mathbb{R}} \|F(\cdot, b)\|_{L^2(\mathbb{R}^+, \frac{da}{a})}^p db\right)^{\frac{1}{p}} = \left(\int_{\mathbb{R}} \left(\int_{\mathbb{R}^+} |F(a, b)|^2 \frac{da}{a}\right)^{\frac{p}{2}} db\right)^{\frac{1}{p}}. \tag{3}$$

Thus, by using the space W^p, we give the definition of the continuous wavelet transform for functions in $L^p(\mathbb{R})$ with respect to an admissible function in $L^1(\mathbb{R}) \cap L^2(\mathbb{R})$.

Definition 4. *Let f be in $L^p(\mathbb{R})$ with $1 < p < \infty$. Consider $a > 0$ and $b \in \mathbb{R}$. Let h be an admissible function in $L^1(\mathbb{R}) \cap L^2(\mathbb{R})$. The continuous wavelet transform of f with respect to h is defined as the map*

$$L_h : L^p(\mathbb{R}, dx) \to W^p$$

so that

$$(L_h f)(a, b) = \int_{\mathbb{R}} f(x) \overline{T_b J_a h(x)} dx = \int_{\mathbb{R}} f(x) \frac{1}{a} \overline{h\left(\frac{x-b}{a}\right)} dx. \tag{4}$$

Note that the continuous wavelet transform can be written as

$$(L_h f)(a, b) = \left[(J_a \overline{h})^\sim * f\right](b), \tag{5}$$

where $*$ means convolution and $h^\sim$ means $h^\sim(x) = h(-x)$.

Remark 2. *According to (5), and since $J_a h \in L^1(\mathbb{R})$ and $f \in L^p(\mathbb{R})$, it follows from Young's Inequality that $(J_a \overline{h})^\sim * f \in L^p(\mathbb{R})$ and $\|(J_a \overline{h})^\sim * f\|_p \leq \|h\|_1 \|f\|_p$. That is,*

$$\|(L_h f)(a, \cdot)\|_p \leq \|h\|_1 \|f\|_p.$$

Additionally, note that from (3),

$$\|L_h f\|_{W^p} = \left(\int_{\mathbb{R}} \|L_h f(\cdot, b)\|_{L^2(\mathbb{R}^+, \frac{da}{a})}^p db\right)^{\frac{1}{p}} = \left(\int_{\mathbb{R}} \left(\int_{\mathbb{R}^+} |(L_h f)(a, b)|^2 \frac{da}{a}\right)^{\frac{p}{2}} db\right)^{\frac{1}{p}},$$

where

$$\|L_h f\|_{W^p} \leq A_p \|f\|_p,$$

and where the constant A_p depends only on p and h. Thus, the continuous wavelet transform is a bounded linear operator, [10].

The inversion formula of the continuous wavelet transform for f in $L^p(\mathbb{R})$ with $1 < p < \infty$ is now given.

Lemma 1. *Consider $f \in L^p(\mathbb{R})$ with $1 < p < \infty$, and $h \in L^1(\mathbb{R}) \cap L^2(\mathbb{R})$ admissible with real values. Then,*

$$f(x) = \frac{1}{C_h} \int_{\mathbb{R}^+} \int_{\mathbb{R}} (L_h f)(a, b) h\left(\frac{x-b}{a}\right) db \frac{da}{a^2}. \tag{6}$$

The equality holds in the L^p sense, and the integrals on the right-hand side have to be taken in the sense of distributions.

Proof. See [10]. □

3. Convergence of the Continuous Wavelet Transform in $L^p(\mathbb{R})$

First, we give a result about the derivative of the continuous wavelet transform with respect to the translation parameter $b \in \mathbb{R}$.

Lemma 2. *If $f \in L^p(\mathbb{R})$ with $1 < p < \infty$ and if $h \in C_0^\infty(\mathbb{R})$ is admissible, then for any integer $n > 0$, $h^{(n)}$ is admissible. Moreover,*

$$\frac{\partial^n}{\partial b^n}(L_h f)(a,b) = \frac{(-1)^n}{a^n}(L_{h^{(n)}} f)(a,b). \tag{7}$$

Proof. From (5), and since $f \in L^p(\mathbb{R})$ and $h \in C_0^\infty(\mathbb{R})$, then $(J_a \overline{h})^\sim * f \in C^\infty(\mathbb{R})$, and

$$\frac{\partial^n}{\partial b^n}\left[(J_a \overline{h})^\sim * f\right](b) = \left[\frac{\partial^n}{\partial b^n}(J_a \overline{h})^\sim * f\right](b) = \frac{(-1)^n}{a^n}\left[(J_a \overline{h^{(n)}})^\sim * f\right](b). \tag{8}$$

This proves Lemma 2. □

Then, we have the following result.

Lemma 3. *Suppose that $h \in C_0^\infty(\mathbb{R})$ is a non-zero function where $\widehat{h}(0) = 0$. Consider f in $L^p(\mathbb{R})$, $1 < p < \infty$. If f is of class C^∞ in a neighborhood of $x = b_0$ in $\mathbb{R}$, then for each non-negative integer n, we have the existence of $\lim_{(a,b) \to (0,b_1)} (W_h^n f)(a,b)$ for each b_1 in a neighborhood of $b_0 \in \mathbb{R}$, where*

$$(W_h^n f)(a,b) := \frac{1}{a}\frac{\partial^n}{\partial b^n}(L_h f)(a,b). \tag{9}$$

Proof. Suppose f is C^∞ in a neighborhood of $x = b_0$ containing $[b_0 - \epsilon, b_0 + \epsilon]$, where $\epsilon > 0$. Take b_1 in $(b_0 - \epsilon/2, b_0 + \epsilon/2)$ and choose b in $(b_0 - \epsilon/2, b_0 + \epsilon/2)$.

Now since $h \in C_0^\infty(\mathbb{R})$, there is $L > 0$ such that $\text{supp}\, h \subset [-L, L]$. Then, for $a \in (0, \epsilon/2L)$, we have $[b - aL, b + aL] \subset [b_0 - \epsilon, b_0 + \epsilon]$. Hence, f is C^∞ in $[b - aL, b + aL]$.

Following Lemma 2, and since $f \in L^p(\mathbb{R})$, it follows from (4) that,

$$(W_h^n f)(a,b) = \frac{1}{a}\frac{(-1)^n}{a^n}\int_{b-aL}^{b+aL} f(x)\frac{1}{a}\overline{h^{(n)}}\left(\frac{x-b}{a}\right)dx = \frac{1}{a}\int_{-L}^{L} f^{(n)}(b+ay)\overline{h(y)}\,dy. \tag{10}$$

Since f is C^∞ at points in the region of integration, then for y in $[-L, L]$,

$$f^{(n)}(b+ay) = f^{(n)}(b) + ay\, f^{(n+1)}(b) + \int_b^{b+ay}(b+ay-t)f^{(n+2)}(t)\,dt.$$

Hence,

$$(W_h^n f)(a,b) = \frac{1}{a}f^{(n)}(b)\int_{-L}^{L}\overline{h(y)}\,dy + f^{(n+1)}(b)\int_{-L}^{L} y\,\overline{h(y)}\,dy + R(a,b),$$

where

$$R(a,b) = \frac{1}{a}\int_{-L}^{L}\left(\int_b^{b+ay}(b+ay-t)f^{(n+2)}(t)\,dt\right)\overline{h(y)}\,dy.$$

Now, set $M = \sup_{x \in [b_0-\epsilon,b_0+\epsilon]}|f^{(n+2)}(x)|$. Then,

$$|R(a,b)| \leq \frac{1}{2}aM\int_{-L}^{L} y^2 |h(y)|\,dy.$$

Thus, $R(a,b) \to 0$ as $(a,b) \to (0,b_1)$ for any b_1 in $(b_0 - \epsilon/2, b_0 + \epsilon/2)$.
Then, since $\hat{h}(0) = 0$ and since $f^{(n+1)}$ is continuous near b_1, we have

$$(\mathcal{W}_h^n f)(a,b) \to f^{(n+1)}(b_1) \int_{-L}^{L} y \overline{h(y)}\, dy \quad \text{as} \quad (a,b) \to (0,b_1). \tag{11}$$

□

4. Main Result 1

Now, let us prove the converse of Lemma 3, which is our first main result.

Theorem 1. *Suppose $h \in C_0^\infty(\mathbb{R})$ satisfies condition (1). Consider f in $L^p(\mathbb{R})$ with $1 < p < \infty$. If, for each non-negative integer n, the limit of $(\mathcal{W}_h^n f)(a,b)$ exists as $(a,b) \to (0,b_1)$ for each b_1 in an open neighborhood of $x = b_0 \in \mathbb{R}$, then f is of class C^∞ in an open neighborhood of $b_0 \in \mathbb{R}$.*

Proof. Suppose that for each non-negative integer n,

$$F_h^n(b_1) := \lim_{(a,b) \to (0,b_1)} (\mathcal{W}_h^n f)(a,b)$$

exists for each b_1 in an open neighborhood containing the closed interval $[b_0 - B, b_0 + B]$, where $B > 0$.

Now, for fixed x in $[b_0 - B, b_0 + B]$ and $y \in \mathbb{R}$, let

$$(\mathcal{I}_h^n f)(a,x,y) = \begin{cases} h(-y)(\mathcal{W}_h^n f)(a, x+ay) & \text{if } a > 0 \\ h(-y) F_h^n(x) & \text{if } a = 0. \end{cases}$$

Note that for x in $[b_0 - B, b_0 + B]$, the function $\mathcal{I}_h^n f$ is well-defined for all $a \geq 0$ and all y in $\mathbb{R}$. Furthermore, for fixed $y \in \mathbb{R}$ and $a \neq 0$, the function $\mathcal{I}_h^n f$ is infinitely differentiable in the variable x by virtue of the definition of $\mathcal{W}_h^n f$.

Then we have the following Lemma (see Appendix A for the proof).

Lemma 4. *For x in $(b_0 - B, b_0 + B)$, let*

$$w(x) = \int_0^\infty \int_{\mathbb{R}} (\mathcal{I}_h^0 f)(a,x,y)\, dy\, da,$$

and let

$$(I_h^n f)(x) = \int_0^\infty \int_{\mathbb{R}} (\mathcal{I}_h^n f)(a,x,y)\, dy\, da.$$

Then for each non-negative integer n,

$$\frac{d^n}{dx^n} w(x) = (I_h^n f)(x). \tag{12}$$

That is, the function w is of class C^∞ on $(b_0 - B, b_0 + B)$.

Back to the proof of Theorem 1, for any x in $\mathbb{R}$ and $\lambda > 0$, define

$$u_\lambda(x) := \int_{\frac{1}{\lambda}}^{\lambda} \int_{\mathbb{R}} h(-y) \frac{1}{a} (L_h f)(a, x+ay)\, dy\, da.$$

Then from Lemma 4, for $x \in (b_0 - B, b_0 + B)$,

$$\lim_{\lambda \to \infty} u_\lambda(x) = w(x).$$

That is, $u_\lambda \to w$ pointwise on $(b_0 - B, b_0 + B)$ as $\lambda \to \infty$.

On the other hand, by (6), we have $u_\lambda \to C_h f$ in the L^p sense as $\lambda \to \infty$. Then, $f = (C_h)^{-1} w$ almost everywhere on $(b_0 - B, b_0 + B)$.

Finally, since from (12) the function w is C^∞ on $(b_0 - B, b_0 + B)$, it follows that f is of class C^∞ on $(b_0 - B, b_0 + B)$. □

5. The Semi-Discrete Wavelet Transform

In this section, we define the semi-discrete wavelet transform (SDWT) of functions $f \in L^p(\mathbb{R})$, and we will prove the local convergence of the SDWT of f via the local regularity of f. For this purpose, we will use the reconstruction formula given in [12]. Thus, we will define the corresponding dilation operator for discrete values.

Definition 5. *For a function $h \in L^1(\mathbb{R}) \cap L^2(\mathbb{R})$, and for fixed $a > 1$, the dilation operator J_{a^m} is now given by*

$$(J_{a^m} h)(x) = \frac{1}{a^m} h\left(\frac{x}{a^m}\right), \quad \text{where} \quad m \in \mathbb{Z}, \quad \text{and} \quad x \in \mathbb{R}. \tag{13}$$

Thus, we have the following definition for the semi-discrete wavelet transform for functions in $L^p(\mathbb{R})$.

Definition 6. *Suppose that h in $L^1(\mathbb{R}) \cap L^2(\mathbb{R})$ is an admissible function. Then, the semi-discrete wavelet transform for a function f in $L^p(\mathbb{R})$ with respect to h is defined as:*

$$(L_h f)(a^m, b) = \left((J_{a^m} \overline{h})^\sim * f\right)(b) = \int_\mathbb{R} f(x) \frac{1}{a^m} \overline{h}\left(\frac{x-b}{a^m}\right) dx, \tag{14}$$

where $a > 1$ is fixed, $m \in \mathbb{Z}$, and $b \in \mathbb{R}$.

See [12] for Remark 3 with N any natural number. In this paper, $N = 1$.

Remark 3. *In order to get a reconstruction formula for the semi-discrete wavelet transform in $L^p(\mathbb{R})$, a function $h \in L^2(\mathbb{R})$ must satisfy the following condition: Given an Unconditional Martingale Difference (UMD) space X with Fourier type $r \in (1, 2]$ and $l := [1/r] + 1$, for all $\alpha \in \{0, 1\}$ with $|\alpha| \leq l$ and $a > 1$, the distributional derivatives $D^\alpha \overline{h}$ are represented by measurable functions, and*

$$Sup_{1 \leq |\omega| < a} \left(\sum_{m \in \mathbb{Z}} a^{2m|\alpha|} |(D^\alpha \overline{\widehat{h}})(a^m \omega)|^2\right)^{1/2} < \infty. \tag{15}$$

Remark 4 (Reconstruction formula, see [12]). *Suppose that $h_1, h_2 \in L^1(\mathbb{R}) \cap L^2(\mathbb{R})$ are admissible and satisfy the condition (15) with*

$$\sum_{m=-\infty}^{\infty} \widehat{h_2}(a^m \omega) \overline{\widehat{h_1}}(a^m \omega) = 1 \tag{16}$$

for almost all $\omega \in \mathbb{R} \setminus \{0\}$. Then for any $f \in L^p(\mathbb{R}), 1 < p < \infty$,

$$f = \frac{1}{2\pi} \sum_{m=-\infty}^{\infty} (J_{a^m} h_2) * (J_{a^m} \widetilde{\overline{h_1}}) * f, \tag{17}$$

where the equality holds in the L^p sense. In this paper, Formulas (15)–(17) based on [12] have been adapted to match with our nomenclature on the wavelet transform definition.

Then we have the following result concerning the continuity of the semi-discrete wavelet transform.

Note 1. *From Definition 6, if $f \in L^p(\mathbb{R})$ and h in $C_0(\mathbb{R})$ is admissible, then $(L_h f)(a^m, b)$ is continuous at (a^{m_1}, b_1) for all $(m_1, b_1) \in \mathbb{Z} \times \mathbb{R}$.*

6. Main Result 2

Now we give our second main result. That is, we will prove the existence of the limit of $(\mathcal{W}_{h_1}^n f)(a^m, b) := \frac{1}{a^m} \frac{\partial^n}{\partial b^n}(L_{h_1} f)(a^m, b)$ as $(a^m, b) \to (0, b_1)$ for any b_1 in a neighborhood of some point $x = b_0$ under the hypothesis that f is of class C^∞ in a neighborhood of $x = b_0$, and where h_1 is admissible in $C_0^\infty(\mathbb{R})$. Note that $a^m \to 0$ if and only if $m \to -\infty$. Thus, we have the following result.

Theorem 2. *Suppose $h_1, h_2 \in C_0^\infty(\mathbb{R})$ are admissible functions that satisfy the condition (16). Consider $f \in L^p(\mathbb{R}), 1 < p < \infty$. Then f is C^∞ in a neighborhood of $x = b_0$ if, and only if for each non-negative integer n,*

$$\lim_{(m,b) \to (-\infty, b_1)} (\mathcal{W}_{h_1}^n f)(a^m, b) \text{ exists for each } b_1 \text{ in a neighborhood of } x = b_0.$$

Proof. First, suppose f is C^∞ in a neighborhood of $x = b_0$. Then by Lemma 3, it follows that for each non-negative integer n,

$$\lim_{(m,b) \to (-\infty, b_1)} (\mathcal{W}_{h_1}^n f)(a^m, b) \text{ exists for each } b_1 \text{ in a neighborhood of } x = b_0.$$

This completes the proof of the first part of Theorem 2.

For the second part, we will use similar arguments to the ones given in the proof of Theorem 1. Suppose then that for each non-negative integer n,

$$\lim_{(m,b) \to (-\infty, b_1)} (\mathcal{W}_{h_1}^n f)(a^m, b) := S_{h_1}^n(b_1)$$

exists for each b_1 in an open neighborhood containing the closed interval $[b_0 - B, b_0 + B], B > 0$.

Then we have the following Lemma (see Appendix A for the proof).

Lemma 5. *For any x in $(b_0 - B, b_0 + B)$, let*

$$v(x) := \sum_{m=-\infty}^{\infty} ((J_{a^m} h_2) * (J_{a^m} \widetilde{h_1}) * f)(x),$$

and let

$$v_n(x) = \sum_{m=-\infty}^{\infty} ((J_{a^m} h_2) * \frac{\partial^n}{\partial x^n}(J_{a^m} \widetilde{h_1}) * f)(x).$$

Then for any non-negative integer n, we have

$$\frac{d^n}{dx^n} v(x) = v_n(x).$$

That is, the function v is of class C^∞ on $(b_0 - B, b_0 + B)$.

Now, back to the proof of Theorem 2, for an integer $M \geq 0$ and any x in $(b_0 - B, b_0 + B)$, define

$$V_M(x) := \sum_{m=-M}^{M} ((J_{a^m} h_2) * (J_{a^m} \widetilde{h_1}) * f)(x). \tag{18}$$

Then by Lemma 5, for any $x \in (b_0 - B, b_0 + B)$,

$$\lim_{M \to \infty} V_M(x) = v(x).$$

That is, $V_M \to v$ pointwise as $M \to \infty$.

On the other hand, from the reconstruction formula given in (17),

$$f(x) = \frac{1}{2\pi} \sum_{m=-\infty}^{\infty} ((J_a^m h_2) * (J_a^m \overline{h_1^{\sim}} * f))(x),$$

hence, we have $V_M \to (2\pi)f$ as $M \to \infty$ for almost every x in $(b_0 - B, b_0 + B)$.

That is, $f = (2\pi)^{-1} v$ pointwise almost everywhere. Thus, by Lemma 5, the function f is of class C^∞ on $(b_0 - \frac{B}{2}, b_0 + \frac{B}{2})$.

This completes the proof of Theorem 2. □

7. Examples

Example 1. *First we give an example for Lemma 3. Let $Q > 1$ be a constant and consider the logistic function*

$$f(x) = \begin{cases} \frac{1}{1+e^{-x}}, & x \in [-Q, Q] \\ 0, & \text{otherwise}. \end{cases}$$

Then $f \in L^p(\mathbb{R})$, $1 < p < \infty$ and f is of class $C^\infty(\mathbb{R})$ in any neighborhood of $x = b_0$ with $b_0 \in (-Q, Q)$. As an admissible function consider the Haar function $h(x)$. Then $\operatorname{supp} h = [0, 1]$, and hence $h \in L^1(\mathbb{R})$.

Then from (10),

$$(W_h^n f)(a, b) = \frac{1}{a} \int_0^1 f^{(n)}(b + ay) \overline{h(y)} \, dy$$

$$= \frac{1}{a} \int_0^{\frac{1}{2}} f^{(n)}(b + ay) \, dy - \frac{1}{a} \int_{\frac{1}{2}}^1 f^{(n)}(b + ay) \, dy$$

$$= \frac{1}{a^2} \left[f^{(n-1)}(b + ay) \right]_0^{\frac{1}{2}} - \frac{1}{a^2} \left[f^{(n-1)}(b + ay) \right]_{\frac{1}{2}}^1$$

$$= \frac{2 f^{(n-1)}(b + \frac{a}{2}) - f^{(n-1)}(b) - f^{(n-1)}(b + a)}{a^2}.$$

By using the Taylor series with integral remainder

$$f^{(n-1)}(b + at) = f^{(n-1)}(b) + at\, f^{(n)}(b) + \frac{1}{2} a^2 t^2 \, f^{(n+1)}(b) + \\ \frac{1}{2} \int_b^{b+at} (b + at - \xi) f^{(n+2)}(\xi) d\xi,$$

and then taking $t = \frac{1}{2}$ and $t = 1$, we have

$$\frac{2 f^{(n-1)}(b + \frac{a}{2}) - f^{(n-1)}(b) - f^{(n-1)}(b + a)}{a^2} \to -\frac{1}{4} f^{(n+1)}(b_1) \quad \text{as} \quad (a, b) \to (0, b_1).$$

This result matches with (11) and shows that for any positive integer n and any b_1 in a neighborhood of $x = b_0$, a limit of $(W_h^n f)(a, b)$ exists as $(a, b) \to (0, b_1)$. Note that despite $h(x)$ having no derivatives, the result is consistent with Lemma 3. This example suggests that the results could apply with other wavelets that are not smooth.

According to [23], we can express $f^{(n+1)}(x)$ as a function of $f(x)$. In this case,

$$\lim_{(a,b) \to (0, b_1)} (W_h^n f)(a, b) = -\frac{1}{4} \sum_{k=1}^{n+2} (-1)^{k-1} (k-1)! \, S(n+2, k) [f(b_1)]^k, \qquad (19)$$

where $S(n+2, k)$ are the Stirling numbers of the second kind.

In fact, logistic function is widely used in the context of artificial neural networks [24–26] because of its mathematical properties. Figures 1–5 show the $(n+1)$-th derivatives of $f(x)$ and the n-th derivatives of $(-\mathcal{W}_h f)(a,b)$ for $n = 0, 1, 2, 6,$ and 7. We are plotting $(-\mathcal{W}_h f)(a,b)$ to illustrate that graphs in 2D and 3D match. Left sides show 2D plots with the same behaviour as the 3D plots of the right sides given the regularity of this function, as is indicated by Lemma 3.

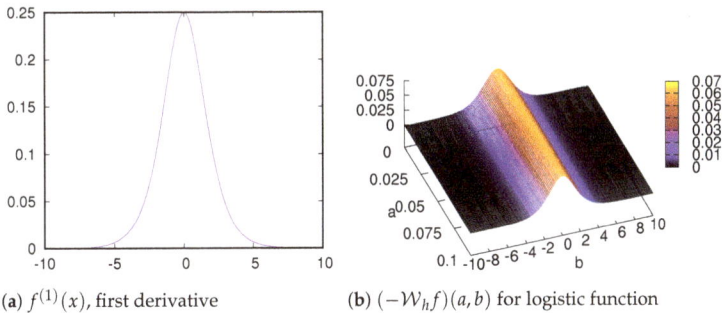

Figure 1. Relationship between $f^{(n+1)}(x)$ and $-\mathcal{W}_h^{(n)} f)(a,b)$, $n = 0$.

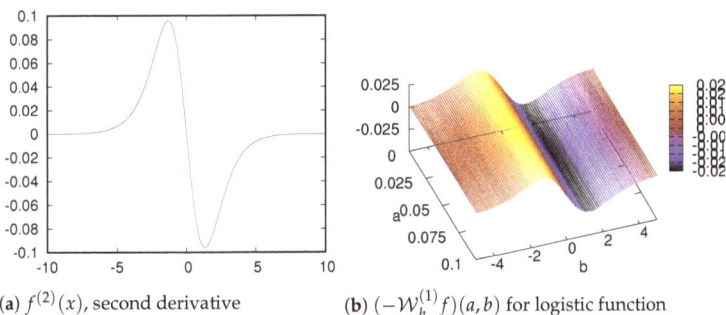

Figure 2. Relationship between $f^{(n+1)}(x)$ and $-\mathcal{W}_h^{(n)} f)(a,b)$, $n = 1$.

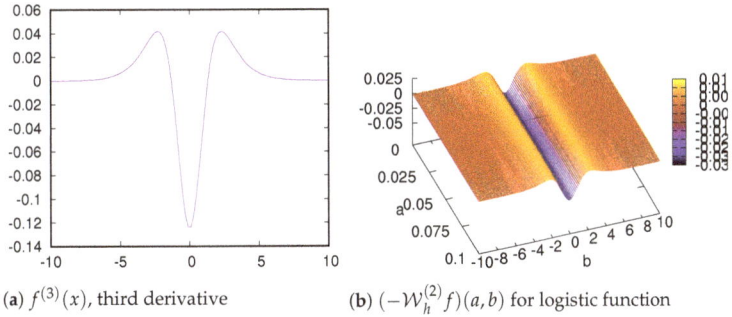

Figure 3. Relationship between $f^{(n+1)}(x)$ and $-\mathcal{W}_h^{(n)} f)(a,b)$, $n = 2$.

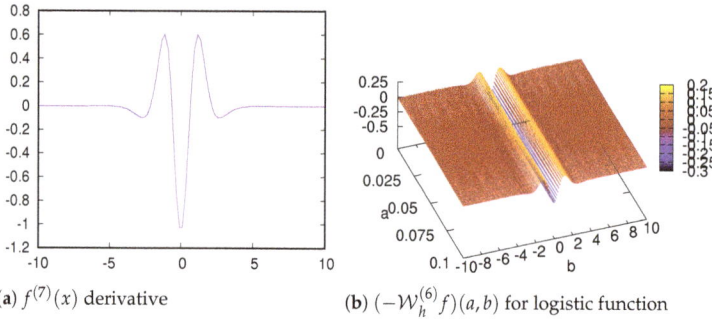

(a) $f^{(7)}(x)$ derivative

(b) $(-\mathcal{W}_h^{(6)} f)(a,b)$ for logistic function

Figure 4. Relationship between $f^{(n+1)}(x)$ and $-\mathcal{W}_h^{(n)} f(a,b)$, $n = 6$.

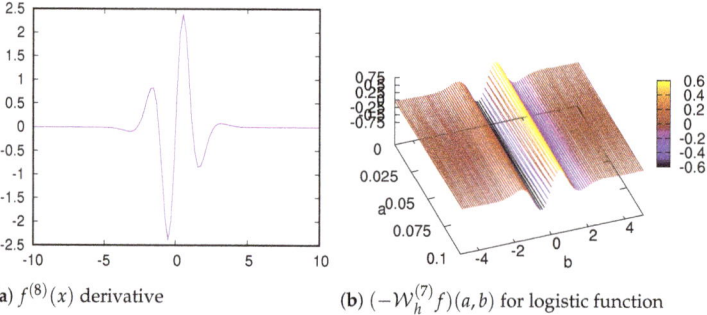

(a) $f^{(8)}(x)$ derivative

(b) $(-\mathcal{W}_h^{(7)} f)(a,b)$ for logistic function

Figure 5. Relationship between $f^{(n+1)}(x)$ and $-\mathcal{W}_h^{(n)} f(a,b)$, $n = 7$.

Table 1 shows some values of $(\mathcal{W}_h^n f)(a,b)$ for points $b_1 = \{0, 2, 4, 8\}$ as $a \to 0$ and for $n = 0, 1, 2, \ldots, 8$. The limit values are consistent (negative values) with those of Figures 1–5. For example, for $n = 0$ and $b_1 = 0$ in Table 1, the value is -0.0625, and the graph of Figure 1 shows a maximum at this point, and moreover, it can be appreciated a consistent behaviour in Figure 1 as $a \to 0$.

For $n = 1$ and $b_1 = 0$, $(\mathcal{W}_h^n f)(a,b) \to 0$, and this is consistent with Figure 2. For $n = 2$ and b_1 moving from 0 to 8, the value of $(\mathcal{W}_h^n f)(a,b)$ tends to zero, and the graph of Figure 3 also shows a vanishing behaviour. As n increases, $f^{(n)}(x)$ and $(\mathcal{W}_h^n f)(a,b)$ have more oscillations (see Figures 4 and 5) but they always keep the regularity, as stated by Lemma 3.

Table 1. $\lim_{(a,b) \to (0,b_1)} (\mathcal{W}_h^n f)(a,b)$ for logistic function.

	b_1			
n	0	2	4	8
0	−0.0625	−0.02624	−0.00441	−0.00008
1	0	0.01999	0.00425	0.00008
2	0.03125	-0.00971	−0.00394	−0.00008
3	0	−0.00519	0.00335	0.00008
4	−0.0625	0.02170	−0.00224	−0.00008
5	0	−0.02660	0.00022	0.00008
6	0.265625	−0.01200	0.00321	−0.00008
7	0	0.13528	−0.00847	0.00007
8	−1.93750	−0.28892	0.01458	−0.00006

Example 2. *Now we give an example for Theorem 2 in the case $b_0 = 0$. Let $h_1 = (1 - x^2) exp^{-\frac{x^2}{2}}$. Consider $f(x) = |x|$ if $|x| \leq 1$ and $f(x) = 0$ otherwise. Then, $supp\, f = [-1, 1]$ and therefore, $f \in L^p(\mathbb{R})$, $1 < p < \infty$. Take $a > 1, b \in \mathbb{R}$ and $m \in \mathbb{Z}$.*

Then from (7), (9) and (10),

$$(\mathcal{W}_{h_1}^n f)(a^m, b) = \frac{1}{a^m} \frac{\partial^n}{\partial b^n}(L_h f)(a^m, b) = \frac{1}{a^m} \frac{(-1)^n}{(a^m)^n}(L_{h^{(n)}} f)(a^m, b)$$

$$= \frac{1}{a^m} \frac{(-1)^n}{(a^m)^n} \int_{b-aL}^{b+aL} f(x) \frac{1}{a^m} \overline{h^{(n)}(\frac{x-b}{a^m})} dx.$$

We have, for $n = 1$,

$$h_1^{(1)}(x) = (-3x + x^3)e^{-\frac{x^2}{2}}$$

and since h_1 is a wavelet with real values,

$$(\mathcal{W}_{h_1}^1 f)(a^m, b) = \frac{-1}{a^{2m}} \int_{b-a^m L}^{b+a^m L} |x| h^{(1)}(\frac{x-b}{a^m}) dx.$$

With a change of variable, $y = \frac{x-b}{a^m}$, then $x = b + a^m y$, and consequently,

$$(\mathcal{W}_{h_1}^1 f)(a^m, b) = \frac{-1}{a^{2m}} \int_{-L}^{L} |b + a^m y| h^{(1)}(y) dy$$

$$= \frac{-1}{a^{2m}} \left[\int_{-L}^{-\frac{b}{a^m}} (-b - a^m y) h^{(1)}(y) dy + \int_{-\frac{b}{a^m}}^{L} (b + a^m y) h^{(1)}(y) dy \right]$$

$$= \frac{-2b}{a^{2m}} \left[(1 - L^2) e^{-\frac{L^2}{2}} - e^{-\frac{b^2}{2a^{2m}}} \right].$$

We analyze $(\mathcal{W}_{h_1}^1 f)(a^m, b)$ involving the limit for $b \to 0$ and $a^m \to 0$ (i.e. $m \to -\infty$). Note that, for $b = 0$,

$$\lim_{m \to -\infty} (\mathcal{W}_{h_1}^1 f)(a^m, 0) = 0$$

while, for $b = a^{2m}$

$$\lim_{m \to -\infty} (\mathcal{W}_{h_1}^1 f)(a^m, a^m) = -2((1 - L^2)e^{-\frac{L^2}{2}} - 1),$$

consequently, this limit does not exist, and f is not C^∞.

Note that in Example 2, we have used a function h_1 that does not have compact support (but it has a fast decay) and the result is consistent with Theorem 2, so the example shows that the results could apply with wavelets with no compact support.

In Figure 6 we show a plot for $f(x)$ in the left side, and a 3D plot in the right side for $\mathcal{W}_{h_1}^{(1)} f)(a^m, b)$ where it is possible to see how the graph loses smoothness and produces "two peaks" close to $b = 0$ while $a^m \to 0$.

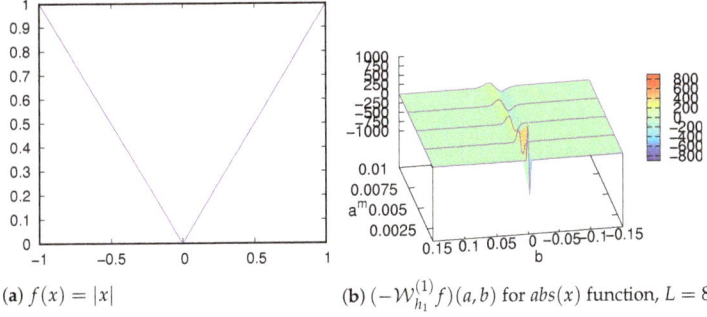

(a) $f(x) = |x|$.

(b) $(-\mathcal{W}_{h_1}^{(1)} f)(a, b)$ for $abs(x)$ function, $L = 8$.

Figure 6. $f(x)$ and $\mathcal{W}_{h_1}^{(1)} f)(a^m, b)$.

Author Contributions: Conceptualization, J.N.-F., S.A.-B. and O.H.-A.; methodology, J.N.-F. and S.A.-B.; software, O.H.-A.; validation, J.N.-F., S.A.-B. and O.H.-A.; formal analysis, J.N.-F., S.A.-B. and O.H.-A.; writing—original draft preparation, J.N.-F., S.A.-B. and O.H.-A. All authors have read and agreed to the published version of the manuscript.

Funding: This research received no external funding.

Acknowledgments: Authors greatly appreciate the reviewers who have dedicated their considerable time and expertise to improve this paper.

Conflicts of Interest: The authors declare no conflict of interest.

Appendix A. Proof of Lemma 4 and Lemma 5

Proof of Lemma 4. (1) First, we prove that the function $\mathcal{I}_h^n f$ is continuous on $\mathbb{R}^+ \times [b_0 - B, b_0 + B] \times \mathbb{R}$.

Let (a_1, x_1, y_1) be any point in $\mathbb{R}^+ \times [b_0 - B, b_0 + B] \times \mathbb{R}$. Note that if $a_1 > 0$, then from (8) and (9), the function $\mathcal{I}_h^n f$ is continuous at (a_1, x_1, y_1).

Now, if a tends to 0, then

$$\lim_{(a,x,y) \to (0, x_1, y_1)} (\mathcal{I}_h^n f)(a, x, y) = \lim_{(a,x,y) \to (0, x_1, y_1)} h(-y)(\mathcal{W}_h^n f)(a, x + ay).$$

Now, since

$$|(a, x + ay) - (0, x_1)|^2 = a^2 + (x - x_1 + ay)^2 \leq a^2 + 2\left[(x - x_1)^2 + a^2 y^2\right]$$
$$= a^2(1 + 2y^2) + 2(x - x_1)^2 \to 0 \quad \text{as} \quad (a, x, y) \to (0, x_1, y_1),$$

it follows that

$$\lim_{(a,x,y) \to (0, x_1, y_1)} (\mathcal{I}_h^n f)(a, x, y) = h(-y_1) \lim_{(a,x,y) \to (0, x_1, y_1)} (\mathcal{W}_h^n f)(a, x + ay)$$
$$= h(-y_1) \lim_{(a,b) \to (0, x_1)} (\mathcal{W}_h^n f)(a, b) = h(-y_1) F_h^n(x_1).$$

(2) Second, we prove that for fixed x in $[b_0 - B, b_0 + B]$, the function $\mathcal{I}_h^n f$ is in $L^1(\mathbb{R}^+ \times \mathbb{R})$. Note that for $a > 0$,

$$(\mathcal{I}_h^n f)(a, x, y) = h(-y)(\mathcal{W}_h^n f)(a, x + ay)$$
$$= h(-y) \frac{1}{a} \frac{\partial^n}{\partial x^n} (L_h f)(a, x + ay) \qquad (A1)$$
$$= h(-y) \frac{1}{a} \frac{(-1)^n}{a^n} (L_{h^{(n)}} f)(a, x + ay).$$

Now, since $h \in C_0^\infty(\mathbb{R})$, then $h \in L^q(\mathbb{R})$ for any $1 \leq q < \infty$. So, choose q so that $\frac{1}{p} + \frac{1}{q} = 1$. Thus, since $f \in L^p(\mathbb{R})$, we have from Hölder's inequality,

$$|(\mathcal{I}_h^n f)(a, x, y)| \leq |h(-y)| \, a^{-2-n+\frac{1}{q}} \|f\|_p \|h^{(n)}\|_q. \qquad (A2)$$

Now, let

$$(\mathcal{G}_h^n f)(a, y) = \begin{cases} |(\mathcal{I}_h^n f)(a, x, y)| & \text{if } 0 < a \leq 1 \\ |h(-y)| \, a^{-2-n+\frac{1}{q}} \|f\|_p \|h^{(n)}\|_q & \text{if } a > 1. \end{cases}$$

Then $|(\mathcal{I}_h^n f)(a, x, y)| \leq (\mathcal{G}_h^n f)(a, y)$ for all $(a, y) \in \mathbb{R}^+ \times \mathbb{R}$.

Hence,

$$\int_{\mathbb{R}^+}\int_{\mathbb{R}}|(\mathcal{G}_h^n f)(a,y)|dyda$$
$$=\int_0^1\int_{\mathbb{R}}|(\mathcal{G}_h^n f)(a,y)|dyda+\int_1^\infty\int_{\mathbb{R}}|(\mathcal{G}_h^n f)(a,y)|dyda$$
$$=\int_0^1\int_{\mathbb{R}}|(\mathcal{I}_h^n f)(a,x,y)|dyda+\int_1^\infty\int_{\mathbb{R}}|h(-y)|\,|a|^{-2-n+\frac{1}{q}}\|f\|_p\|h^{(n)}\|_q\,dyda.$$

Suppose now that $supp\,h\subset[-d,d]$ for some $d>0$. Then

$$\int_0^\infty\int_{\mathbb{R}}|(\mathcal{G}_h^n f)(a,y)|dyda=\int_0^1\int_{-d}^d|(\mathcal{I}_h^n f)(a,x,y)|dyda$$
$$+\|f\|_p\|h^{(n)}\|_q\left(\int_{-d}^d|h(-y)|dy\right)\left(\int_1^\infty a^{-2-n+\frac{1}{q}}da\right). \tag{A3}$$

Since the function $\mathcal{I}_h^n f(\cdot,x,\cdot)$ is continuous on $[0,1]\times[-d,d]$, and $\int_1^\infty a^{-2-n+\frac{1}{q}}da<\infty$ for any non-negative integer n and $1\le q<\infty$, it follows that $\mathcal{G}_h^n f\in L^1(\mathbb{R}^+\times\mathbb{R})$. Hence, $(\mathcal{I}_h^n f)(\cdot,x,\cdot)\in L^1(\mathbb{R}^+\times\mathbb{R})$.

(3) Finally, note that for $n=0$, $a>0$ and $x\in(b_0-B,b_0+B)$, we have from (A1),

$$\frac{\partial}{\partial x}(\mathcal{I}_h^0 f)(a,x,y)=(\mathcal{I}_h^1 f)(a,x,y).$$

Hence, since $(\mathcal{I}_h^0 f)(\cdot,x,\cdot)\in L^1(\mathbb{R}^+\times\mathbb{R})$, $\frac{\partial}{\partial x}(\mathcal{I}_h^0 f)(a,x,y)$ exists and $|(\mathcal{I}_h^1 f)(a,x,y)|\le(\mathcal{G}_h^1 f)(a,y)$ for all (a,y), where $(\mathcal{G}_h^1 f)(a,y)$ is integrable, it follows that

$$\frac{d}{dx}\int_{\mathbb{R}^+}\int_{\mathbb{R}}(\mathcal{I}_h^0 f)(a,x,y)dyda\quad\text{exists, and}$$

$$\frac{d}{dx}\int_{\mathbb{R}^+}\int_{\mathbb{R}}(\mathcal{I}_h^0 f)(a,x,y)dyda=\int_{\mathbb{R}^+}\int_{\mathbb{R}}\frac{\partial}{\partial x}(\mathcal{I}_h^0 f)(a,x,y)dyda.$$

That is,

$$\frac{d}{dx}w(x)=(I_h^1 f)(x).$$

By using the same argument we get,

$$\frac{d^n}{dx^n}w(x)=\frac{d}{dx}\int_{\mathbb{R}^+}\int_{\mathbb{R}}(\mathcal{I}_h^{n-1} f)(a,x,y)dyda=(I_h^n f)(x),$$

for any non-negative integer n. This completes the proof of Lemma 4. □

Proof of Lemma 5. (1) Since $f\in L^p(\mathbb{R})$, and $h_1\in C_0^\infty(\mathbb{R})$,

$$(\mathcal{W}^n{}_{h_1}f)(a^m,b)=\frac{1}{a^m}\left(\frac{\partial^n}{\partial b^n}(J_{a^m}\widetilde{h_1})*f\right)(b)$$

then $(\mathcal{W}^n{}_{h_1}f)(a^m,b)$ in C^∞ for any b in $\mathbb{R}$. Furthermore, the limit

$$\lim_{(m,b)\to(-\infty,b_1)}(\mathcal{W}^n{}_{h_1}f)(a^m,b)=S_{h_1}^n(b_1),$$

exists for any b in $[b_0-B,b_0+B]$.

The function $(\mathcal{W}^n{}_{h_1}f)(a^m,b)$ converges uniformly to $S_{h_1}^n(b)$ in $[b_0-B,b_0+B]$ and $(\mathcal{W}^n{}_{h_1}f)(a^m,b)$ is a bounded function for $m<0$. Consequently, it is uniformly bounded.

So, there exist $C_W^n > 0$ such that

$$|(\mathcal{W}^n_{h_1} f)(a^m, b)| < C_W^n,$$

for b in $[b_0 - B, b_0 + B]$ and any $m < 0$.

(2) Next we prove that for x in $[b_0 - B, b_0 + B]$, the series

$$\sum_{m=-\infty}^{\infty} ((J_{a^m} h_2) * \frac{\partial^n}{\partial x^n}(J_{a^m} \overline{\tilde{h_1}}) * f)(x)$$

converges uniformly. For this purpose, they are divided into three parts, as follows,

$$\sum_{m=-\infty}^{\infty} |((J_{a^m} h_2) * \frac{\partial^n}{\partial x^n}(J_{a^m} \overline{\tilde{h_1}}) * f)| = \\ \left(\sum_{m=-\infty}^{-M-1} + \sum_{m=-M}^{-M} + \sum_{m=M+1}^{\infty} \right) |((J_{a^m} h_2) * \frac{\partial^n}{\partial x^n}(J_{a^m} \overline{\tilde{h_1}}) * f)|. \quad (A4)$$

First consider m a negative integer.
Since $supp\ h_2 \subset [-d, d]$, then $supp\ h_2(\frac{x-\cdot}{a^m}) \subset [x - a^m d, x + a^m d]$. Let $M > 0$ be such that for $m < -M$, $[x - a^m d, x + a^m d] \subset [b_0 - B, b_0 + B]$, then $a^m d \leq \frac{B}{2}$.

$$((J_{a^m} h_2) * \frac{\partial^n}{\partial b^n}(J_{a^m} \overline{\tilde{h_1}}) * f)(x) = \int_{-\infty}^{\infty} h_2(\frac{x-b}{a^m}) \frac{1}{a^m} \frac{\partial^n}{\partial b^n}(J_{a^m}(\overline{\tilde{h_1}}) * f)(b) db \\ = \int_{-\infty}^{\infty} h_2(\frac{x-b}{a^m}) \mathcal{W}^n_{h_1}(a^m, b) db$$

For $m < -M$ we have the following estimation,

$$\left| \int_{-\infty}^{\infty} \frac{a^m}{a^m} h_2(\frac{x-b}{a^m}) \mathcal{W}^n_{h_1}(a^m, b) db \right| \leq C_W^n a^m \int_{-\infty}^{\infty} \frac{1}{a^m} |h_2(\frac{x-b}{a^m})| db = C_W^n a^m \|h_2\|_1.$$

This gives the uniform convergence of the series for $m < -M$.
Now, if m is a positive integer,

$$((J_{a^m} h_2) * \frac{\partial^n}{\partial b^n}(J_{a^m} \overline{\tilde{h_1}}) * f)(x) = \int_{-\infty}^{\infty} \frac{1}{a^m} h_2(\frac{x-b}{a^m}) \frac{(-1)^n}{a^{mn}} \left[(J_{a^m} \overline{h_1^{(n)}})^{\sim} * f \right](b) db$$

From Remark 2 and Young's inequality it follows that,

$$\left| \int_{-\infty}^{\infty} \frac{1}{a^m} h_2(\frac{x-b}{a^m}) \frac{(-1)^n}{a^{mn}} \left[(J_{a^m} \overline{h_1^{(n)}})^{\sim} * f \right](b) db \right| \leq \frac{1}{a^{mn}} \|h_2\|_1 \|h_1^{(n)}\|_1 \|f\|_p$$

It gives the uniform convergence of the series for $m > M$.
Consequently, the series (A4) converge uniformly and absolutely.
(3) Finally, since the series (A4) converge uniformly, then it is possible to derivate term by term. Hence,

$$\frac{d}{dx} \sum_{m=-\infty}^{\infty} ((J_{a^m} h_2) * (J_{a^m} \overline{\tilde{h_1}}) * f)(x) = \sum_{m=-\infty}^{\infty} ((J_{a^m} h_2) * \frac{\partial}{\partial x}(J_{a^m} \overline{\tilde{h_1}}) * f)(x)$$

That is,

$$\frac{d}{dx} v(x) = \sum_{m=-\infty}^{\infty} ((J_{a^m} h_2) * \frac{\partial}{\partial x}(J_{a^m} \overline{\tilde{h_1}}) * f)(x) = v_1(x).$$

Hence, for any non-negative integer n,

$$\frac{d^n}{dx^n}v(x) = \sum_{m=-\infty}^{\infty} ((J_{a^m}h_2) * \frac{\partial^n}{\partial x^n}(J_{a^m}\overline{\widetilde{h_1}}) * f)(x) = v_n(x).$$

This proves Lemma 5. □

References

1. Navarro, J. The one dimensional regularity of the continuous wavelet transform applied to weak solutions. *Pioneer J. Math. Math. Sci.* **2012**, *5*, 95–111.
2. Navarro, J.; Elizarraraz, D. Convergence of the continuous wavelet transform with rotations in higher dimensions. *Adv. Oper. Theory* **2020**, *5*, 143–166. [CrossRef]
3. Ashurov, R.; Butaev, A. On continuous wavelet transform of distributions. *Appl. Math. Lett.* **2011**, *24*, 1578–1583. [CrossRef]
4. Wilson, M. *Weighted Littlewood-Paley Theory and Exponential-Square Integrability*; Lecture Notes in Mathematics; Springer: Berlin, Germany, 2008; Volume 1924.
5. Wilson, M. How fast and in what sense does the Calderon reproducing formula converge? *J. Fourier Anal. Appl.* **2010**, *16*, 768–785. [CrossRef]
6. Weisz, F. Inversion formula for the continuous wavelet transform. *Acta Math. Hungar.* **2013**, *138*, 237–258. [CrossRef]
7. Li, K.; Sun, W. Pointwise convergence of the Calderon reproducing formula. *J. Fourier Anal.* **2012**, *18*, 439–455. [CrossRef]
8. Ashurov, R. Convergence of the continuous wavelet transform on the entire Lebesgue set of L_p functions. *Int. J. Wavelets Multiresolut. Inf.* **2011**, *9*, 675–683. [CrossRef]
9. Pathak, R.S. The wavelet transform of distributions. *Tohoku Math. J.* **2004**, *56*, 411–421. [CrossRef]
10. Perrier, V.; Basdevant, C. Besov norm in terms of the continuous wavelet transform. Applications to structure functions. *Math. Models Methods Appl. Sci.* **1996**, *6*, 649–664. [CrossRef]
11. Daubechies, I. *Ten Lectures on Wavelets*; SIAM: Montpelier, VT, USA, 1992.
12. Kaiser, C.; Weis, L. Wavelet transform for functions with values in UMD spaces. *Stud. Math.* **2008**, *186*, 101–126. [CrossRef]
13. Rao, T.; Sikić, H.; Song, R. Application of Carleson's Theorem to wavelet inversion. *Control Cybern.* **1994**, *23*, 761–771.
14. Nie, L.; Wu, S.; Lin, X.; Zheng, L.; Rui, L. Approximate derivative calculated by using continuous wavelet transform. *J. Chem. Inf. Comp. Sci.* **2002**, *42*, 274–283. [CrossRef] [PubMed]
15. Xueguang, S.; Chaoxiong, M. A general approach to derivative calculation using wavelet transform. *Chem. Int. Lab. Syst.* **2003**, *69*, 157–165.
16. Firdous, A.S. Implementation of wavelet solutions to second order differential equations with Maple. *Appl. Math. Sci.* **2012**, *127*, 6311–6326.
17. Abdesselem, D.; Wajdi, B.; Chokri, B. Wavelet neural networks for DNA sequence classification using the genetic algorithms and the Least Trimmed Square. *Proc. Comp. Sci.* **2016**, *96*, 418–427.
18. Zaied, M.; Jemai, O.; Amar, C.B. Training of the Beta wavelet networks by the frames theory: Application to face recognition. In *2008 First Workshops on Image Processing Theory, Tools and Applications*; IEEE: New York, NY, USA, 2008; pp. 1–6.
19. Borgi, M.A.; Labate, D.; El'Arbi, M.; Ben Amar, C. Shearlet Network-based Sparse Coding Augmented by Facial Texture Features for Face Recognition. In *Image Analysis and Processing, Proceedings of the 17th International Conference on Image Analysis and Processing, Naples, Italy, 9–13 September 2013*; Petrosino, A., Ed.; Springer: Berlin/Heidelber, Germany, 2013; pp. 611–620.
20. Navarro, J.; Elizarraraz, D. Smothness of wek solutions under lineal partial differential operators with constant coefficients via the convergence of the n-dimensional continuous shearlet transform. *Int. Trans. Spec. Funct.* **2019**, *32*, 166–191.
21. Navarro, J.; Herrera, O. Fast Convergence of the Two Dimensional Discrete Shearlet Transform. *Comp. Sist.* **2020**, *24*, 469–480.
22. Sunmonu, A. Wavelet neural network model for yield spread forecasting. *Mathematics* **2017**, *5*, 2–15.
23. Minai, A.A.; Williams, R.D. On the Derivatives of the Sigmoid. *Neural Netw.* **1993**, *6*, 845–853. [CrossRef]
24. Haykin, S. *Neural Networks and Learning Machines*, 3rd ed.; University McMaster Ed.: Hamilton, ON, Canada, 2009.
25. TensorFlow: Large-Scale Machine Learning on Heterogeneous Systems. Available online: www.tensorflow.org (accessed on 15 December 2020).
26. Keras. Available online: github.com/fchollet/keras (accessed on 15 December 2020).

Article

Boundary Values in Ultradistribution Spaces Related to Extended Gevrey Regularity

Stevan Pilipović [1,†], Nenad Teofanov [1,†] and Filip Tomić [2,*,†]

1. Faculty of Sciences, Department of Mathematics and Informatics, University of Novi Sad, 21000 Novi Sad, Serbia; stevan.pilipovic@dmi.uns.ac.rs (S.P.); nenad.teofanov@dmi.uns.ac.rs (N.T.)
2. Faculty of Technical Sciences, Department of Fundamental Sciences, University of Novi Sad, 21000 Novi Sad, Serbia
* Correspondence: filip.tomic@uns.ac.rs
† These authors contributed equally to this work.

Abstract: Following the well-known theory of Beurling and Roumieu ultradistributions, we investigate new spaces of ultradistributions as dual spaces of test functions which correspond to associated functions of logarithmic-type growth at infinity. In the given framework we prove that boundary values of analytic functions with the corresponding logarithmic growth rate towards the real domain are ultradistributions. The essential condition for that purpose, known as stability under ultradifferential operators in the classical ultradistribution theory, is replaced by a weaker condition, in which the growth properties are controlled by an additional parameter. For that reason, new techniques were used in the proofs. As an application, we discuss the corresponding wave front sets.

Keywords: ultradifferentiable functions; ultradistributions; extended Gevrey regularity; boundary values of analytic functions; wave front sets

MSC: 46F20; 46E10; 35A18

1. Introduction

In this paper we describe certain intermediate spaces between the spaces of Schwartz distributions and any space of Gevrey ultradistributions as boundary values of analytic functions. More precisely, we continue to investigate a new class of ultradifferentiable functions and their duals ([1–4]) following Komatsu's approach [5,6]. We refer to [7] and the references therein for another equally interesting approach.

The derivatives of such ultradifferentiable functions are controlled by the two-parameter sequences of the form $M_p^{\tau,\sigma} = p^{\tau p^\sigma}$, $p \in \mathbf{N}$, $\tau > 0$, $\sigma > 1$. For that reason we call them extended Gevrey functions. It turns out that such functions can be used in the study of a class of strictly hyperbolic equations and systems. In particular, the extended Gevrey class associated with the sequence $M_p^{1,2} = p^{p^2}$ is used in the analysis of the regularity of the corresponding Cauchy problem in [8]. It captures the regularity of the coefficients in the space variable (with low regularity in time), so that the corresponding Cauchy problem is well posed in appropriate solution spaces.

Actually, the growth rate of sequence $M_p^{\tau,\sigma}$ implied a change in the growth of the expression h^p in the classical definition (see [5]). Hence, instead of that expression, we use h^{p^σ}, which essentially changes the corresponding proofs in the analysis of new ultradistribution spaces. Indeed, the extra exponent σ which appears in the power of term h implies that the extended Gevrey classes are different from any Carleman class C^L; cf. [9]. This difference is essential for many calculations—for example, in the proof of the inverse closedness property; cf. [10].

We especially emphasize the role of the Lambert W function that appears in the theory of new ultradistribution spaces for the first time. This is the essential contribution of our approach. The properties of new ultradistribution spaces described in terms of the Lambert function and its asymptotic properties show that our approach is naturally included in the general theory of ultradistributions positioning the new spaces; let us call them extended Gevrey ultradistributions, between classical distributions and Komatsu type ultradistributions.

Distributions as boundary values of analytic functions are investigated in many papers; see [11] for the historical background and the relevant references therein. We point out a nice survey for distribution and ultradistribution boundary values given in the book [9]. The essence of the existence of a boundary value is the determination of the growth condition under which an analytic function $F(x + iy)$, observed on a certain tube domain with respect to y, defines an (ultra)distribution as y tends to 0. The classical result can be roughly interpreted as follows: if $F(x + iy) \leq C|y|^{-M}$ for some $C, M > 0$ then $F(x + i0)$ is in the Schwartz space $\mathcal{D}'(U)$ in a neighborhood U of x. (see Theorem 3.1.15 in [9]). For Gevrey ultradistributions, sub-exponential growth rate of analytic function F of the form $|F(x+iy)| \leq Ce^{k|y|^{-1/(t-1)}}$ for some $C, k > 0$ and $t > 1$ implies the boundary value result. The function in the exponent precisely describes the asymptotic behavior of the associated function to the Gevrey sequence $p!^t$, $p \in \mathbf{N}$; cf. [6,12]. In general, such representations are provided if test functions admit almost analytic extensions in the non-quasianalytic case related to Komatsu's condition $(M.2)$ (see [13]).

Different results concerning boundary values in the spaces of ultradistributions can be found in [5,6,11,13,14]. Even now this topic for ultradistribution spaces is interesting (cf. [15–18]). Especially, we have to mention [19]. At the end of this introduction we will briefly comment on the approach in this paper and our approach.

Extended Gevrey classes $\mathcal{E}_{\tau,\sigma}(U)$ and $\mathcal{D}_{\tau,\sigma}(U)$, $\tau > 0$, $\sigma > 1$, are introduced and investigated in [1–4,10,20]. The derivatives of functions in such classes are controlled by sequences of the form $M_p^{\tau,\sigma} = p^{\tau p^\sigma}$, $p \in \mathbf{N}$. Although such sequences do not satisfy Komatsu's condition $(M.2)$, the corresponding spaces consist of ultradifferentiable functions; that is, it is possible to construct differential operators of infinite order and prove their continuity properties on the test and dual spaces.

Our main intention in this paper is to establish the sufficient condition when the elements of dual spaces can be represented as boundary values of analytic functions. We follow the classical approach to boundary values given in [11] and carry out necessary modifications in order to use it in the analysis of spaces developed in [1–4]. Here, for such spaces, plenty of non-trivial constructions are established. In particular, we analyze the corresponding associated functions as a main tool in our investigations.

Moreover, we apply these results in the description of related wave front sets. The wave front set $\mathrm{WF}_{\tau,\sigma}(u)$, $\tau > 0$, $\sigma > 1$, of a Schwarz distribution u is analyzed in [2–4,10,20]. In particular, it is proved that they are related to the classes $\mathcal{E}_{\tau,\sigma}(U)$. We extend the definition of $\mathrm{WF}_{\tau,\sigma}(u)$ to a larger space of ultradistributions by using their boundary value representations. This allows us to describe intersections and unions of $\mathrm{WF}_{\tau,\sigma}(u)$ (with respect to τ) by using specific functions with logarithmic type behavior.

Let us comment on another very interesting concept of construction of a large class of ultradistribution spaces. In [19,21,22] and several other papers the authors consider sequences of the form $k!M_k$, where they presume a fair number of conditions on M_k and discuss in details their relations. For example, consequences of the composition of ultradifferentiable functions determined by different classes of such sequences are discussed. Moreover, they consider weighted matrices, that is, a family of sequences of the form $k!M_k^\lambda$, $k \in \mathbb{N}$, $\lambda \in \Lambda$ (partially ordered and directed set), and make the unions, again considering various properties such as compositions and boundary values. Their analysis follows the approach of [7,23]. In essence, an old question of ultradistribution theory was the analysis of unions and intersections of ultradifferentiable function spaces. This is very well elaborated in quoted papers. The main reason why our classes are not covered by the quoted papers is the factor $h^{|\alpha|^\sigma}$, $\sigma > 1$, in the seminorm (4). For that reason our conditions on the weight sequence $(\widetilde{(M.2)}')$ and $\widetilde{(M.2)}$ given below) differ from the corresponding ones in the quoted papers. As we already explained, our growth rate is not just another point of view, since the basic facts used in the proofs are related to a new investigations involved by the Lambert W function. Actually, the precise estimates of our paper can be used for the further extensions in weighted matrix approach, since the original idea for our approach is quite different and based on the relation between $[n^s]!$ and $n!^s$ in the estimate of derivatives ($[n^s]$ means integer value not exceeding n^s, $s \in (0,1)$; cf. [1,2]).

The paper is organized as follows: We end the introduction with some notation. In Section 2 we introduce the necessary background on the spaces of extended Gevrey functions and their duals, spaces of ultradistributions. Our main result, Theorem 1, is given in Section 3. Wave front sets in the framework of our theory are discussed in Section 4. Finally, in Appendix A we prove a technical result concerning the associated functions $T_{\tau,\sigma,h}(k)$ and recall the basic continuity properties of ultradifferentiable operators on extended Gevrey classes, in a certain sense analogous to stability under the ultradifferentiable operators in the classical theory.

Notation

We denote by $\mathbf{N}$, $\mathbf{Z}_+$, $\mathbf{R}$ and $\mathbf{C}$ the sets of nonnegative integers, positive integers, real numbers and complex numbers, respectively. For a multi-index $\alpha = (\alpha_1, \ldots, \alpha_d) \in \mathbf{N}^d$, we write $\partial^\alpha = \partial^{\alpha_1} \ldots \partial^{\alpha_d}$, $D^\alpha = (-i)^{|\alpha|} \partial^\alpha$ and $|\alpha| = |\alpha_1| + \cdots + |\alpha_d|$. The open ball $B_r(x_0)$ has radius $r > 0$ and center at $x_0 \in \mathbf{R}^d$; $\partial_{\bar{z}} = (\partial_{\bar{z}_1}, \ldots, \partial_{\bar{z}_n})$ where $\partial_{\bar{z}_j} = \frac{1}{2}(\partial_{x_j} + i\partial_{y_j})$, $j = 1, \ldots, d$, $z = x + iy \in \mathbf{C}^d$. By Hartogs's theorem, $f(z)$, $z \in \Omega$, Ω is open in $\mathbf{C}^d$, and is analytic if it is analytic with respect to every coordinate variable z_j.

Throughout the paper we always assume $\tau > 0$ and $\sigma > 1$.

2. Test Spaces and Duals

We are interested in $M_p^{\tau,\sigma}$, $p \in \mathbf{N}$, sequences of positive numbers such that, for some $C > 1$, the following conditions are satisfied:

(M.1) $\quad (M_p^{\tau,\sigma})^2 \leq M_{p-1}^{\tau,\sigma} M_{p+1}^{\tau,\sigma}$, $\quad p \in \mathbf{N}$;

$\widetilde{(M.2)} \quad M_{p+q}^{\tau,\sigma} \leq C^{p^\sigma + q^\sigma + 1} M_p^{2^{\sigma-1}\tau,\sigma} M_q^{2^{\sigma-1}\tau,\sigma}$, $\quad p,q \in \mathbf{N}$;

$\widetilde{(M.2)}' \quad M_{p+1}^{\tau,\sigma} \leq C^{p^\sigma+1} M_p^{\tau,\sigma}$, $\quad p \in \mathbf{N}$;

(M.3)' $\quad \displaystyle\sum_{p=1}^{\infty} \frac{M_{p-1}^{\tau,\sigma}}{M_p^{\tau,\sigma}} < \infty$.

We notice that (M.1) and (M.3)' are usual conditions of logarithmic convexity and non-quasianalyticity, respectively, and when $\sigma = 1$ and $\tau > 0$ the conditions $\widetilde{(M.2)}'$ and $\widetilde{(M.2)}$ become the standard conditions of stability under differential and ultradifferential operators, (M.2)' and (M.2), respectively (see [5]). In the sequel we consider the sequence $M_p^{\tau,\sigma} = p^{\tau p^\sigma}$, $p \in \mathbf{N}$, which fulfills the above mentioned conditions (see Lemma 2.2 in [1]). This particular choice slightly simplifies our exposition. Clearly, by choosing $\sigma = 1$ and $\tau > 1$ we recover the well known Gevrey sequence $p!^\tau$.

Recall [4], the associated function related to the sequence $p^{\tau p^\sigma}$ is defined by

$$T_{\tau,\sigma,h}(k) = \sup_{p \in \mathbf{N}} \ln \frac{h^{p^\sigma} k^p}{p^{\tau p^\sigma}}, \quad k > 0. \qquad (1)$$

For $h = \sigma = 1$ and $\tau > 1$, $T_{\tau,1,1}(k)$ is the associated function of the Gevrey sequence $p!^\tau$.

In the next lemma we derive the precise asymptotic behavior of the function $T_{\tau,\sigma,h}$ associated with the sequence $p^{\tau p^\sigma}$. This in turn highlights the essential difference between $T_{\tau,\sigma,h}$ and the associated functions determined by Gevrey type sequences.

We first introduce some notation. The Lambert W function is defined as the inverse function of ze^z, $z \in \mathbf{C}$, wherefrom

$$x = W(x)e^{W(x)}, \quad x \geq 0.$$

We denote its principal (real) branch by $W(x)$, $x \geq 0$ (see [24,25]). It is a continuous, increasing and concave function on $[0, \infty)$, $W(0) = 0$, $W(e) = 1$, and $W(x) > 0$, $x > 0$. It can be shown that W can be represented in the form of the absolutely convergent series

$$W(x) = \ln x - \ln(\ln x) + \sum_{k=0}^{\infty} \sum_{m=1}^{\infty} c_{km} \frac{(\ln(\ln x))^m}{(\ln x)^{k+m}}, \quad x \geq x_0 > e,$$

with suitable constants c_{km} and x_0. Thus the following estimates hold:

$$\ln x - \ln(\ln x) \leq W(x) \leq \ln x - \frac{1}{2}\ln(\ln x), \quad x \geq e, \tag{2}$$

with the equality in (2) if and only if $x = e$.

For given $\sigma > 1$, $\tau, h > 0$, let

$$\mathcal{R}(h,k) := h^{-\frac{\sigma-1}{\tau}} e^{\frac{\sigma-1}{\sigma}} \frac{\sigma-1}{\tau\sigma} \ln k = h^{-\frac{\sigma}{\tau\sigma'}} e^{\frac{1}{\sigma'}} \frac{1}{\tau\sigma'} \ln k, \quad k > e,$$

where

$$\frac{1}{\sigma} + \frac{1}{\sigma'} = 1, \quad \text{i.e.} \quad \sigma' = \frac{\sigma}{\sigma-1}.$$

Lemma 1. *Let $h > 0$, and let $T_{\tau,\sigma,h}$ be given by (1). Then there exist constants $B_1, B_2, b_1, b_2 > 0$ such that*

$$B_1 k^{b_1 \left(\frac{\ln k}{\ln(\ln k)}\right)^{\frac{1}{\sigma-1}}} \leq \exp\{T_{\tau,\sigma,h}(k)\} \leq B_2 k^{b_2 \left(\frac{\ln k}{\ln(\ln k)}\right)^{\frac{1}{\sigma-1}}}, \quad k > e.$$

More precisely, if

$$c_1 = \left(\frac{\sigma-1}{\tau\sigma}\right)^{\frac{1}{\sigma-1}}, \quad \text{and} \quad c_2 = h^{-\frac{\sigma-1}{\tau}} e^{\frac{\sigma-1}{\sigma}} \frac{\sigma-1}{\tau\sigma},$$

then there exist constants $A_1, A_2 > 0$ such that

$$A_1 k^{\frac{1}{2}\frac{\sigma-1}{\sigma} c_1 \left(\frac{\ln k}{\ln(c_2 \ln k)}\right)^{\frac{1}{\sigma-1}}} \leq \exp\{T_{\tau,\sigma,h}(k)\} \leq A_2 k^{c_1 \left(\frac{\ln k}{\ln(c_2 \ln k)}\right)^{\frac{1}{\sigma-1}}}, \quad k > e.$$

Proof. Lemma 1 can be proved by following the arguments used in the proof of Theorem 2.1 in [4]. There it is shown that for given $h > 0$, $\tau > 0$ and $\sigma > 1$ the following inequalities hold:

$$\tilde{A}_{\tau,\sigma,h} \exp\left\{\left(\frac{\ln k}{(2^{\sigma-1}\tau W(\mathcal{R}(h,k)))^{\frac{1}{\sigma}}\sigma'}\right)^{\sigma'}\right\} \leq e^{T_{\tau,\sigma,h}(k)}$$

$$\leq A_{\tau,\sigma,h} \exp\left\{\left(\frac{\ln k}{(\tau\sigma' W(\mathcal{R}(h,k)))^{\frac{1}{\sigma}}}\right)^{\sigma'}\right\}, \quad k > e,$$

for some $A_{\tau,\sigma,h}, \tilde{A}_{\tau,\sigma,h} > 0$. Moreover, in the view of (2), it follows that

$$W^{-\frac{\sigma'}{\sigma}}(\mathcal{R}(h,k))(\ln k)^{\sigma'} \asymp \left(\frac{\ln k}{\ln(C_h \ln k)}\right)^{\frac{\sigma'}{\sigma}} \ln k, \quad k \to \infty,$$

with $C_h := h^{-\frac{\sigma-1}{\tau}} e^{\frac{\sigma-1}{\sigma}} \frac{\sigma-1}{\tau\sigma} = h^{-\frac{\sigma}{\tau\sigma'}} e^{\frac{1}{\sigma'}} (\tau\sigma')^{-1}$.

Details are left for the reader. □

We define (following the classical approach [5]):

$$T^*_{\tau,\sigma,h}(k) = \sup_{p \in \mathbb{N}} \ln \frac{h^{p^\sigma} k^p}{p^{p(\tau p^\sigma - 1 - 1)}}, \quad k > 0. \tag{3}$$

It turns out that $T^*_{\tau,\sigma,h}(k)$ enjoys the same asymptotic behavior as $T_{\tau,\sigma,h}$; cf. Lemma A1 (a) in Appendix A. This is another difference between our approach and the classical ultradistribution theory, where T^* plays an important role.

Next we recall the definition of spaces $\mathcal{E}_{\tau,\sigma}(U)$ and $\mathcal{D}_{\tau,\sigma}(U)$, where U is an open set in $\mathbb{R}^d$ ([1]).

Let $K \subset\subset \mathbb{R}^d$ be a regular compact set. Then, $\mathcal{E}_{\tau,\sigma,h}(K)$ is the Banach space of functions $\phi \in C^\infty(K)$ such that

$$\|\phi\|_{\mathcal{E}_{\tau,\sigma,h}(K)} = \sup_{\alpha \in \mathbb{N}^d} \sup_{x \in K} \frac{|\partial^\alpha \phi(x)|}{h^{|\alpha|^\sigma} |\alpha|^{\tau |\alpha|^\sigma}} < \infty. \tag{4}$$

We have

$$\mathcal{E}_{\tau_1,\sigma_1,h_1}(K) \hookrightarrow \mathcal{E}_{\tau_2,\sigma_2,h_2}(K), \quad 0 < h_1 < h_2, \ 0 < \tau_1 < \tau_2, \ 1 < \sigma_1 < \sigma_2,$$

where $\hookrightarrow$ denotes the strict and dense inclusion.

The set of functions from $\mathcal{E}_{\tau,\sigma,h}(K)$ supported by K is denoted by $\mathcal{D}^K_{\tau,\sigma,h}$. Next,

$$\mathcal{E}_{\{\tau,\sigma\}}(U) = \varprojlim_{K \subset\subset U} \varinjlim_{h \to \infty} \mathcal{E}_{\tau,\sigma,h}(K), \tag{5}$$

$$\mathcal{E}_{(\tau,\sigma)}(U) = \varprojlim_{K \subset\subset U} \varprojlim_{h \to 0} \mathcal{E}_{\tau,\sigma,h}(K), \tag{6}$$

$$\mathcal{D}_{\{\tau,\sigma\}}(U) = \varinjlim_{K \subset\subset U} \mathcal{D}^K_{\{\tau,\sigma\}} = \varinjlim_{K \subset\subset U} \left(\varinjlim_{h \to \infty} \mathcal{D}^K_{\tau,\sigma,h} \right), \tag{7}$$

$$\mathcal{D}_{(\tau,\sigma)}(U) = \varinjlim_{K \subset\subset U} \mathcal{D}^K_{(\tau,\sigma)} = \varinjlim_{K \subset\subset U} \left(\varprojlim_{h \to 0} \mathcal{D}^K_{\tau,\sigma,h} \right). \tag{8}$$

Spaces in (5) and (7) are called Roumieu type spaces, and (6) and (8) are Beurling type spaces. Note that all the spaces of ultradifferentiable functions defined by Gevrey type sequences are contained in the corresponding spaces defined above.

For the corresponding spaces of ultradistributions we have:

$$\mathcal{D}'_{\{\tau,\sigma\}}(U) = \varprojlim_{K \subset\subset U} \varprojlim_{h \to 0} (\mathcal{D}^K_{\tau,\sigma,h})', \quad \mathcal{D}'_{(\tau,\sigma)}(U) = \varprojlim_{K \subset\subset U} \varinjlim_{h \to \infty} (\mathcal{D}^K_{\tau,\sigma,h})'.$$

Topological properties of all those spaces are the same as in the case of Beurling and Roumieu type spaces given in [5].

We will use abbreviated notation τ, σ for $\{\tau, \sigma\}$ or (τ, σ). Clearly,

$$\mathcal{D}'(U) \hookrightarrow \mathcal{D}'_{\tau,\sigma}(U) \hookrightarrow \varprojlim_{t \to 1} \mathcal{D}'_t(U),$$

where $\mathcal{D}'_t(U) = \mathcal{D}'_{t,1}(U)$ denotes the space of Gevrey ultradistributions with index $t > 1$. More precisely, if (for $\sigma > 1$) we put

$$\mathcal{D}^{(\sigma)}(U) = \varprojlim_{\tau \to 0} \mathcal{D}_{\tau,\sigma}(U), \quad \text{and} \quad \mathcal{D}^{\{\sigma\}}(U) = \varinjlim_{\tau \to \infty} \mathcal{D}_{\tau,\sigma}(U),$$

then

$$\mathcal{D}'(U) \hookrightarrow \mathcal{D}'^{\{\sigma\}}(U) \hookrightarrow \mathcal{D}'^{(\sigma)}(U) \hookrightarrow \varprojlim_{t \to 1} \mathcal{D}'_t(U),$$

where $\mathcal{D}'^{(\sigma)}(U)$ and $\mathcal{D}'^{\{\sigma\}}(U)$ are dual spaces of $\mathcal{D}^{(\sigma)}(U)$ and $\mathcal{D}^{\{\sigma\}}(U)$, respectively.

Thus we are dealing with intermediate spaces between the space of Schwartz distributions and spaces of Gevrey ultradistributions. In the next section we show the boundary value result in the given framework. This, however, asks for the use of new techniques.

3. Main Result

The condition $(M.2)$ (also known as the stability under the ultradifferentiable operators), essential for the boundary value theorems in the framework of ultradistribution spaces [5,13], is in our approach replaced by the condition $\widetilde{(M.2)}$. We note that in [19] a more general condition than $(M.2)$ is considered. In the case of the sequence $M_p^{\tau,\sigma} = p^{\tau p^\sigma}$, $p \in \mathbf{N}$, the asymptotic behaviour given in Lemma 1 is essentially used to prove our main result as follows.

Theorem 1. *Let $\sigma > 1$, U be an open set in $\mathbf{R}^d$, Γ an open cone in $\mathbf{R}^d$ and $\gamma > 0$. Assume that $F(z), z \in Z$ is an analytic function, where*

$$Z = \{z \in \mathbf{C}^d \mid \operatorname{Re} z \in U, \operatorname{Im} z \in \Gamma, |\operatorname{Im} z| < \gamma\},$$

and such that

$$|F(z)| \leq A|y|^{-H\left(\frac{\ln(1/|y|)}{\ln(\ln(1/|y|))}\right)^{\frac{1}{\sigma-1}}}, \quad z = x + iy \in Z,$$

for some $A, H > 0$ (resp. for every $H > 0$ there exists $A > 0$). Then

$$F(x + iy) \to F(x + i0), \quad y \to 0, \ y \in \Gamma, \tag{9}$$

in $\mathcal{D}'^{(\sigma)}(U)$ (resp. $\mathcal{D}'^{\{\sigma\}}(U)$).

More precisely, if

$$|F(z)| \leq A \exp\{T_{(2^\sigma-1)\tau,\sigma,H}(1/|y|)\} \quad z = x + iy \in Z, \tag{10}$$

for some $A, H > 0$ (resp. for every $H > 0$ there exists $A > 0$) then (9) holds in $\mathcal{D}'_{(\tau/2^{\sigma-1},\sigma)}(U)$ (resp. $\mathcal{D}'_{\{\tau/2^{\sigma-1},\sigma\}}(U)$).

Proof. Let $K \subset\subset U$ and $\varphi \in \mathcal{D}^K_{\tau/2^{\sigma-1},\sigma}$. Moreover, let $\kappa \in \mathcal{D}_{\tau/2^{\sigma-1},\sigma}(\mathbf{R}^d)$ be such that $\operatorname{supp} \kappa \subseteq \overline{B(0,2)}$, $\kappa = 1$ on $B(0,1)$.

In the sequel we denote $m_p = p^{\tau((2p)^{\sigma-1}-1)}$, $p \in \mathbf{N}$. Clearly, m_p is an increasing sequence and $m_p \to \infty$ as $p \to \infty$.

Fix $h > 0$, and let

$$\kappa_\alpha(y) = \kappa(4hm_{|\alpha|}y), \quad \alpha \in \mathbf{N}^d, \ y \in \mathbf{R}^d.$$

Note that

$$\operatorname{supp} \kappa_\alpha \subseteq \{y \in \mathbf{R}^d \mid |y| \leq 1/(2hm_{|\alpha|})\}, \tag{11}$$

and for $j = 1, \ldots, d$,

$$\operatorname{supp} \partial_{y_j} \kappa_\alpha \subseteq \{y \in \mathbf{R}^d \mid 1/(4hm_{|\alpha|}) \leq |y| \leq 1/(2hm_{|\alpha|})\}, \quad \alpha \in \mathbf{N}^d. \tag{12}$$

Let

$$\Phi(z) = \sum_{\alpha \in \mathbf{N}^d} \frac{\partial^\alpha \varphi(x)}{|\alpha|^{\tau|\alpha|}}(iy)^\alpha \kappa_\alpha(y), \quad z = x + iy \in \mathbf{C}^d. \tag{13}$$

Clearly, Φ is a smooth function in $\mathbb{R}^{2d}$ and $\Phi(x) = \varphi(x)$ for $x \in K$.

Fix $Y = (Y_1, \ldots, Y_d) \in \Gamma$, $Y \neq 0$, $|Y| < \gamma$, and set

$$Z_Y = \{x + itY \mid x \in K, \ t \in (0,1]\}. \tag{14}$$

In order to use Stoke's formula (see [13]) we need to estimate Φ and its derivatives on Z_Y. To that end we had to adjust the standard technique in a nontrivial manner.

Let us show that there exists $A_h > 0$ such that

$$|\Phi(z)| \leq A_h \|\varphi\|_{\mathcal{E}_{\tau/2^{\sigma-1},\sigma,h'}}, \quad h > 0, \ z \in Z_Y. \tag{15}$$

Note that (11) implies

$$|tY|^{|\alpha|}|\kappa_\alpha(tY)| \leq \frac{1}{(2hm_{|\alpha|})^{|\alpha|}} = \frac{|\alpha|^{\tau|\alpha|}}{(2h)^{|\alpha|}|\alpha|^{2^{\sigma-1}\tau|\alpha|^\sigma}}, \quad t \in (0,1], \ \alpha \in \mathbf{N}^d,$$

and therefore we obtain

$$|\Phi(z)| \leq \sum_{\alpha \in \mathbf{N}^d} \frac{|\partial^\alpha \varphi(x)|}{|\alpha|^{\tau|\alpha|}} |tY|^{|\alpha|}|\kappa_\alpha(tY)| \leq \sum_{\alpha \in \mathbf{N}^d} \frac{|\partial^\alpha \varphi(x)|}{(2h)^{|\alpha|}|\alpha|^{2^{\sigma-1}\tau|\alpha|^\sigma}}$$

$$\leq \|\varphi\|_{\mathcal{E}_{\tau/2^{\sigma-1},\sigma,h}} \sum_{\alpha \in \mathbf{N}^d} \frac{h^{|\alpha|^\sigma}|\alpha|^{(\tau/2^{\sigma-1})|\alpha|^\sigma}}{(2h)^{|\alpha|}|\alpha|^{2^{\sigma-1}\tau|\alpha|^\sigma}} = A_h \|\varphi\|_{\mathcal{E}_{\tau/2^{\sigma-1},\sigma,h'}},$$

where $A_h = \sum_{\alpha \in \mathbf{N}^d} \frac{h^{|\alpha|^\sigma - |\alpha|}}{2^{|\alpha|}|\alpha|^{\tau_0|\alpha|^\sigma}} < \infty$ for $\tau_0 = \tau(2^{\sigma-1} - \frac{1}{2^{\sigma-1}}) > 0$. Hence (15) follows.

Next we estimate $\partial_{\bar{z}_j}\Phi(z), j \in \{1,\ldots,d\}$, when $z \in Z_Y$. More precisely, we show that for a given $h > 0$, there exists $B_h > 0$ such that

$$|\partial_{\bar{z}_j}\Phi(z)| \leq B_h \|\varphi\|_{\mathcal{E}_{\tau/2^{\sigma-1},\sigma,h}} \exp\{-T_{(2^\sigma-1)\tau,\sigma,h}(1/|tY|)\}, \quad z \in Z_Y. \tag{16}$$

By (11) and (12) it is sufficient to prove (16) for

$$1/(4hm_{|\alpha|}) \leq |tY| \leq 1/(2hm_{|\alpha|}), \quad 0 < t \leq 1, \ \alpha \in \mathbf{N}^d. \tag{17}$$

Note that for $z \in Z_Y$ we have

$$\partial_{\bar{z}_j}\Phi(z) = \frac{1}{2}\bigg(\sum_{\alpha \in \mathbf{N}^d} \frac{\partial^{\alpha+e_j}\varphi(x)}{|\alpha|^{\tau|\alpha|}} i^{|\alpha|}(tY)^\alpha \kappa_\alpha(tY)$$

$$+ \sum_{\alpha \in \mathbf{N}^d} \frac{\partial^\alpha \varphi(x)}{|\alpha|^{\tau|\alpha|}} \alpha_j i^{|\alpha|+1} t^{|\alpha|} Y^{\alpha-e_j} \kappa_\alpha(tY)$$

$$+ \sum_{\alpha \in \mathbf{N}^d} \frac{\partial^\alpha \varphi(x)}{|\alpha|^{\tau|\alpha|}} i^{|\alpha|+1} t^{|\alpha|+1} Y^\alpha 4hm_{|\alpha|} \cdot (\partial_{y_j}\kappa)(4hm_{|\alpha|}tY)\bigg) = \frac{1}{2}(S_1 + S_2 + S_3)(z).$$

We will show that there exists a constant $B_h > 0$ such that

$$\exp\{T_{(2^\sigma-1)\tau,\sigma,h}(1/|tY|)\}|S_1(z)| \leq B_h \|\varphi\|_{\mathcal{E}_{\tau/2^{\sigma-1},\sigma,h'}}, \quad z \in Z_Y.$$

The estimates for S_2 and S_3 can be obtained in a similar way.

Let $C_h = C\max\{h, h^{2^{\sigma-1}}\}$ where $C > 0$ is the constant from $\widetilde{(M.2)'}$. Using

$$(p+1)^\sigma \leq 2^{\sigma-1}(p^\sigma + 1), \quad p \in \mathbf{N},$$

we obtain

$$\frac{h^{|\beta|^\sigma}}{|tY|^{|\beta|}|\beta|^{(2^\sigma-1)\tau|\beta|^\sigma}}|S_1(z)| \le C_h\|\varphi\|_{\mathcal{E}_{\tau/2^{\sigma-1},\sigma,h}}$$

$$\left(\sum_{\substack{\alpha\in\mathbf{N}^d\\|\alpha|\le|\beta|}} + \sum_{\substack{\alpha\in\mathbf{N}^d\\|\alpha|>|\beta|}}\right)\frac{h^{|\beta|^\sigma}C_h^{|\alpha|^\sigma}|\alpha|^{(\tau/2^{\sigma-1})|\alpha|^\sigma}}{|\beta|^{(2^\sigma-1)\tau|\beta|^\sigma}|\alpha|^{\tau|\alpha|}}|tY|^{|\alpha|-|\beta|}|\kappa_\alpha(tY)|$$

$$= C_h\|\varphi\|_{\mathcal{E}_{\tau/2^{\sigma-1},\sigma,h}}(I_{1,\beta}+I_{2,\beta}), \quad \beta\in\mathbf{N}^d, z\in Z_Y.$$

It remains to show that $\sup_{\beta\in\mathbf{N}^d}I_{1,\beta}$ and $\sup_{\beta\in\mathbf{N}^d}I_{2,\beta}$ are finite.
First we estimate $I_{1,\beta}$. Note that for $|\alpha|\le|\beta|$, the left-hand side in (17) implies

$$|tY|^{|\alpha|-|\beta|}|\kappa_\alpha(tY)| \le (4hm_{|\alpha|})^{|\beta|-|\alpha|} \le \frac{(4h)^{|\beta|}m_{|\beta|}^{|\beta|}}{h^{|\alpha|}m_{|\alpha|}^{|\alpha|}}$$

$$\le \frac{(4h)^{|\beta|}|\alpha|^{\tau|\alpha|}|\beta|^{2^{\sigma-1}\tau|\beta|^\sigma}}{h^{|\alpha|}|\alpha|^{2^{\sigma-1}\tau|\alpha|^\sigma}}, \quad t\in(0,1], \alpha,\beta\in\mathbf{N}^d. \quad (18)$$

Again, when $\tau_0 = \tau(2^{\sigma-1}-\frac{1}{2^\sigma-1})$, by (18) we have

$$I_{1,\beta} \le \frac{(4h)^{|\beta|}h^{|\beta|^\sigma}}{|\beta|^{(2^{\sigma-1}-1)\tau|\beta|^\sigma}}\sum_{\alpha\in\mathbf{N}^d}\frac{C_h^{|\alpha|^\sigma}}{h^{|\alpha|}|\alpha|^{\tau_0|\alpha|^\sigma}} = C_h'\frac{(4h)^{|\beta|}h^{|\beta|^\sigma}}{|\beta|^{(2^{\sigma-1}-1)\tau|\beta|^\sigma}}, \quad \beta\in\mathbf{N}^d.$$

Hence, we conclude $\sup_{\beta\in\mathbf{N}^d}I_{1,\beta} \le C_h'\exp\{T_{(2^{\sigma-1}-1)\tau,\sigma,h}(4h)\} < \infty$.
To estimate $I_{2,\beta}$ we first note that for $|\alpha|>|\beta|$ the right-hand side in (17) implies

$$|tY|^{|\alpha-\beta|}|\kappa_\alpha(tY)| \le (1/(2hm_{|\alpha|}))^{|\alpha-\beta|} \le 1/((2h)^{|\alpha-\beta|}m_{|\alpha-\beta|}^{|\alpha-\beta|})$$

$$\le \frac{|\alpha|^{\tau|\alpha|}}{(2h)^{|\alpha-\beta|}|\alpha-\beta|^{2^{\sigma-1}\tau|\alpha-\beta|^\sigma}}, \quad t\in(0,1],\ \alpha,\beta\in\mathbf{N}^d. \quad (19)$$

Set $C_h'' = C\max\{C_h, C_h^{2^{\sigma-1}}\}$. Using $\widetilde{(M.2)}$, (19) and (A4), for $\beta\in\mathbf{N}^d$, we have

$$I_{2,\beta} \le \sum_{\substack{\alpha\in\mathbf{N}^d\\|\alpha|>|\beta|}}\frac{h^{|\beta|^\sigma}C_h^{|\alpha|^\sigma}|\alpha|^{(\tau/2^{\sigma-1})|\alpha|^\sigma}}{|\beta|^{(2^\sigma-1)\tau|\beta|^\sigma}(2h)^{|\alpha-\beta|}|\alpha-\beta|^{2^{\sigma-1}\tau|\alpha-\beta|^\sigma}}$$

$$\le C\sum_{\substack{\alpha\in\mathbf{N}^d\\|\alpha|>|\beta|}}\frac{h^{|\beta|^\sigma}(C_h'')^{|\alpha-\beta|^\sigma}(C_h'')^{|\beta|^\sigma}|\alpha-\beta|^{\tau|\alpha-\beta|^\sigma}|\beta|^{\tau|\beta|^\sigma}}{|\beta|^{(2^\sigma-1)\tau|\beta|^\sigma}(2h)^{|\alpha-\beta|}|\alpha-\beta|^{2^{\sigma-1}\tau|\alpha-\beta|^\sigma}}$$

$$\le \frac{(C_h''h)^{|\beta|^\sigma}}{|\beta|^{\tau(2^\sigma-2)|\beta|^\sigma}}C\sum_{\delta\in\mathbf{N}^d}\frac{(C_h'')^{|\delta|^\sigma}}{(2h)^{|\delta|}|\delta|^{(2^{\sigma-1}-1)\tau|\delta|^\sigma}} = C_h'''\frac{(C_h''h)^{|\beta|^\sigma}}{|\beta|^{\tau(2^\sigma-2)|\beta|^\sigma}}.$$

In particular, $\sup_{\beta\in\mathbf{N}^d}I_{2,\beta} \le C_h'''\exp\{T_{(2^\sigma-2)\tau,\sigma,C_h''h}(1)\} < \infty$.
Now, Stoke's formula gives

$$\langle F(x+i0),\varphi(x)\rangle = \int_K F(x+iY)\Phi(x+iY)dx$$

$$+ 2i\sum_{j=1}^d Y_j\int_0^1\int_K \partial_{\bar{z}_j}\Phi(x+itY)F(x+itY)dtdx, \quad (20)$$

and we have used the assumptions in Theorem 1, and inequalities (15) and (16).

Note that for $H = h$, (10) and (15) imply that there exists $A_h > 0$ such that

$$|F(x+iY)\Phi(x+iY)| \leq A_h \|\varphi\|_{\mathcal{E}_{\tau/2^{\sigma-1},\sigma,h}} \exp\{T_{(2^\sigma-1)\tau,\sigma,h}(1/|Y|)\}$$
$$= A'_h \|\varphi\|_{\mathcal{E}_{\tau/2^{\sigma-1},\sigma,h}}, \quad x \in K, \quad (21)$$

where $A'_h = A_h \exp\{T_{(2^\sigma-1)\tau,\sigma,h}(1/|Y|)\}$.

Moreover, (10) and (16) imply that there exists $B_h > 0$ such that

$$|\partial_{\bar{z}_j}\Phi(z)F(z)| \leq B_h \|\varphi\|_{\mathcal{E}_{\tau/2^{\sigma-1},\sigma,h}}, \quad 1 \leq j \leq d, z \in Z_Y. \quad (22)$$

Now (20)–(22) imply

$$|\langle F(x+i0), \varphi(x)\rangle| \leq B'_h \|\varphi\|_{\mathcal{E}_{\tau/2^{\sigma-1},\sigma,h}},$$

for suitable constant $B'_h > 0$. This completes the proof of the second part of theorem, and the first part follows immediately. □

Remark 1. *In order to show that any ultradistribution f is locally (on a bounded open set U) the sum of boundary values of analytic functions defined in the corresponding cone domains Γ_j, $j = 1, \ldots, k$, one should proceed as in the classical theory. We multiply f by a cutoff test function κ_U equal to 1 over U, and obtain $f_0 = f\kappa_U$ equals f on U. Then we divide $\mathbb{R}^n \setminus \{0\}$ into regular non overlapping cones $\Gamma_{j0}, j = 1, \ldots, k$, dual cones of Γ_j, and define*

$$F_j(z) = \langle f_0(t), \int_{\Gamma_{j0}} \exp\{2\pi i(z-t)\eta\}d\eta\rangle, \quad z \in \mathbb{R}^n + i\Gamma_j, \quad j = 1, \ldots, k.$$

Now one can get the growth conditions for $F_j, j = 1, \ldots, k$, and show that

$$f_0 = \sum_{j=1}^{k} \lim_{y \to 0, y \in \Gamma_j} F_j(x+iy), \quad x \in \mathbb{R}^n.$$

The details will be given in a separate contribution where we will consider L^p versions of new ultradistributions spaces similar to the corresponding ones in [11].

4. Wave Front Sets

In this section we analyze wave front sets $\mathrm{WF}_{\tau,\sigma}(u)$ related to the classes $\mathcal{E}_{\tau,\sigma}(U)$ introduced in Section 2. We refer to [2–4,10,20] for properties of $\mathrm{WF}_{\tau,\sigma}(u)$ when u is a Schwartz distribution.

We begin with the definition.

Definition 1. *Let $\tau > 0$, $\sigma > 1$, U open set in $\mathbb{R}^d$ and $(x_0, \xi_0) \in U \times \mathbb{R}^d \setminus \{0\}$. Then for $u \in \mathcal{D}'_{\{\tau,\sigma\}}(U)$ (respectively $\mathcal{D}'_{(\tau,\sigma)}(U)$), $(x_0, \xi_0) \notin \mathrm{WF}_{\{\tau,\sigma\}}(u)$ (resp. $(x_0, \xi_0) \notin \mathrm{WF}_{(\tau,\sigma)}(u)$) if and only if there exists a conic neighborhood Γ of ξ_0; a compact neighborhood K of x_0; and $\phi \in \mathcal{D}_{\{\tau,\sigma\}}(U)$ (respectively $\phi \in \mathcal{D}_{(\tau,\sigma)}(U)$) such that $\mathrm{supp}\,\phi \subseteq K$, $\phi = 1$ on some neighborhood of x_0 and*

$$|\widehat{\phi u}(\xi)| \leq A \exp\{-T_{\tau,\sigma,h}(|\xi|)\}, \quad \xi \in \Gamma,$$

for some $A, h > 0$ (resp. for any $h > 0$ there exists $A > 0$).

We will write $\mathrm{WF}_{\tau,\sigma}(u)$ for $\mathrm{WF}_{(\tau,\sigma)}(u)$ or $\mathrm{WF}_{\{\tau,\sigma\}}(u)$.

Remark 2. *Note that $\mathrm{WF}_{\tau,1}(u) = \mathrm{WF}_\tau(u)$, $\tau > 1$, are Gevrey wave front sets investigated in [12].*

Moreover (cf. [3]), for $0 < \tau_1 < \tau_2$ and $\sigma > 1$ we have

$$\mathrm{WF}(u) \subset \mathrm{WF}_{\tau_2,\sigma}(u) \subset \mathrm{WF}_{\tau_1,\sigma}(u) \subset \bigcap_{t>1} \mathrm{WF}_t(u) \subset \mathrm{WF}_A(u), \quad u \in \mathcal{D}'(U),$$

where WF_A denotes the analytic wave front set.

Let

$$\mathrm{WF}^{\{\sigma\}}(u) = \bigcap_{\tau>0} \mathrm{WF}_{\tau,\sigma}(u), \quad u \in \mathcal{D}'^{\{\sigma\}}(U),$$

and

$$\mathrm{WF}^{(\sigma)}(u) = \bigcup_{\tau>0} \mathrm{WF}_{\tau,\sigma}(u), \quad u \in \mathcal{D}'^{(\sigma)}(U).$$

For such wave front sets we have the following corollary which is an immediate consequence of Lemma 1.

Corollary 1. *Let $u \in \mathcal{D}'^{\{\sigma\}}(U)$ (resp. $\mathcal{D}'^{(\sigma)}(U)$), $\sigma > 1$. Then $(x_0, \xi_0) \notin \mathrm{WF}^{\{\sigma\}}(u)$ (resp. $(x_0, \xi_0) \notin \mathrm{WF}^{(\sigma)}(u)$) if and only if there exists a conic neighborhood Γ of ξ_0; a compact neighborhood K of x_0; and $\phi \in \mathcal{D}^{\{\sigma\}}(U)$ (resp $\phi \in \mathcal{D}^{(\sigma)}(U)$) such that $\mathrm{supp}\,\phi \subseteq K$, $\phi = 1$ on some neighborhood of x_0 and*

$$|\widehat{\phi u}(\xi)| \le A|\xi|^{-H\left(\frac{\ln|\xi|}{\ln(\ln|\xi|)}\right)^{\frac{1}{\sigma-1}}}, \quad \xi \in \Gamma,$$

for some $A, H > 0$ (resp. for any $H > 0$ there exists $A > 0$).

We write $u(x) = F(x + i\Gamma 0)$ if $u(x)$ is obtained as boundary value of the analytic function F as $y \to 0$ in Γ. Recall (cf. [9])

$$\Gamma_0 = \{\xi \in \mathbf{R}^d \mid y \cdot \xi \ge 0 \text{ for all } y \in \Gamma\}$$

denotes the dual cone of Γ.

To conclude the paper we prove the following theorem.

Theorem 2. *Let the assumptions of Theorem 1 hold, and let $u(x) = F(x + i\Gamma 0) \in \mathcal{D}'^{(\sigma)}(U)$ (resp. $\mathcal{D}'^{\{\sigma\}}(U)$). Then*

$$\mathrm{WF}^{(\sigma)}(u) \subseteq U \times \Gamma_0, \quad (\text{resp. } \mathrm{WF}^{\{\sigma\}}(u) \subseteq U \times \Gamma_0).$$

More precisely, if $u(x) = F(x + i\Gamma 0) \in \mathcal{D}'_{\{\tau/2^{\sigma-1},\sigma\}}(U)$ (resp. $\mathcal{D}'_{(\tau/2^{\sigma-1},\sigma)}(U)$) then

$$\mathrm{WF}_{\{(2^\sigma-1)\tau,\sigma\}}(u) \subseteq U \times \Gamma_0, \quad (\text{resp. } \mathrm{WF}_{((2^\sigma-1)\tau,\sigma)} \subseteq U \times \Gamma_0).$$

Proof. Fix $x_0 \in U$ and $\xi_0 \notin \Gamma_0 \backslash \{0\}$. Then there exists $Y = (Y_1, \ldots, Y_d) \in \Gamma$, $|Y| < \gamma$, such that $Y \cdot \xi_0 < 0$. Moreover, there exists conical neighborhood V of ξ_0 and constant $\gamma_1 > 0$ such that $Y \cdot \xi \le -\gamma_1 |\xi|$, for all $\xi \in V$. To see that, note that there exists $B_r(\xi_0)$ such that $Y \cdot \xi < 0$ for all $\xi \in B_r(\xi_0)$. The assertion follows for $V = \{s\xi \mid s > 0, \xi \in B_r(\xi_0)\}$ and $\gamma_1 = \inf_{\xi \in V, |\xi|=1} (-Y) \cdot \xi$.

Let $\tau > 0$ and $\tau_0 = (2^\sigma - 1)\tau$. If $u(x) = F(x + i\Gamma 0) \in \mathcal{D}'_{\tau/2^{\sigma-1},\sigma}(U)$ as in Theorem 1, then

$$|F(z)| \le A \exp\{T_{\tau_0,\sigma,h_1}(1/|y|)\}, \quad z = x + iy \in Z, \tag{23}$$

for suitable constants $A, h_1 > 0$.

Choose $\varphi \in \mathcal{D}^K_{\tau/4^{\sigma-1},\sigma}$ such that $\varphi = 1$ in a neighborhood of x_0 and let Z_Y be as in (14). Then there exists Φ (see (13)) such that

$$|\Phi(z)| \leq A_1, \quad \text{and} \quad |\partial_{\overline{z_j}} \Phi(z)| \leq A_2 \exp\{-T_{\tau_0/2^{\sigma-1},\sigma,h_2}(1/|tY|)\}, \tag{24}$$

$z \in Z_Y$, $1 \leq j \leq d$, for suitable constants $A_1, A_2, h_2 > 0$.

Note that formula (20) implies

$$\widehat{(\varphi u)}(\xi) = \langle u(x)e^{-ix\cdot\xi}, \varphi(x)\rangle = \int_K F(x+iY)e^{-i(x+iY)\cdot\xi}\Phi(x+iY)dx$$

$$+ 2i \sum_{j=1}^{d} Y_j \int_0^1 \int_K \partial_{\overline{z_j}}\Phi(x+itY)F(x+itY)e^{-i(x+itY)\cdot\xi}dtdx, \quad \xi \in V. \tag{25}$$

Using (23) and (24) we have

$$|F(x+iY)\Phi(x+iY)e^{-i(x+iY)\xi}| \leq B e^{-\gamma_1|\xi|}, \quad x \in K, \xi \in V, \tag{26}$$

for some $B > 0$.

Moreover, for $z \in Z_Y$ and $\xi \in V$ we have

$$|F(z)\partial_{\overline{z_j}}\Phi(z)e^{-iz\cdot\xi}|$$
$$\leq C\exp\{T_{\tau_0,\sigma,h_1}(1/|tY|) - T_{\tau_0/2^{\sigma-1},\sigma,h_2}(1/|tY|) - t\gamma_1|\xi|\}$$
$$\leq C_1 \exp\{-T_{\tau_0,\sigma,c_{h_1,h_2}}(1/(t\gamma_1)) - t\gamma_1|\xi|\} \leq C_2 \exp\{-T_{\tau_0,\sigma,c'_{h_1,h_2}}(|\xi|)\}, \tag{27}$$

for suitable constants $C_1, C_2, c_{h_1,h_2}, c'_{h_1,h_2} > 0$, where we have used inequalities (A2) and (A3).

Finally, using (25)–(27) we obtain

$$|\widehat{(\varphi u)}(\xi)| \leq B_1(e^{-\gamma_1|\xi|} + \exp\{-T_{\tau_0,\sigma,c'_{h_1,h_2}}(|\xi|)\}) \leq B_2 \exp\{-T_{\tau_0,\sigma,c'_{h_1,h_2}}(|\xi|)\},$$

for $\xi \in V$ and for suitable constant $B_2 > 0$. This completes the proof. □

5. Conclusions

Various classes of (ultra)distributions are commonly introduced as topological duals of suitable test function spaces, or as equivalence classes of certain Cauchy sequences of smooth functions. Another approach is given through their representations as finite sums of boundary values of analytic functions. We refer to [11] for a history, motivation and a detailed study of the subject. In this paper, we give a characterization of analytic functions whose boundary values are elements of intermediate spaces between the spaces of Schwartz distributions and any space of Gevrey ultradistributions. Test function spaces for such spaces of ultradistributions are related to the so-called extended Gervey regularity studied by the authors in [1–4,10,20]. We note that the extended Gevrey classes are different from any Carleman class which appears to be essential for many calculations, leading to the use of novel tools and techniques. In particular, we have used asymptotic properties of the Lambert W function in order to describe appropriate logarithmic growth rate in our calculations. This tool appears in the theory of new ultradistribution spaces for the first time (see also [4]). Since we relaxed the condition of stability under ultradifferentiable operators, to prove our main result, Theorem 1, we had to preform nontrivial changes in proofs of related results of classical theory (cf. [13]). This methodology could be used in other situations as well. For example, in future research we will consider the Paley–Wiener theorem for the new spaces of ultradistributions. This, in turn, will be used to prove the structure theorems in terms of boundary values of analytic functions; cf. Remark 1. We will also study other classes of two parameter sequences $M_p^{\tau,\sigma}$, apart from $p^{\tau p^\sigma}$, $p \in \mathbf{N}$, $\tau > 0$, $\sigma > 1$. This will be done in the spirit of Komastu [5].

Author Contributions: Individual contributions of the authors were equally distributed. Conceptualization, methodology, writing—original draft preparation and writing—review and editing, S.P., N.T. and F.T. All authors have read and agreed to the published version of the manuscript.

Funding: This research was funded by Ministry of Education, Science and Technological Development, Republic of Serbia, project numbers 451-03-68/2020-14/200125 and 451-03-68/2020-14/200156; the Serbian Academy of Sciences and Arts, project F10; and MNRVOID of the Republic of Srpska, project 19.032/961103/19.

Conflicts of Interest: The authors declare no conflict of interest. The funders had no role in the writing of the manuscript, or in the decision to publish the results.

Appendix A

In the following Lemma we study $T_{\tau,\sigma,h}(k)$ in some detail.

Lemma A1. *Let $h > 0$, and $T_{\tau,\sigma,h}$ be given by (1), and let $T^*_{\tau,\sigma,h}$ be given by (3). Then*

(a) *If $h_1 < h_2$ then $T_{\tau,\sigma,h_1}(k) < T_{\tau,\sigma,h_2}(k)$, $k > 0$. Moreover, for any $h > 0$ there exists $H > h$ such that*

$$T_{\tau,\sigma,h}(k) \leq T^*_{\tau,\sigma,h}(k) \leq T_{\tau,\sigma,H}(k), \quad k > 0. \tag{A1}$$

(b) *For $h_1, h_2 > 0$ there exists $C, c_{h_1,h_2} > 0$ such that*

$$T_{\tau,\sigma,h_1}(k) + T_{\tau,\sigma,h_2}(k) \leq T_{\tau/2^{\sigma-1},\sigma,c_{h_1,h_2}}(k) + \ln C \quad k > 0, \tag{A2}$$

(c) *For every $h > 0$ there exists $H > 0$ such that*

$$T_{\tau,\sigma,H}(l) \leq T_{\tau,\sigma,h}(1/k) + kl, \quad k,l > 0. \tag{A3}$$

Proof. (a) Notice that for arbitrary $h > 0$,

$$\ln \frac{h^{p^\sigma} k^p}{p^{\tau p^\sigma}} \leq \ln \frac{p^p h^{p^\sigma} k^p}{p^{\tau p^\sigma}} \leq \ln \frac{(Ch)^{p^\sigma} k^p}{p^{\tau p^\sigma}}, \quad k > 0,$$

where for the second inequality we use that for every $\sigma > 1$ there exists $C > 1$ such that $p^p \leq C^{p^\sigma}$, $p \in \mathbf{N}$ (see the proof of Proposition 2.1. in [1]). Now (A1) follows by putting $H = Ch$.

(b) Let $h_1, h_2 > 0$. We will use the following simple inequality

$$p^\sigma + q^\sigma \leq (p+q)^\sigma \leq 2^{\sigma-1}(p^\sigma + q^\sigma), \quad p,q \in \mathbf{N}. \tag{A4}$$

Since, $h_1^{p^\sigma} h_2^{q^\sigma} \leq (h_1 + h_2)^{p^\sigma + q^\sigma}$ we conclude that

$$h_1^{p^\sigma} h_2^{q^\sigma} \leq (h_1 + h_2)^{(p+q)^\sigma} \quad \text{when} \quad h_1 + h_2 \geq 1$$

and

$$h_1^{p^\sigma} h_2^{q^\sigma} \leq (h_1 + h_2)^{(1/2^{\sigma-1})(p+q)^\sigma} \quad \text{when} \quad 0 < h_1 + h_2 < 1.$$

Hence, there exists $0 < c_\sigma \leq 1$ such that

$$\ln \frac{h_1^{p^\sigma} k^p}{p^{\tau p^\sigma}} + \ln \frac{h_2^{q^\sigma} k^q}{q^{\tau q^\sigma}} \leq \ln \frac{(C(h_1+h_2)^{c_\sigma})^{(p+q)^\sigma} k^{p+q}}{(p+q)^{(\tau/2^{\sigma-1})(p+q)^\sigma}} + \ln C, \quad p,q \in \mathbf{N},$$

where $C > 0$ is constant appearing in $\widetilde{(M.2)}$. Now (A2) follows after taking supremums over $p, q \in \mathbf{N}$.

(c) Recall (see [6]) that there exists $A > 0$ such that $kl = \sup_{p \in \mathbf{N}} \ln \dfrac{A^p k^p l^p}{p^p}$. Note that for every $\sigma > 1$ there exists $0 < C < 1$ such that $\dfrac{1}{p^p} \geq C^{p^\sigma}$, $p \in \mathbf{N}$.

Then for arbitrary $h > 0$ we have

$$T_{\tau,\sigma,h}(1/k) + kl = \sup_{p,q \in \mathbf{N}} \ln \dfrac{h^{p^\sigma}}{k^p p^{\tau p^\sigma}} \dfrac{A^q k^q l^q}{q^q} \geq \sup_{p,q \in \mathbf{N}, p=q} \ln \dfrac{(A'Ch)^{p^\sigma} l^p}{p^{\tau p^\sigma}} = T_{\tau,\sigma,H}(l), \quad k,l > 0,$$

where $A' = \min\{1, A\}$. This proves (A3). □

Finally, we discuss certain stability and embedding properties of $\mathcal{E}_{\tau,\sigma}(U)$ given by (5) and (6). Analogous considerations hold when the spaces $\mathcal{D}_{\tau,\sigma}(U)$ from (7) and (8) are considered instead.

Let $a_\alpha \in \mathcal{E}_{(\tau,\sigma)}(U)$ (resp. $a_\alpha \in \mathcal{E}_{\{\tau,\sigma\}}(U)$), where U is an open set in $\mathbf{R}^d$. Then we say that

$$P(x, \partial) = \sum_{|\alpha|=0}^{\infty} a_\alpha(x) \partial^\alpha$$

is an ultradifferential operator of class (τ, σ) (resp. $\{\tau, \sigma\}$) on U if for every $K \subset\subset U$ there exists constant $L > 0$ such that for any $h > 0$ there exists $A > 0$ (resp. for every $K \subset\subset U$ there exists $h > 0$ such that for any $L > 0$ there exists $A > 0$) such that

$$\sup_{x \in K} |\partial^\beta a_\alpha(x)| \leq A h^{|\beta|^\sigma} |\beta|^{\tau|\beta|^\sigma} \dfrac{L^{|\alpha|^\sigma}}{|\alpha|^{\tau 2^{\sigma-1}|\alpha|^\sigma}}, \quad \alpha, \beta \in \mathbf{N}^d.$$

We refer to [2] for the proof of the following continuity and embedding properties.

Proposition A1.

(a) Let $P(x, \partial)$ be an ultradifferential operator of class (τ, σ) (resp. $\{\tau, \sigma\}$). Then $P(x, \partial): \mathcal{E}_{\tau,\sigma}(U) \longrightarrow \mathcal{E}_{\tau 2^{\sigma-1},\sigma}(U)$ is a continuous linear mapping; the same holds for

$$P(x, \partial): \varinjlim_{\tau \to \infty} \mathcal{E}_{\tau,\sigma}(U) \longrightarrow \varinjlim_{\tau \to \infty} \mathcal{E}_{\tau,\sigma}(U).$$

(b) Let $\sigma_1 \geq 1$. Then for every $\sigma_2 > \sigma_1$

$$\varinjlim_{\tau \to \infty} \mathcal{E}_{\tau,\sigma_1}(U) \hookrightarrow \varprojlim_{\tau \to 0^+} \mathcal{E}_{\tau,\sigma_2}(U).$$

(c) If $0 < \tau_1 < \tau_2$, then

$$\mathcal{E}_{\{\tau_1,\sigma\}}(U) \hookrightarrow \mathcal{E}_{(\tau_2,\sigma)}(U) \hookrightarrow \mathcal{E}_{\{\tau_2,\sigma\}}(U), \quad \sigma > 1,$$

and

$$\varinjlim_{\tau \to \infty} \mathcal{E}_{\{\tau,\sigma\}}(U) = \varinjlim_{\tau \to \infty} \mathcal{E}_{(\tau,\sigma)}(U),$$

$$\varprojlim_{\tau \to 0^+} \mathcal{E}_{\{\tau,\sigma\}}(U) = \varprojlim_{\tau \to 0^+} \mathcal{E}_{(\tau,\sigma)}(U), \quad \sigma > 1.$$

Consequently we obtain that

$$\varinjlim_{t \to \infty} \mathcal{E}_t(U) \hookrightarrow \mathcal{E}_{\tau,\sigma}(U) \hookrightarrow C^\infty(U), \quad \tau > 0, \sigma > 1,$$

where $\mathcal{E}_t(U)$ is Gevrey space with index $t > 1$.

References

1. Pilipović, S.; Teofanov, N.; Tomić, F. On a class of ultradifferentiable functions. *Novi Sad J. Math.* **2015**, *45*, 125–142.
2. Pilipović, S.; Teofanov, N.; Tomić, F. Beyond Gevrey regularity. *J. Pseudo-Differ. Oper. Appl.* **2016**, *7*, 113–140. [CrossRef]
3. Pilipović, S.; Teofanov, N.; Tomić, F. Beyond Gevrey regularity: Superposition and propagation of singularities. *Filomat* **2018**, *32*, 2763–2782. [CrossRef]
4. Pilipović, S.; Teofanov, N.; Tomić, F. A Paley-Wiener theorem in extended Gevrey regularity. *J. Pseudo-Differ. Oper. Appl.* **2020**, *11*, 593–612. [CrossRef]
5. Komatsu, H. Ultradistributions, I: Structure theorems and a characterization. *J. Fac. Sci. Univ. Tokyo Sect. IA Math.* **1973**, *20*, 25–105.
6. Komatsu, H. *An Introduction to the Theory of Generalized Functions, Lecture Notes*; Department of Mathematics Science University of Tokyo: Tokyo, Japan, 1999.
7. Braun, R.W.; Meise, R.; Taylor, B.A. Ultra-differentiable functions and Fourier analysis. *Results Math.* **1990**. *17*, 206–237. [CrossRef]
8. Cicognani, M.; Lorenz, D. Strictly hyperbolic equations with coefficients low-regular win time and smooth in space. *J. Pseudo-Differ. Oper. Appl.* **2018**, *9*, 643–675. [CrossRef]
9. Hörmander, L. *The Analysis of Linear Partial Differential Operators I*; Springer: Berlin/Heidelberg, Germany, 1990.
10. Teofanov, N.; Tomić, F. Inverse closedness and singular support in extended Gevrey regularity. *J. Pseudo-Differ. Oper. Appl.* **2017**, *8*, 411–421. [CrossRef]
11. Carmichael, R.; Kaminski, A.; Pilipović, S. *Boundary Values and Convolution in Ultradistribution Spaces*; World Scientific Publishing Co. Pte. Ltd.: Hackensack, NJ, USA, 2007.
12. Rodino, L. *Linear Partial Differential Operators in Gevrey Spaces*; World Scientific: Singapore, 1993.
13. Pilipović, S. Structural theorems for ultradistributions. *Dissertationes Math. Rozpr. Math.* **1995**, *340*, 223–235.
14. Pilipović, S. Microlocal properties of ultradistributions. Composition and kernel type operators. *Publ. Inst. Math.* **1998**, *64*, 85–97.
15. Debrouwere, A.; Vindas, J. On the non-triviality of certain spaces of analytic functions. Hyperfunctions and ultrahyperfunctions of fast growth. *Rev. R. Acad. Cienc. Exactas Fís. Nat. Ser. A Mat. RACSAM* **2018**, *112*, 473–508. [CrossRef]
16. Dimovski, P.; Pilipović, S.; Vindas, J. Boundary values of holomorphic functions in translation- invariant distribution spaces. *Complex Var. Elliptic Equ.* **2015**, *60*, 1169–1189. [CrossRef]
17. Fernańdez, C.; Galbis, A.; Gómez-Collado, M.C. (Ultra)distributions of Lp-growth as boundary values of holomorphic functions. *Rev. R. Acad. Cienc. Exactas Fís. Nat. Ser. A Mat. RACSAM* **2003**, *97*, 243–255.
18. Vučković, Đ.; Vindas, J. Ultradistributional boundary values of harmonic functions on the sphere. *J. Math. Anal. Appl.* **2018**, *457*, 533–550. [CrossRef]
19. Fürdös, S.; Nenning, D.N.; Rainer, A.; Schindl, G. Almost analytic extensions of ultradifferentiable functions with applications to microlocal analysis. *J. Math. Anal. Appl.* **2020**, *481*, 123451. [CrossRef]
20. Teofanov, N.; Tomić, F. Ultradifferentiable functions of class $M_p^{\tau,\sigma}$ and microlocal regularity, Generalized functions and Fourier analysis. In *Advances in Partial Differential Equations*; Birkhäuser, Basel, Switzerland, 2017; pp. 193–213.
21. Kriegl, A.; Michor, P.W.; Rainer, A. The convenient setting for quasianalytic Denjoy–Carleman differentiable mappings. *J. Funct. Anal.* **2011**, *261*, 1799–1834. [CrossRef]
22. Rainer, A.; Schindl, G. Composition in ultradifferentiable classes. *Studia Math.* **2014**, *224*, 97–131. [CrossRef]
23. Meise, R.; Vogt, D. Characterization of convolution operators on spaces of C^∞-functions admitting a continuous linear right inverse. *Math. Ann.* **1987**, *279*, 141–155. [CrossRef]
24. Corless, R.M.; Gonnet, G.H.; Hare, D.E.G.; Jeffrey, D.J.; Knuth, D.E. On the Lambert W function. *Adv. Comput. Math.* **1996**, *5*, 329–359. [CrossRef]
25. Hoorfar, A.; Hassani, M. Inequalities on the Lambert W function and hyperpower function. *J. Inequalities Pure Appl. Math.* **2008**, *9*, 5–9.

MDPI
St. Alban-Anlage 66
4052 Basel
Switzerland
Tel. +41 61 683 77 34
Fax +41 61 302 89 18
www.mdpi.com

Mathematics Editorial Office
E-mail: mathematics@mdpi.com
www.mdpi.com/journal/mathematics

www.ingramcontent.com/pod-product-compliance
Lightning Source LLC
LaVergne TN
LVHW070600100526
838202LV00012B/524